Ensuring Inequality

ENSURING INEQUALITY

The Structural Transformation of the African-American Family

Donna L. Franklin

New York   Oxford
OXFORD UNIVERSITY PRESS 1997

Oxford University Press

Oxford   New York
Athens   Aukland   Bangkok   Bogotá   Bombay
Buenos Aires   Calcutta   Cape Town   Dar es Salaam   Delhi
Florence   Hong Kong   Istanbul   Karachi
Kuala Lumpur   Madras   Madrid   Melbourne
Mexico City   Nairobi   Paris   Singapore
Taipei   Tokyo   Toronto

and associated companies in
Berlin   Ibadan

Published by Oxford University Press, Inc.,
198 Madison Avenue, New York, New York 10016

Oxford is a registered trademark of Oxford University Press

Library of Congress Cataloging-in-Publication Data

Franklin, Donna L.
Ensuring inequality : the structural transformation of the
African-American family / Donna L. Franklin.
p.   cm.   Includes bibliographical references and index.
ISBN 0–19–510078–6
1. Afro-American families—History.
2. Fatherless family—United States—History.
3. Single-parent family—United States—History.
4. Poverty—United States.   I. Title.
E185.86.F68   1997   306.85'089'96073—dc20   96–7930

3 5 7 9 8 6 4 2

Printed in the United States of America
on acid-free paper

For my parents, Donald and Helen Franklin,
whose love and belief sustained me;

my grandmother, Blanche Ballard,
a queen among women; and

in memory of my brother, Glen Anthony Franklin

CONTENTS

FOREWORD

The publication of this book could not be more timely. In the face of a rising number of solo-parent families and out-of-wedlock births, the nation is embroiled in a debate about family values. In August 1996 Congress passed and the president of the United States signed a controversial welfare reform bill that effectively ends the federal entitlement to subsistence income for poor families in need. Assumptions about the breakdown of the American family and the factors that have contributed to it are featured in both the debate over family values and the welfare-reform legislation.

Donna Franklin points out that even though a national opinion poll reveals that a substantial majority of Americans believe that children are better off if one parent stays home, there is little support for the idea that welfare mothers should be compensated for staying at home. One possible explanation for this position was provided by the Harvard sociologist Theda Skocpol. She stated that "when mothers' pensions became federally subsidized with Aid to Dependent Children in 1935, Americans still presumed a mother's place was in the home. But in the late twentieth century, they no longer do. Across the class structure, father and mother alike hold paid employment. People will no longer accept a welfare system that ostensibly pays poor mothers to stay home."[1]

Conservatives call for work and responsible parenthood. But we have yet to create social policies that make it possible for all Americans, poor and nonpoor, to work while raising their children. Meanwhile, the number of solo-parent nonworking families continue to grow, and it is asserted that welfare is the single most important contributing factor, even though scientific evidence consistently contradicts this claim.[2] Since the 1994 congressional elections, welfare mothers have been publicly demonized by many conservative politicians.

As I pointed out in my book, *When Work Disappears: The World of the New Urban Poor*, the increasing attacks on welfare mothers are part of a larger reaction to the growing problems of social dislocation in our nation's inner cities.[3] Even though the number of white AFDC recipients was roughly equal to the number of black recipients in 1995, many people associate welfare with young, unmarried black mothers having babies. The increasing number of African-American AFDC recipients has been linked in public discourse to such larger problems as the dissolution of the family and the decline in family values. It is argued that welfare exacerbates these problems, and that ending welfare would force people to assume personal and family responsibility, thereby reversing the trend of rising inner-city dislocations, including family breakups.

However, as shown in this book, the issues involved in the decline of nuclear black families are far more complex than those involved in the simplistic welfare arguments. Professor Franklin identifies and shows the cumulative effects of five factors that have transformed the African-American family structure over time. These five historical factors include slavery, the northern migration that resulted in the loss of communal institutions, AFDC policies, decreasing job opportunities for lower-class black men, and social isolation in neighborhoods of high poverty concentration.

In addition to these five factors, the structure of black families, like that of white and other ethnic families, has also been affected by changing values in our society that increased the independence and autonomy of all women, by changes in traditional gender roles not only within the family but in the workplace as well, and by more liberal attitudes toward out-of-wedlock births and single parenthood. As Professor Franklin puts it, "these changes have placed the traditional nuclear family under much greater strain and have predictably had the most devastating impact on African-American families."

Professor Franklin feels that it is important for policymakers to address the problems of many African-American families with an understanding that the high levels of nonmarriage are very likely irreversible and that therefore changes in public policy should be directed at ways to strengthen relations within the family, including the mother-child dyad. For example, "If the mother is drug-free, motivated to be a good mother, and considered fit to rear her child," states Franklin, "resources should be directed at fortifying the mother-child dyad by strengthening the mother's parenting skills."

Nonetheless, regardless of the structure of African-American families—whether solo-parent or nuclear—the survival of many of them as viable and healthy units will depend on social policies that make it possible for parents to work while caring for their children. Others, particularly middle class and professional black families, have the social and economic resources that strengthen family relations and provide a healthy environment for child development.

The African-American family is not a monolithic entity. Sixty-five percent of those families with children under eighteen whose level of educational attainment features a bachelor's degree and 69 percent of those with a graduate/professional degree are married-couple units. The corresponding figures for those with only a high school degree (or GED) or who have not graduated from high school are 45.8 percent and 37.9 percent respectively.[4] And in many ghetto neighborhoods the proportion of married-couple families is even lower. For example, in the inner-city neighborhoods of Chicago only one-quarter of the families with children under eighteen are husband-wife families.[5] These are the families, many of whom are on welfare, especially in need of progressive social policies that make it possible for the parents to work while caring for their children. It is very important that work opportunities be provided for both men and women.

As I pointed out in *The Truly Disadvantaged,* comprehensive economic policies that "enhance employment opportunities among the truly disadvantaged—both men and women—are needed."[6] The central problem facing inner-city workers is that changes in the economy have shifted the demand for labor away from low-skilled workers.[7] Despite claims by conservative analysts that low-skilled workers fail to take advantage of labor-market opportunities,[8] available evidence strongly suggests that it is harder for low-skilled inner-city workers to find employment today.[9] For example, the anthropologists Katherine Newman and Chauncy Lennon found that during a five-month period there were fourteen applicants for every individual who was hired in fast food businesses in Harlem. They also found that among those applicants who were not hired, three-quarters had not found a single job a year later. They concluded that the people of Harlem pounding the pavement looking for work far exceeded the number of jobs to be found.[10]

With the new welfare reform legislation we have created a situation in which long-term AFDC recipients in the inner city will flood a pool already filled with jobless adults looking for work. Indeed, according to one report, given the current rate of growth in the New York City economy, if every new job were given to the city's current welfare recipients, it would take twenty-one years to absorb them into the economy.[11]

A similar point was made by Donna Franklin. She points out that

a study released in 1995 by the Manhattan Borough President found that at any given time about 50,000 jobs, of all types (not just entry level), are available in New York city If they were all filled by welfare recipients, 300,000 more jobs would be needed for the remaining adults on welfare, and an additional 200,000 jobs would be needed for other unemployed New Yorkers. Thus while the welfare discussions have shifted to the problematic behaviors of nonworking black mothers, the opportunities for all low-wage workers have been deteriorating and the black poor have increasingly been isolated in neighborhoods of concentrated poverty.

But the problem for many lower-income African-American families is not simply the creation of jobs, however basic this is to their own economic survival. Franklin's comprehensive analysis reveals the need for a combination of social interventions to overcome the severe consequences of ghetto life, consequences that impede healthy family relations. These include the development of community-based family services agencies to "combat the effects of isolation and helplessness of low-income mothers and to enhance their coping skills related to living in urban poverty"; the expansion of the network of social services to increase "pregnant women's access to prenatal care and information on early childhood nutrition"; the creation of innovative and more effective approaches for children placed in foster care; the economic revitalization of the inner city through enterprise zones and community development corporations; and black self-help efforts, "which must include the participation of more affluent blacks who are willing to establish and maintain links with the poorest blacks."

I would add one additional intervention to this list—the creation of public sector jobs. Franklin recognizes the need for "government endeavors directed specifically at inner cities." The gap between the number of low-skilled workers and the supply of low-skilled jobs is so great in some urban areas that public-sector employment will be needed to supplement private sector hiring. Without the infusion of public-sector jobs it will be difficult to prevent the creation of a large number of homeless welfare families when they reach the time limit for receiving welfare.

The challenge facing America is great. We not only have to increase our commitment to confront the problems associated with the structural transformation of the African-American family, we also need to develop a greater understanding of the complex set of factors that caused this transformation. The reading of this comprehensive book by all concerned citizens is an important step in helping to achieve both of these objectives.

Harvard University   WILLIAM JULIUS WILSON

Notes

1. Theda Skocpol, "Bury It," *The New Republic.* August 12, 1996, 21.

2. See, for example, Greg J. Duncan, "Testimony Before the Subcommittee on Human Resources of the Committee on Ways and Means Hearing on Early Childbearing," U.S. Congress, Washington, D.C., 1994; Saul D. Hoffman, Greg J. Duncan, and Ronald B. Mincy, "Marriage and Welfare Use Among Young Women: Do Labor Market, Welfare and Neighborhood Factors Account for Declining Rates of Marriage Among Black and White Women?" Paper presented at the annual meeting of the American Economic Association, New Orleans, Louisiana, December, 1991; Greg J. Duncan and Saul D. Hoffman, "Teenage Underclass Behavior and Subsequent Poverty: Have the Rules Changed?" in *The Urban Underclass*, ed. Christopher Jencks and Paul E. Peterson (Washington, D.C., Brookings Institution, 1991), 155–74; and Mary Jo Bane and David Ellwood, *The Dynamics of Dependence and the Routes to Self-Sufficiency* (Cambridge, Mass.: Urban Systems Research and Engineering, 1983).

3. William Julius Wilson, *When Work Disappears: The World of the New Urban Poor* (New York: Knopf, 1996).

4. U.S. Bureau of the Census, "Characteristics of the Black Population" (Washington, D.C.: Government Printing Office, 1990).

5. Wilson, *When Work Disappears.*

6. William Julius Wilson, *The Truly Disadvantaged: The Inner City, the Underclass, and Public Policy* (Chicago: University of Chicago Press, 1987), 150.

7. Sheldon Danziger and Peter Gottschalk, *America Unequal* (Cambridge, Mass.: Harvard University Press, 1995).

8. See, for example, Lawrence Mead, *Beyond Entitlement: The Social Obligations of Citizenship* (New York: The Free Press, 1986), and Lawrence Mead, *The New Politics of Poverty: The Working Poor in America* (New York: Basic Books, 1992).

9. Danziger and Gottschalk, *America Unequal.*

10. Katherine Newman and Chauncy Lennon, "Finding Work in the Inner City: How Hard is it Now? How Hard will it be for AFDC Recipients?" Russell Sage Foundation Working Paper #76, October 1995.

11. Alan Finder, "Welfare Recipients in Big Cities Outnumber Jobs They Might Fill," *New York Times*, August 25, 1996, 1, 17.

ACKNOWLEDGMENTS

In his best-selling book, *The Celestine Prophecy*, James Redfield writes, "Whenever people cross our paths, there is always a message for us. Chance encounters do not exist. . . . If we have a conversation with someone who crosses our path and we do not see a message pertaining to our current questions, it does not mean there was not a message. It only means we missed it for some reason." During the years when I was working on this book, countless people crossed my path, and I had the opportunity to ask numerous questions. Although I may have missed many of the messages, the most important ones were given to me by Barbara Solomon, Dolores Norton, and William J. Wilson.

Barbara Solomon is responsible for launching me into my academic career. She guided me through both graduate degrees and chaired my doctoral committee. In addition, she gave my name to the Search Committee at the University of Chicago when they called requesting qualified applicants. By successfully combining a strong marriage, motherhood (four children, to be exact), and a highly productive academic career, and just being a kind and caring individual, she gave me the message to reach for my dreams.

If Barbara demonstrated that you could combine marriage, motherhood, and a career, Dodie Norton showed me that you could successfully juggle single parenting and unwieldy academic responsibilities. When I arrived at The University of Chicago in 1982, just out of a marriage and a first-time single parent, she always managed to find the time in her hectic schedule to be encouraging and understanding. In addition, any written materials I gave her were read carefully and critically, and returned within a short period of time. Dodie gave me the message that I could have a successful academic career in spite of any obstacles that were put in my path.

In 1984 the black faculty at the University of Chicago convened a conference to commemorate the work of Professor Allison Davis. Davis, a pioneer researcher on African-Americans, had retired quietly without any recognition of his years of exemplary service and scholarship. (Professor Davis died shortly after this conference was held; it was almost as if he were waiting for his colleagues to acknowledge their debt to him.) This conference offered me the opportunity to cross paths with messengers like the late St. Clair Drake and John Hope Franklin. With hindsight, I realize that encountering these great minds was an important factor in the formation of my ideas for this book.

In working with the faculty committee on the Davis conference, I had an opportunity to become better acquainted with some of my colleagues at the university. The first was Bill Wilson. If Barbara and Dodie taught me that I could successfully juggle the disparate areas of my life, he showed me how much you could get accomplished if you had a supportive mate. Bill, a generous man, not only read my dissertation in the early stages of our professional relationship, but assisted me in organizing my ideas so that I could get some publications out of it. Bill gave me the message that I could achieve my goals if I were focused, hard working, and disciplined.

The other colleague with whom I became better acquainted as the result of working on the conference committee was Ann Dibble Jordan (then known as Ann Cook). Ann had been working in the Chicago Lying-In Hospital for more than twenty years as a social worker and field instructor for social work students at the university. She worked directly with black mothers who came into the hospital for obstetrical care and unselfishly shared her valuable insights into some of the complexities of the family patterns found among black women living in poverty neighborhoods. Many of the ideas that flowed from our conversations have probably found their way into this book.

The year following the conference, Bill made the decision to pull together an interdisciplinary group of faculty to conduct research on poverty in the city of Chicago. When he invited me to join the team as a co-investigator, I realized that this was the opportunity of a lifetime. It was my participation in this project, that crystallized my ideas for the book.

During the four years of the project, Bill invited scholars with national reputations to present papers on issues related to the black family. The list of guest presenters included individuals from both sides of the ideological spectrum—scholars such as Elijah Anderson, Mary Jo Bane, Lawrence Mead, Glen Loury, Greg

Duncan, Tamara Hareven, and the late Michael Harrington, to name a few. The stimulating question-and-answer periods forced me to articulate my own arguments and, more importantly, to think about whether my evidence sustained these arguments. I also had the opportunity to meet and confer with some of the individuals who served on the project's advisory board, such as Eleanor Holmes Norton and Lee Rainwater.

In 1987, I was invited by Professor Peggy Dilworth-Anderson to make the featured presentations, along with Linda Burton, at the Third Annual Life Span Family Conference at the University of North Carolina at Greensboro. During the question and answer session, a question about the Moynihan Report and the "matriarchal" structure of the black family provoked some of the strongest reactions from conference attendees. I also noticed that black and white participants had different reactions to Moynihan's analysis. Whereas there was strong disagreement among the blacks in attendance with the contents of the Moynihan Report, the white audience members seemed to be in agreement with it. I left this conference with the message that there were many more questions than answers on the complicated subject of black family structure.

It was Richard English, however, the Dean of the School of Social Work at Howard University, who gave me the message that I should write a book and with that the first opportunity to begin work on it. He invited me to be a Visiting Professor at Howard during the 1989–90 academic year. The inducements were clear: first, a chance to get better acquainted with members of his faculty whose substantive area of study was the black family (e.g., Harriet McAdoo and Joyce Ladner); and second, access to two important archives—the National Archives and the Moreland Spingarn Archives.

I will be forever grateful to Jerry Cates, then a member of Howard's faculty, who personally escorted me on my first trip to the National Archives and gave me my initial introduction to the use of the system. Without his support, I am not sure I would have persevered. Some of the figures in the book that provide the most convincing evidence on the economic vulnerability of black families when compared with white families during the 1930s in five northern cities were found in the National Archives. These data were found in an obscure place in the archives; therefore this is probably the first time this information has been reproduced in print.

Meeting Leon Dash and reading his book, *When Children Want Children*, was yet another stimulus in organizing my ideas for this book. (Leon won a Pulitzer Prize for his next project.) In this book, Leon traced the patterns of adolescent childbearing he found in Washington, D.C., to sharecropping in the South. I was initially both fascinated by and skeptical of his journalistic ("unscientific") approach to establishing these linkages. I wondered whether more scholarly investigations had been conducted on this topic. When I discussed my concerns with Leon, he directed me to Charles S. Johnson's book, *Shadow of the Plantation*. This turned out to be a critically important book in shaping my understanding of how sharecropping influenced the family patterns of African Americans.

Isabel Wilkerson, another Pulitzer Prize–winning black journalist (the first black female), wrote a comprehensive story for the *New York Times* on an innovative welfare-to-work program in Chicago. This program was established to train former welfare recipients, primarily women, in construction jobs. Isabel's report documented the challenges American cities will face as they try to put welfare mothers to work and was one of the earliest to appear in the print media. My summary of her report appears in the book's final chapter. It was also helpful to discuss this project: how she got the story, some of her candid reactions to the program and its participants, why she felt the program wasn't more successful, and her hopefulness about welfare reform.

The Urban and Family Life Conference convened in 1991 at the University of Chicago and research findings from Wilson's project were presented. Not only was the paper that I presented with Susan Smith carefully critiqued by Linda Burton, but I also got messages from some audience members that I might need to reexamine some of my thinking on the book. I also remember having an energizing luncheon discussion with Erol Ricketts, Ron Ferguson (Harvard's John F. Kennedy School of Government), and Ron Mincy (currently at the Ford Foundation). This exchange was particularly helpful in further developing my ideas for this book.

I have benefited enormously from the comments of colleagues who read the earliest drafts of this manuscript: Mimi Abramovitz, Walter Allen, Thomas Holt, Margaret Rosenheim, Rosemary Sarri, and Adele Logan Alexander for the chapter on slavery. I must give a special thanks to two individuals, however, Laurence E. Lynn and Martin Rein. They both read chapters and wrote a plethora of critical comments—always urging me on. It was Marty who really inspired me to get it finished, in spite of this anxiety. Others who gave me important messages either directly or indirectly were Clifford Alexander, Gina Barclay-McLaughlin, Mary Becker, Robert Booker, Karen Crawford, Eloise Cornelius, Vera Dexter, Laura Epstein, Karen Frehl, Eileen Gambrill, Chris Gamwell, Sharon Hicks-Bartlett, Barbara Ransby, Aisha Ray, Theda Skocpol, Diana Slaughter-Dafoe, Susan Smith, and Michael Sosin.

Aaron Geib, Dana Gambill, and Mario Prietto patiently endured and responded swiftly to the vagaries of my requests for rare books, journals that were no longer in circulation, and any and all of the documentation that was needed for the book. In addition, Dana drafted all of the tables for the book. I would also like to thank Rino Patti, the dean at the University of Southern California, for his support during the final phase of the book. Finally, I would like to express my profound appreciation to Dolores Cross, the president of Chicago State University, who offered me a Distinguished Visiting Professorship in the Department of Sociology, with a reduced academic work load, so that I could continue work on the book; Gene Tanke and Jessie Combre for their editorial assistance; Gioia Stevens, my editor at Oxford, for both her persistence and her patience during my periods of ambivalence; and Faith Childs, my literary agent, for going beyond the call of duty in providing guidance and support.

Many close friends and family members have contributed to this effort as well. My sisters, Vicki, April, and Stephani have nurtured, reassured, and cared for me during this process. My brother Greg provided support and admiration. (My siblings have truly been the "wind beneath my wings.") My niece Alexis organized my office and tried to keep everything categorized for me. I thank Bart for moving to Chicago so that he could share the parenting responsibilities for Myisha, and for becoming a friend. Once he arrived, I realized that although I was still a single parent, I was no longer a solo parent. I appreciate Reggie's clairvoyance and intuitive insights, and I thank my closest friends—Dodie, Elizabeth, Fran, J.R., Jessie, Marion, Pam, Reuben, Shepard, Stephen, and Donna—for their honest appraisal and sometimes for just being there.

I have been fortunate enough to have parents and a grandmother who have followed my efforts with interest and love—this book is dedicated to them. My deepest gratitude, however, is reserved for my daughter Myisha. She is the one who had to live with me and endure my obsession with this book on a daily basis. She willingly sacrificed my attention so that I could devote unrestricted energies to this book. At the same time she "normalized" my life by pulling me out of the project when I needed a break. She has been the most extraordinary gift. I would want her in my life even if she were not my daughter.

INTRODUCTION

Exponential increases in the number of children who are growing up in father-absent families have evoked concern in the minds of the American public that traditional family values are on the decline. Reactions to these anomalous trends have even begun to appear in newspapers and popular journals.[1] Proposed changes in public welfare policies would discourage unmarried mothers from having families. And the compromise advanced by a bipartisan coalition of governors has empowered some states even to deny welfare benefits to single mothers under the age of eighteen.

Currently, African-American women, compared with white women, are more likely to bear children as teenagers, less likely to ever marry, more likely to experience marital instability, and more likely to become parents outside of marriage.[2] As a result, a much higher proportion of African-American women are likely to become single parents and enter poverty. Furthermore, when the fathers are absent in African-American families, more than half of those families live in poverty, compared to about one-quarter of white father-absent families.[3]

Why do the marriage and family experiences of African-Americans differ from those of white Americans? How are we to explain the evolution of the African-American family over the past three centuries? More specifically, how do we explain the disproportionate number of unmarried adolescent black mothers? What are the implications of these changes in family structure?

Alexis de Tocqueville visited the United States in 1831 and made some observations regarding the institution of marriage and slavery:

> There exists, indeed, a profound and natural antipathy between the institution of marriage and that of slavery. A man does not marry when he cannot exercise marital authority, when his children must be born his equal, irrevocably destined to the wretchedness of their father; when, having no power over their fate, he can neither know the duties, the privileges, the hopes, nor the cares which belong to the paternal relation. It is easy to perceive that every motive which incites the freedman to a lawful union is lost to the slave by the simple fact of his slavery.[4]

Racial differences in marriage and family experiences have existed over time: These changes did not begin in the last two decades or even the past half-century, they have been 300 years in the making. However, the more recent pronounced changes in the family formation patterns of African-Americans represent a dramatic departure from the family life that was documented by scholars during an earlier period.

When David Ellwood critiqued the "situation" versus "culture" arguments on poverty, he characterized them as the "most confused and perplexing intellectual histories of any topic related to the disadvantaged."[5] These polemical discussions have been confusing because they have not taken into account the historical, cultural, and social evolution of the African-American family.

It is the purpose of this book to contribute to this debate by providing a more comprehensive historical study of the evolution of black family life than has been offered in the past. My premise is that a full understanding of the contemporary African-American family requires attention to its entire historical development. This understanding, if grasped by policymakers, would alter current approaches to the problem.

The problems of the African American family are a reflection of the broader social problems in the populace. Whenever American has undergone a moral dilemma, it has the greatest impact on the most vulnerable citizens. Samuel Johnson once observed that, "A decent provision for the poor is the true test of civilization."[6] By that gauge, how society provides for the most disadvantaged mothers and their children tells us something about our basic values as a society.

The most recent gauge of American civility is the passage of the Republican welfare legislation that would cut $56 billion in spending and give states new powers to remove millions of poor mothers and their children from the welfare rolls. This legislation passed overwhelming in the House and the Senate. The House approved the measure 328 to 101, the Senate approved a similar version by a vote of 74 to 24, and President Clinton signed the measure on August 22, 1996.

In endorsing the Republican bill, Mr. Clinton has acquiesced in the most sweeping reversal of domestic social policy since the New Deal.

Prior Explanatory Frameworks

A number of formulations have been advanced over the past century to explain the differences between black and white family structures. Scholarly explanations of the origins and evolution of the black family can be divided into four groups. The first is the anthropological and African-origin approach, whose earliest proponents were George W. Williams and Carter G. Woodson. These scholars argued that it was the African heritage of black Americans that most influenced their beliefs and practices. In recent years, there has been a resurgence in the scholarship linking African-American family patterns with their African legacy.[7]

Melville Herskovits carried this analysis further than other scholars in his book *The Myth of the Negro Past*. When Herskovits discussed the causes underlying the "matriarchal Negro family," he traced this phenomenon to the polygynous West African societies. In his view, this social organization had important implications for understanding kinship groups and the strength of the bond between the black mother and her children. In polygynous African societies, the "responsibilities of upbringing, discipline, and supervision are much more the province of the mother than of the father."[8]

The second approach is sociological, and was put forward by E. Franklin Frazier, W. E. B. DuBois, and Daniel P. Moynihan, all of whom both blamed slavery for disrupting black family life and are generally credited with developing the "matriarchal argument" to describe the black family structure. According to their view, the institution of slavery destroyed the African heritage (although DuBois was ambivalent and changed his position over time), undermined the authority of the black male, and thus contributed to the development of the matrifocal family structure.

The third approach developed out of the arguments of scholars who were principally historians and opposed the idea of the matriarchy. These include Herbert Gutman, John Blassingame, Eugene Genovese, Robert Fogel, Stanley Engerman, and Orville Burton. When these historians studied the institution of slavery, they generally agreed with the sociological school that slavery was a source of the family problems of African-Americans. However, Gutman, Blassingame, and Genovese deviated from the earlier tradition in that they viewed black culture as a synthesis of the slaves' African heritage and white culture. The disagreements among these scholars are discussed in chapter 1.

The fourth approach is the most recent development and is being set forth primarily by social scientists who have rejected earlier sociological traditions. These scholars abandoned Moynihan's matriarchal thesis and reevaluated the "disorganization" of the black family within the context of the northern migration of African-Americans within the United States. This analysis places blame on the more recent social forces that have been linked to blacks' difficult transition from the rural South to life in an urban environment. Diminishing employment opportunities, especially for black males, have also been cited as a major factor in the changing African-American family structure.[9] One example of this approach can be found in a paper by Frank Furstenberg, Theodore Hershberg, and John Modell which asserts that Gutman's statistics support their contention that the "female-headed family . . . emerged, not as a legacy of slavery but as a result of the destructive conditions of northern urban life."[10] Books on the northern migration have likewise focused renewed attention on life in the urban North as a major factor in the changes found in black marriage and family patterns.[11]

Another dimension of black family life that has to do with family structure, but is rarely included in this discussion, is the issue of adolescent childbearing among African-Americans. Although adolescent childbearing did not emerge as a social problem until the 1970s, in fact a greater proportion of black teenagers, when compared to whites, have historically become parents.[12] The study of adolescent childbearing is rarely integrated into the study of the structure and family patterns of African-Americans and is usually investigated as an isolated phenomena. I will include this most important dimension.

These rival explanations of differences in family structure among blacks are not so much wrong as incomplete. The arguments blaming "slavery only," "migration only," and the "male marriageable pool," or the independent investigation of adolescent childbearing among African-Americans are insufficient to explain much of the variance in family structure between whites and blacks. Furthermore, these explanatory approaches have not been applied to understanding the poverty found among black mother-only families who reside in inner-city neighborhoods.

The Framework of This Book

Arguments that focus on recent social forces, which are insufficient to explain much of the variance in poor blacks' family structure, only serve to perpetuate the development of policies that will continue to be ineffective in addressing their needs. This book has developed a comprehensive approach that takes into consideration the additive and cumulative effects of various factors on the black family over time. The black family is traced from slavery to its contemporary state. In addition, this book incorporates the historical evolution of adolescent childbearing in its study of the causal circumstances that have transformed African-American family structure.

Part I of this book examines the experiences of the black family through World War II; Part II describes the events affecting it from the 1950s through the 1980s; and the final chapter discusses what can be done to break the cycle of poverty among the most disadvantaged African-Americans.

Chapter 1 provides a historical context for examining the impact of slavery on the African-American family, offering a critical analysis of the historical scholarship on the institution of slavery. The major ideas set forth by each of the eminent scholars are examined, with special attention to the contributions of DuBois, Frazier, Fogel, Gutman, Genovese, and Blassingame.

Chapter 2 examines the imprint that sharecropping left on black family life. The Freedman's Bureau attempted to impose patriarchal authority on the black family rather than to facilitate the egalitarian relations that had existed during slavery. A rural proletariat emerged with a distinctive set of family formation patterns, produced by slavery and exacerbated by the sharecropping system.

Chapter 3 examines the emergence of public benefits for mother-only families. Societal notions about the deserving and undeserving poor guided the development of social policies for the poorest single mothers. When the New Deal policies were developed, agricultural labor and domestic service—the occupations in which black women were overrepresented—were not covered. The only New Deal program that most black mothers qualified for was also the most stigmatizing—Aid to Dependent Children (ADC). The differing characteristics of white and black women on welfare during this period are also discussed.

Chapter 4 focuses on the hardships black families faced as they made the transition from an agrarian to an urban existence. The economic disaster of the Great Depression, coupled with the demographic shift of blacks to urban areas, had a devastating impact on the black family. With a high rate of family desertion by black fathers as they encountered numerous obstacles to finding employment in the North, the 1930s was the decade in which mother-only black families had the greatest increase. The beginnings of a class stratification within the black community are discussed along with the emergence of "underclass" patterns of behavior among the poorest blacks.

Chapter 5 highlights the effect of World War II on the African-American family. Although defense industries contributed to growth in the economy during the war, once the war ended and these industries shut down, government policies that had been created to ensure fair employment practices were abandoned. Most of the gains blacks made during the wartime boom were wiped out. Postwar economic dislocations stranded many families, especially blacks, in new communities where job opportunities dwindled. Evidence presented in this chapter documents a high rate of black marital disintegration and an increase in the number of births to unmarried black women and adolescents.

Chapter 6 discusses changes in public policies, especially on housing and welfare, that had a devastating impact on the black family. This period witnessed not only the construction of the first high-density public housing projects, but the initiation of "suitable homes" policies by AFDC administrators that placed black mothers receiving welfare under surveillance. Urban ghettos became increasingly isolated from mainstream society, and the social and economic gaps between the black "haves" and "have-nots" widened.

Chapter 7 considers the events of the 1960s, which include the impact of the Moynihan Report and the evolution of the National Welfare Rights Organization. Two elements that are generally overlooked in discussions on the report are covered: the tensions between black women and men that spilled over into the public sphere for the first time; and Moynihan's recommendation that black males retreat to an "utterly masculine world . . . a world away from women, a world run by strong men of unquestioned authority."[13] The examination of the NWRO sheds light on the tensions between black men and women during this period, in that George Wiley took a paternalistic view of the abilities of poor women and excluded them from leadership roles in the NWRO.

Chapter 8 discusses poverty researchers' observations of some dramatic recent changes in the behavioral patterns of the most disadvantaged blacks who are residing in poverty neighborhoods. These persons are becoming increasingly involved in street crime, becoming more disconnected from the formal labor market, experiencing longer spells of poverty, and becoming increasingly dependent on welfare. Concepts like "social isolation," "concentration effects," and "the urban "underclass" have appeared in the lexicon on poverty to explain the emerging phenomena. The explanations set forth in the social science literature are critically analyzed.

Chapter 9 reopens the old debate on the consequences of family structure for African-American children, the community, and the nation as a whole. It addresses some of the questions most often debated: What are the underlying issues in welfare reform? Are black mothers willing to work? What do we do about the most disadvantaged black mothers? What can be done to break the cycle of poverty?

Notes

1. See, for example, Barbara Dafoe Whitehead, "Dan Quayle was Right," *Atlantic Monthly*, April 1993 47–50; Margaret L. Usdansky, "Single Motherhood: Stereotypes vs. Statistics," *New York Times*, February 11, 1996, E4.

2. Reynolds Farley and Walter Allen, *The Color Line and the Quality of Life in America* (New York: Oxford University Press, 1988); Thomas Espenshade, "The Recent Decline of American Marriage: Blacks and Whites in Comparative Perspective," in *Contemporary Mar-*

riage: Comparative Perspectives of a Changing Institution, ed. Kingsley Davis and A. Gross-bard-Schechtman (New York: Russell Sage Foundation, 1986), 53–90; Neil G. Bennett, David E. Bloom, and Patricia H. Craig, "The Divergence of Black and White Marriage Patterns," *American Journal of Sociology* 3(November 1989):692–722.

3. Department of Commerce, *Poverty in the United States: 1991* (Washington, D.C.: Department of Commerce, 1991), 1.

4. Quoted in Herbert Gutman, *The Black Family in Slavery and Freedom 1750–1925* (New York: Vintage, 1976), xxi.

5. David Ellwood, *Poor Support: Poverty in the American Family* (New York: Basic Books, 1988), 195.

6. Quoted in Jack Rothman, "Tinkering Won't Work on Welfare." *Los Angeles Times,* January 18, 1996, B9.

7. For additional sources on the African legacy found among slaves see, for example, Sidney W. Mintz and Richard Price, *The Birth of African-American Culture: An Anthropological Perspective* (Boston: Beacon Press, 1992) and Melville Herskovitz, *Myth of the Negro Past* (Boston: Beacon Press, 1941). Scholars reconsidering the influence of the African legacy on the family formation patterns of African-Americans include Caroline Bledsoe, "Transformation in Sub-Saharan African Marriage and Fertility," *Annals of the American Academy of Political and Social Science* 510 (July 1990):115–125, and Niara Sudarkasa, "Interpreting the African Heritage in Afro-American Family Organization," *Black Families,* ed. Harriette McAdoo (Beverly Hills: Sage Publications, 1981):37–53. For an ethnographic analysis of a Mississippi community which concluded an African heritage most influenced the black family, see Demitri B. Shimkin, Edith Shimkin, and Dennis Frate, eds., *The Extended Family in Black Societies* (The Hague: Mouton, 1978). Finally, for an examination of the ethnic and cultural aspects of race and family, see Andrew T. Miller, "Social Science, Social Policy, and the Heritage of African-American Families," in *The "Underclass" Debate: Views from History,* ed. Michael Katz (Princeton: Princeton University Press, 1993):254–292. For a valuable discussion on matrifocality, especially his definition, see N. Tanner, "Matrifocality in Indonesia and Africa and among Black Americans," in *Women, Culture, and Society,* eds. M. Z. Rosaldo and L. Lamphere.

8. Herskovitz, *Myth of the Negro Past,* 169.

9. For example, William J. Wilson reviews the literature on the transferral of poverty and welfare dependency from the South to the North and contends that more recent social forces are primarily responsible for northern poverty, e.g., the "male marriageable pool"; *The Truly Disadvantaged: The Inner City, the Underclass, and Public Policy* (Chicago, University of Chicago Press, 1987). When Paul Lammermeier studied seven cities in the Ohio Valley, he suggested reappraising E. Franklin Frazier's studies of the black family in urban cities "in light not of a cultural holdover from slavery . . . but as the result of urban life caused by poverty and discrimination;" "The Urban Black Family in the Nineteenth Century: A Study of Black Family Structure in the Ohio Valley, 1850–1880," *Journal of Marriage and the Family* 35(August 1973). Elizabeth Pleck found in her studies of the city of Boston that female-headed households were a product of the urban economic structure. She asserted that "the combined effects of poverty, sterility, and declining community regulation

of family life" produced greater marital instability among black urban families; *Black Migration and Poverty: Boston, 1865–1900* (New York: Academic Press, 1979).

10. Frank F. Furstenberg, Jr., Theodore Hershberg, and John Modell, "The Origins of the Female-Headed Black Family: The Impact of the Urban Experience," in *Philadelphia: Work, Space, Family and Group Experience in the Nineteenth Century*, ed. Theodore Hershberg (New York: Oxford University Press, 1981).

11. James Grossman, *Land of Hope: Chicago, Black Southerners, and the Great Migration* (Chicago: University of Chicago Press, 1989); Nicholas Lemann, *The Promised Land: The Great Migration and How It Changed America* (New York: Knopf, 1991).

12. Donna Franklin, "Race, Class and Adolescent Pregnancy: An Ecological Analysis." *American Journal of Orthopsychiatry* 58 (July, 1988):339–54.

13. Lee Rainwater and William L. Yancey, *The Moynihan Report and the Politics of Controversy* (Cambridge, Mass: The M.I.T. Press, 1967), 88.

PART I

CHAPTER ONE

SLAVERY: A REEXAMINATION OF ITS IMPACT

I shall forgive the white South much in its final judgment day: I shall forgive its slavery, for slavery is a world-old habit; I shall forgive its fighting for a well-lost cause, and for remembering that struggle with tender tears: I shall forgive its so-called "pride of race." . . . *but one thing I shall never forgive, neither in this world nor the world to come: its wanton and continued and persistent insulting of black womanhood which it sought and seeks to prostitute to its lust.*

W. E. B. DuBois, Darkwater: Voices from Within the Veil

Eliza Grayson was a former Mississippi slave whose husband had died while fighting in the Union Army. In 1893 she applied to the federal government for a widow's pension. A portion of the interview Julius Lemkowitz conducted with her in the Pension Office is as follows:

"Elisha Grayson and I were Mr. Montgomery's slaves before the war," Grayson told the interviewer. "We were married by Jerry Benjamin some time before the war; I cannot say when." "Who is Jerry Benjamin? . . . Was he a preacher?" Lemkowitz inquired. "He was no preacher; but being the head man on the plantation and a member of the church he married me and Elisha." "Whose permission did you get to marry? . . .

Could Jerry Benjamin read and write?" They had their master's permission, she answered, and the headman was literate. The Graysons' first son had died three months after birth but a second son, Spencer, survived. "How many children have you had before your marriage to Elisha Grayson, and who is their father?" "I had one by my master's son, Frank Montgomery," Mrs. Grayson stated, without further comment.

"After the birth of that child" and before marriage, the interviewer continued, "have you lived or cohabited with any man?" "No sir," she assured him. "I never lived with any man after that until I took up with Elisha Grayson."

"How long after your marriage to Elisha Grayson was Spencer born?" "I do not know," Mrs. Grayson replied, "but we did not 'get' him till after our marriage." Hadn't she cohabited with Elijah Hall, a married man, before Elisha enlisted in the Union Army? "No, sir." Only several years after her husband left the plantation did she "commence cohabitating" with Elijah Hall. "I was a faithful wife as long as Elisha Grayson was at home."

In answer to a query about her other children, Eliza Grayson listed four with Hall's last name, and of the remaining two, she explained, "I have had to do with several men and I cannot say really who their fathers are." Since the birth of her last child by Hall, over ten years ago, she swore, "that no man has ever touched me." The inquiry closed with the question, "By whom can you prove that your first child was by your master's son?" "By Hanson Clay, if he is living."[1]

In the aftermath of slavery, the case of Eliza Grayson is one of the first public records to disclose the effects of racial and sexual exploitation on the marriage and family patterns of African-Americans. The dialogue also reveals the complexity of concepts such as "illegitimacy," "infidelity," and "rape" when applied to the sexual conduct of former slaves and their masters.

Contemporary Debate

Four central questions have influenced the scholarly discourse on slavery: Was there a distinct slave culture in which slaves shared common views of various aspects of their lives?[2] To what extent was this culture influenced by whites? By the slaves' African heritage? Finally, did distinct family formation patterns emerge from this culture?[3]

Current debate has focused mainly on recent social forces as causes of weakened marital ties among African-Americans.[4] For example, William J. Wilson, in interpreting the history of the African-American family, has written that "[historical research] demonstrates that neither slavery, nor economic deprivation, nor the migration to urban areas affected black family structure by the first quarter of the twentieth century." Wilson constructed his argument by citing Gutman's landmark work. Gutman concluded that the black households he studied from 1725 to 1925 had two-parent families and a majority of the children were born into two-parent households.[5]

Not only have historians challenged Gutman's analyses but also social scientists—such as Andrew Cherlin, who recently asserted that "too little attention [has been given] to the historical roots of recent changes" in the family patterns of African-Americans.[6] Preston, Lim, and Morgan concurred with Cherlin's assertion

when they analyzed a public use sample from the census data of 1910, made
available in 1989:

> Frazier's account of more fluid and less formal marital arrangements in the
> rural south at the turn of the century, based on ethnographic observations
> and a skeptical use of census and other data is more accurate. Accordingly
> the role of slavery and its aftermath, and perhaps also the legacy of West
> African family traditions, deserve more than a footnote in histories of the
> evolution of the black family.[7]

After presenting the early historical research, I will reexamine more recent formulations that provide divergent perspectives on the culture that emerged among
slaves and shaped their sex mores and family formation patterns. And, while the
slave families in the antebellum era were remarkably stable, this chapter explores
various historical analyses of why the family patterns of slaves differed from whites
during the period are significant.

Some of the significant analyses in the literature on slavery have categorized
scholars as "traditional," "revisionist," or "neorevisionist." In my view, these ru-
dimentary groupings obscure some crucial nuances found in the scholarly discourse.[8] I focus, accordingly, on certain ideas set forth by DuBois, Frazier, Stampp,
Elkins, Fogel, Genovese, Gutman, and Blassingame, and some of the counterviews
that have emerged to challenge their scholarship.

Early Explanations of the Effects of Slavery

In writing *The Philadelphia Negro* at the turn of the century, DuBois dated nearly
all of his analyses from the arrival of people of African descent in the city and in
a section on family structure, he drew on the African experience. In 1909 he
observed that although black slaves could not "trace an unbroken social history
from Africa" he insisted there was a "distinct nexus existed between Africa and
America." He then urged that the study of historical evidence might uncover "the
unbroken thread of African and American history."[9] It was Carter G. Woodson,
however, who argued forcibly that it was the African heritage of black Americans
that most influenced their beliefs and practices.[10]

Melville Herskovits carried this analysis further than other scholars in *The Myth
of the Negro Past*. When Herskovits discussed the causes underlying the "matriarchal
Negro family," he traced this phenomenon to the polygynous West African societies. In his view, this social organization had important implications for understanding kinship groups and the strength of the bond between the black mother
and her children. In polygynous African societies, he said, the "responsibilities of
upbringing, discipline, and supervision are much more the province of the mother

than of the father."[11] Numerous other scholars have recently reaffirmed the general unity of African culture and the fact that it influenced the family systems of blacks in America.[12]

In *The Negro American Family*, however, DuBois moved away from the emphasis on African heritage of blacks to provide a balanced picture of family life, in reaction against invectives that were being directed at the sexual mores of many blacks.[13] The book's objective was to "show a greater internal differentiation of social conditions" among blacks; he asserted that the failure to recognize class differences is the "cause of much confusion." He described the family lives of thirteen rural and urban families in order to portray the emergence of the "better classes." DuBois reflected his generation's view of social class in his description of poor families as the "lowest type of a country family" and of two of the most stable families with larger incomes as the "higher type of Negro families."[14]

Slavery was DuBois's explanation for the "disorganization" he found among the poorest black families.[15] He pointed to sharp differences between the family patterns of house servants and those of field hands during slavery. Among the former, "religion and marriage rites received more attention and the Negro monogamic family rose as a dependent offshoot of their feudal slave regime." Among the latter, especially those who survived a ruthless overseer, "there was no family life, no meals, no marriages, no decency, only an endless round of toil and a wild debauch at Christmas time."

DuBois also noted that slavery had a crippling effect on the slave father, who lacked the authority to govern or protect his family. In DuBois's view, "his wife could be made his master's concubine, his daughter could be outraged, his son whipped, or he himself sold away without being able to protest or lift a preventing finger." He asserted that the position of the mother was also undermined. Whether field hand or house servant, she could spend little or no time in her own home, so "her children had little care or attention." According to DuBois, she was "often the concubine of the master or his sons," and she could be separated from her family at any time by the "master's command or by his death or debts."

In DuBois's view, a weakened black family emerged from slavery with a dual set of sexual mores. One pattern, which emerged from the house servants, was monogamic with stable two-parent families. Another set of sexual mores was associated with field hands, and these family patterns were described as single parents and children born to unwed mothers. DuBois attributes these differences in sex mores among blacks to the institution of slavery: "[T]he great body of field hands were raped of their own sex customs and provided with no binding new ones."[16]

E. Franklin Frazier, examining family formation patterns among rural black women, extended the formulations of DuBois. He focused on the high rate of nonmarital births among blacks, but replaced DuBois's concept of the monogamic family and dual sex mores with the concept of a dual family structure (two-parent and single parent). In making this transition Frazier borrowed DuBois's idea that such differences emerged from the occupational structure on the plantations: field hands were more likely to be single parents; artisans and house servants had a more stable two-parent family structure. Frazier went beyond DuBois to describe black women emerging as a more controlling force in the slave household—self-reliant, self-sufficient, and lacking a "spirit of subordination to masculine authority."[17]

The Emergence of the "Sambo" Thesis

Kenneth Stampp and Stanley Elkins have more recently produced two major histories of slavery that are consistent with the analyses of DuBois and Frazier but emphasize the demoralizing aspects of slavery with little attention to the strengths reported by DuBois and Frazier. Like Du Bois and Frazier, Stampp moved away from emphasizing the slaves' African heritage when he described the social disorganization created by the institution of slavery:

> In Africa, the Negroes had been accustomed to a strictly regulated family and a rigidly enforced moral code. But in America the disintegration of their social organization removed the traditional sanctions which had encouraged them to respect their old customs . . . The slaves had lost their native culture without being able to find a workable substitute and therefore lived in a kind of cultural chaos.[18]

With the destruction of family life and the rigid moral code that had prevailed in Africa, the consequences were "an air of impermanence" in the typical slave family. This ephemeral status was further exacerbated by a custom employed by a great majority of slaveholders, who, according to Stampp, gave preference to business over sentiment and broke up families when under financial pressure. Stampp did agree with Frazier that the slave family was matriarchal and that "the male slave's only crucial function within the family was that of siring offspring." Slave parents, in Stampp's view, regarded their children with indifference; "sexual promiscuity was widespread."[19] He argued further that a slave would be assured of his master's affection only if he conformed to the rules of conduct that governed his relations with his master and carefully observed "the fine line between friskiness and insubordination, between cuteness and insolence"; a slave had to adopt the pose of a "fawning dependent," a relationship that robbed slaves of their self-confidence and promoted "infantilization."[20]

Building on Stampp's description of the repressive power of the masters, Stanley Elkins argues that this power was so great that it reduced the slave to an infantile dependence on the master. His book, *Slavery: a Problem in American Institutional and Intellectual Life*, infused new life into the debate on the black family by introducing the "Sambo" proposition: Slavery not only emasculated the black man and undermined his parental and spousal authority, but his personality was also altered and he was reduced to a docile and dependent "Sambo."

> For the Negro child, in particular, the plantation offers no really satisfactory father image other than the master. The "real" father was virtually without authority over his child, since discipline, parental responsibility, and control of rewards and punishments all rested in others' hands; the slave father could not even protect the mother of his children except by appealing directly to the master. Indeed, the mother's own role loomed far larger for the slave child than did that of the father.[21]

In this view the African slaves could have resisted the forces that were embedded in the institution of slavery only if they had had "some sort of alternative force of moral and psychological orientation." However, slaves lived in "social isolation," and the "problem of the Negro in slavery times involved the virtual absence of such forces."[22] Elkins's implicit characterization of the slave as docile, emasculated, and compliant has continued to shape the stereotypical images of African-American males in popular literary descriptions.

The Moynihan Report and the Emergence of a Counterview

In 1965 the Moynihan Report set off an extraordinary series of critical reactions to the "class-culture" thesis it contained.[23] Moynihan's analysis of the mid-twentieth-century black family had a colossal impact on the generation of scholars who were emerging at that time. Moynihan quoted Frazier and described a "lower-class" subculture found in the African-American community. Moynihan expressed concern that marital dissolution, out-of-wedlock-births, and reliance on welfare were increasing among African-Americans. It was the content of this report that provoked the next series of scholarly investigations into the impact of slavery on the African-American family.[24] (Chapter 7 gives a comprehensive analysis of the Moynihan Report.)

A group of historians emerged during the 1970s catalyzed by the Moynihan report to challenge many of the ideas set forth by scholars who had studied the aftermath of slavery and its effect on the African-American family. In carefully constructed and persuasive arguments on slave survival strategies, they criticized earlier scholars for underestimating the extent to which slaves were able to shape their own culture and for minimizing the extent to which the African heritage was incorporated into that culture. For example, Frazier, Stampp, and Elkins had argued that the institution of slavery had destroyed the African heritage (DuBois changed his position over time). Fogel and Engerman, Gutman, Blassingame, and Genovese challenged this paradigm and instead viewed the slave culture as a synthesis of the slaves' African heritage and the whites' culture.[25] These historians utilized differing methods, however, when analyzing slave culture. Fogel and Engerman incorporated methods from the disciplines of economics and history, whereas Gutman, Blassingame, and Genovese employed conventional historical methods.

Econometrics and the Analysis of Slave Culture

Robert Fogel and Stanley Engerman were some of the first scholars to apply econometric practice to the study of slavery. Their book, *Time on the Cross: The Economics of American Negro Slavery*, provoked considerable controversy with its new conclusions about slavery, which constituted "an entirely new portrayal of slavery's past" and challenged "virtually every assumption that has been made about the management of slaves, their work habits, their domestic welfare."[26]

In an attempt to challenge one of the major ideas set forth by Moynihan, one of the myths this book attempted to dispute was the belief that slave breeding, sexual exploitation, and promiscuity destroyed the black family. Fogel and Engerman argued instead that the family was the basic unit of social organization under slavery and "it was in the economic interest of planters to encourage the stability of slave families and most of them did so."[27]

Fogel and Engerman, examining a sample of records from thirty plantations around New Orleans and a small census sample, agreed with other historians studying the slave family that it was not "merely a copy of the white family" but was, in addition, influenced by their African heritage and their "particular socioeconomic characteristics." The result was a family life with characteristics that were, if not restricted to, at least more frequent among black than white families." They also asserted that "it is not true that the typical slave family was matriarchal in form . . . and the male slave's only crucial function within the family was that of siring offspring."[28]

According to Fogel and Engerman, planters recognized husbands as heads of families. In an attempt to challenge the prevailing ideas about slave women as the more controlling force during slavery, they presented evidence from the city of Charleston as an example that it was slave men, not slave women, who occupied virtually all the managerial positions on the plantations.

According to Fogel and Engerman, the family was the main instrument for promoting the increase of the slave population. Planters believed that fertility rates would be highest when the family was the strongest. Planters promoted the stability of the slave families by combining a system of rewards for marriage and sanctions against adultery and divorce. Although slave marriages were explicitly denied under legal codes, they were promoted and recognized under plantation codes.

What emerges from Fogel and Engerman is a portrayal of planters as moral individuals with humanistic values who conducted good business practices; and this characterization of the planter has come under vociferous attack. The authors have defended themselves in two ways: They have asserted that not all planters lived by the moral codes of their day and that slave women were not exploited sexually by white males because only 9.9 percent of the rural black population were mulatto in 1860. Critics have replied that it is impossible to quantify sexual exploitation.

On a related issue, Fogel and Engerman considered the role of planters in the destabilization of slave families by using 5,000 records of the interstate sale of slaves in New Orleans. Many historians had argued that many slave families were separated and sometimes obliterated when they were sold by slaveholders who chose business over sentiment when they were experiencing financial strains. While the authors concede that the records "contain no statements regarding whether or not slaves were sold without husbands (or wives) or were separated from their spouses as a consequence of being traded," they nevertheless assert that slave families were rarely separated.[29] Blassingame argues that such an assertion is like "flipping a coin and ignoring all the times it comes up tails."[30]

Qualitative Historians' Counterview on Slave Culture

Another group of historians shared Fogel and Engerman's disenchantment with the existing paradigm on the slave family but launched their challenge using a descriptive rather than a quantitative approach. John Blassingame, Herbert Gutman, and Eugene Genovese agreed that historians and sociologists had misunderstood the slave family and argued that the black family emerged from bondage with a remarkable degree of stability.[31]

Writing from a Marxist perspective, Genovese used sources that included use of fugitive autobiographies and the interviews of thousands of former slaves conducted in the 1920s and 1930s by scholars at Fisk University and the WPA Writers' Project. He asserted that the slaves "created impressive norms of family life, including as much of a nuclear family norm as conditions permitted, and that they entered the postwar social system with a remarkably stable base." Many families became "indifferent or demoralized," Genovese argues, "but those with a strong desire for family stability were able to set norms for life in freedom that could serve their own interests and function reasonably within the wider social system of a white-dominated America."[32]

In Genovese's view, the masters understood the strength of the marital and family ties among their slaves as "a powerful means of social control." He introduced the idea of paternalism as a way of discussing the influence the planters were able to exert over their slaves. Genovese believed that religious tenets rationalized paternalism but at the same time for the slave defined specific limits to white hegemony.

> Southern paternalism may have reinforced racism as well as class exploitation but it also unwittingly invited its victims to fashion their own interpretation of the social order it was intended to justify. And the slaves, drawing on a Christian religion that was supposed to ensure their compliance and docility, rejected the essence of slavery by protecting their rights and values as human beings.[33]

Primarily utilizing published autobiographies of runaway slaves, Blassingame's was the first major reinterpretation of slavery to follow Elkins's book.[34] Blassingame accepted Elkins's Sambo as realistic, but would give us two others—Jack, the trickster, and Nat, the rebel.[35] He argued that slaves were not devoid of institutional support, and he recognized the influence of masters. Blassingame's major departure from Elkins was to place more emphasis on the role of the white church in promoting sexual fidelity among married slaves and in attempting to restrain masters from breaking up families. He maintains that the African slaves' beliefs and practices were transformed by their Christianization and that the slave family served as a buffer to the harsh realities of slavery.[36] In Blassingame's view, although the slave family was frequently broken, it was able to survive on the plantation without becoming totally dependent on and submissive to the master.

Blassingame's initial descriptions of the slave family reflected the influence of Frazier's ideas about the dual family structure. Departing from Frazier, though, he did not limit the development of the male-absent families primarily to field hands, but found monogamous families among all occupational slave groups. He also pointed to the strength of the monogamous family in the autobiographies of former slaves.

Blassingame agreed with other historians that the black family had been weakened by the institution of slavery, but attributed this destabilization to the master's intrusive sexual exploitation of the slaves. According to Blassingame, the white man's pursuit of black women frequently destroyed any possibility that "comely black girls could remain chaste for long."[37] Frederick Douglass likewise declared that the "slave woman is at the mercy of the fathers, sons or brothers of her master."[38]One of the reasons that these interracial unions were so destructive to family life is that there were legal prohibitions against black-white marriages.[39]

In contrast, Gutman, who did not analyze the role of the masters and the white

Christian church in the slave family's development, portrayed the slave family based on records of six large slaveholdings located mainly in black counties, selected because they had exceptional records. Through a careful analysis of plantation birth registers, marriage applications received by Union officers following emancipation, and documents containing the direct testimony of former slaves, Gutman reconstructed the slave family and kinship structure and showed an adaptive African-American culture that was created without any significant influence by slaveowners. African-American slaves developed independently with distinctive kin and family arrangements that fostered a new culture of social and communal obligations, which provided the social basis for the African-American community over time and across space.[40]

The Impact of Slave Culture on Family Formation Patterns

The issue of the distinct family formation patterns found among slaves was also analyzed by scholars during this period. Gutman viewed family formation patterns as shaped by enslavement, stating that "much indirect evidence suggests a close relationship between the relatively early age of a slave woman at the birth of a first child, prenuptial intercourse . . . and the economic needs of slaveowners.[41] Genovese seems to agree with Gutman on how the early childbearing patterns emerged among slaves, but views them within the context of marriage: "Many slaves, if not most, married in their mid-teens or later, possibly earlier than most well-to-do whites. . . . Most masters let the slaves pick their own partners at their own pace and relied on natural desires to accomplish reasonably early mating."[42]

Although Genovese did not comment directly on this matter, my inference from his writing is that he perceived these early childbearing patterns as emerging out of a "paternalistic compromise." Paul Escott captured the major thrust and complexity of Genovese's argument when he stated that Genovese "asserted the moral independence and cultural unity of the slaves, yet always emphasized more strongly the pervasive and controlling influence of the masters."[43]

Gutman carried this argument further, maintaining that slave births were viewed differently by slaves and their owners.[44] The owner viewed the birth of a slave child primarily from an economic standpoint; for slaves it was more reflective of social and familial beliefs that bound slave men and women together in affective kin groups. Gutman nevertheless asserted, "Doubtless they realized that if they had children early, their owners would have both economic and ethical reasons to allow them to remain together."[45]

Within the institution of slavery, the slaves developed their own standards of morality and sexual propriety, standards that deviated from those prevailing among influential whites.[46] For example, Genovese noted that even the "more conservative parents who married their daughters off young did not get hysterical if their unmarried daughters got pregnant. . . . A slave girl's chances to get the man she wanted did not slip much because she had an illegitimate child."[47] Whereas European and American values focused on establishing paternity, distinct norms among slaves emphasized marriage while refraining from stigmatizing women who gave birth outside of marriage.[48]

According to Genovese, the objective of the slave women was to live respectably and happily with one man; virginity at marriage carried only small prestige. Slaves also had a clear prohibition against postmarital philandering, which ranked as a serious offense. Leon Litwack lent support to Genovese's observation when he quoted the owner of a Georgia plantation as stating, "The Negroes had their own ideals of morality, and held to them very strictly; they did not consider it wrong for a girl to have a child before she married, but afterwards were extremely severe upon anything like infidelity on her part."[49]

Gutman has provided one of the more incisive analyses of why prenuptial intercourse, which was common among both indentured servants and slaves, survived much longer among slaves:

> Reproducing the slave labor required only the simple biological dyad "mother and child." The social dyads "husband and wife" and "father and child" were not essential. Neither was the completed nuclear family. But many owners, who did little to discourage prenuptial intercourse among their slaves, nevertheless encouraged the formation of completed slave families. . . . Slave women mostly counted in the calculation of their owners as mothers, and slave men counted as laborers.[50]

Drew Faust provided support to this observation and elaborated on how the slaveowner used the family unit as a means of social control, commenting that the correlation between positive family ties and a reduction in escape attempts did not go unnoticed by the slaveowner.[51]

Thomas L. Webber summarized the viewpoint shared by most of the historians who studied slavery during this period:

> American slaves fashioned a new culture from both the culture fountain of African past and the crucible of their experiences under slavery in the South. Slave culture had at its heart a set of cultural themes, forms of artistic expression, a religion, a family pattern, and a commonly structure which set blacks apart from whites and enabled them to form and control a world of their own values and definitions.[52]

In Webber's view, the plantation owners used all the instruments of power at their disposal to shape slaves into their image of a "good" slave.

The difference among the historians of this period are the degree to which they believed that the culture that arose among slaves was a form of resistance to their environmental conditions. Blassingame, Gutman and Genovese disagreed on the role of external forces in producing the family norms and sexual mores of the slaves. Blassingame recognized the influence of the planters and viewed them as avaricious but emphasized the role of the white church in restraining planters from breaking up families and in promoting marital fidelity among slaves. Genovese, on the other hand, perceived a stronger impact of plantation owners and overseers on slave family life than did Blassingame. While he agreed with Blassingame that families were broken up by the slave trade, Genovese argued that such sales were either delayed or avoided, not because of the good will of the planters but because of the resentment that such sales would cause among the slaves. Genovese viewed planters as mainly concerned about undermining the "morale of the labor force."[53] Genovese described the sexual mores of slaves as rather contemporary regarding sexual freedom for single female slaves and more Victorian regarding such freedom for married female slaves. Gutman presents the clearest portrait of slaves who were not influenced by the planters, and he found more stability and uniformity in the slave family than did Blassingame or Genovese. He also downplayed the interaction between planters and slaves and emphasized the fusion of the experiences of the slaves in the New World and their African heritage.

Variability in the Slave Family Structure

Disparities in the findings of historians who have studied slave culture have demonstrated that the methodological approach is an important factor in the conclusions that are generated.[54] An econometric analysis conducted by Stephen Crawford is one of the more definitive in asserting that the plantation's size, not the slaves' occupation, as proposed by DuBois and Frazier, primarily determined the quality of slave family life.[55] This study is viewed as rigorous in that when Crawford applied statistical analyses to the interviews with former slaves conducted by Fisk University scholars in 1929 and the WPA Writers' Project in the 1930s, he was able to demonstrate that the views of the two groups were quite similar. Constructing a distribution of households in which 742 slaves under age thirteen were raised, Crawford found that on such matters as the stability of the family, the occupation of the slaves, the usage of leisure time, and the severity and type of punishment, the experiences of slaves on smaller plantations differed significantly from that of slaves living on large ones.

Crawford initially did not control for plantation size, reporting that 66 percent lived in two-parent families, 24 percent in single-parent families, and 10 percent lived alone or in the master's quarters. When he controlled for the size of the plantation, however, Crawford found that single-parent families were 50 percent more prevalent on plantations with fifteen or fewer slaves than on large ones. He found that about 60 percent of the single-parent households had been created because families had been separated by slavery, in particular by the slave trade.

Studies controlling for plantation size have shown how earlier historians might have conceptualized experiences of the slave family differently, even when using similar sources such as the narratives of former slaves. Orville Burton's investigation of the narratives of the experiences of nineteenth-century black and white families in Edgefield, South Carolina, confirmed Crawford's findings: Small slaveowners were more susceptible to economic crises that resulted in the separation of slaves through sale or rental. Also, whites who had one or two slaves might have had sexual relations with them, whereas on large plantations the "slave communities served as a buffer against white oppression."[56]

Richard Steckel analyzed a larger and more representative sample of data and likewise controlled for plantation size.[57] He discovered that the proportion of women who bore children was substantially lower on plantations with 100 or more slaves than on those with just a few. Steckel explained that although the masters encouraged marriage, they also insisted on maintaining the rigid labor discipline of the gang system.[58] But on slave plantations too small to sustain a gang system, slaves were permitted to fraternize with slaves on other farms and to marry slaves belonging to other owners. As a result, slave women on small farms typically married younger, had longer childbearing periods, and were less likely to remain childless than the women on the big gang-system farms.[59]

Crawford's earlier analysis had provided an alternative interpretation of the way plantation size influenced the slaves' family patterns. He found that in one out of every six of the single slave mothers, the father was white. He also found that the probability of having a white father was also higher on small plantations.[60] When Steckel analyzed data in the manuscript schedules of the 1860 census, his findings were consistent with those of Crawford. Using a more powerful statistical technique and a larger sample than could be obtained from the interviews with former slaves used by Crawford, Steckel found that on average, one out of every ten slave children was mulatto. He also demonstrated that this proportion likely to be was seven times as high on a farm of ten slaves engaged in mixed farming than it was on a cotton plantation of seventy-five slaves in the deep South. According to Steckel, the proportion of mulatto children was highest on small slave units in large predominately white cities and lowest on large plantations in the rice-growing region where the density of whites was low. The findings of Crawford, Burton, and Steckel show us why single parents were more prevalent and two-parent families under greater pressure on small plantations.[61]

The experiences of Jane Peterson, a slave women on a small plantation, illustrate the slave woman's vulnerability to sexual exploitation by the planter:

> Aunt Jane Peterson, old friend of mine, come to visit me nearly every year after she got so old. She told me things took place in slavery times. She was in Virginia till after freedom. She had two girls and a boy with a white daddy. She told me all abut how that come. She said no chance to run off or ever get off, you had to stay and take what come. She never got to marry till after freedom. Then she had three more black children by her husband. She said she was the cook. Old Master say, "Jane, go to the lot and get the eggs." She was scared to go and scared not to go. He'd beat her out there, put her head between the slip gap where they let hogs into the pasture from the lot down back of the barn. She say, "Old Missus whip me. This ain't right." He'd laugh. Said she bore three of his children in a room in the same house his family lived in. She lived in the same house. She had a room so she could build fires and cook breakfast by four o'clock sometimes, she said. She was so glad freedom comes on and soon as she heard it she took her children and was gone. . . . Part white children sold for more than black children. They used them for house girls.[62]

Slavery and Early Childbearing Patterns

In discussing the sexual practices of slaves, Gutman asserted that the essential value of adult women rested on their capacity to reproduce the labor force. The institution of slavery put a premium on females who began to bear children early, both inside and outside marriage. The issue of whether or not slavery produced the early childbearing patterns found among slave women is a thorny one, and the calculations of the age at first birth of slave women have varied.[63] The strongest evidence for the earlier childbearing patterns found among slaves comes from Richard Steckel when he compared slave fertility behaviors with those of whites during the same period. He found that slaves' mean age at first birth was lower than whites' by 2.1 years in probate data comparison and 1.3 years in plantation record data comparison.[64]

At the same time, Steckel challenged Gutman's generalizations about sexual mores among adolescent slaves. He argued that slave women who eventually bore children abstained from sexual intercourse for a substantial period after they became fertile. The average age of slave women at the birth of their first child was about twenty-one, while the average age of menarche was about fourteen and a half. If adolescent slave women had been having sexual intercourse regularly from the onset of menses, as Gutman suggested, they would on average have had a child by the age of sixteen or seventeen. According to Steckel's calculations, the average interval of adolescent abstention from sexual intercourse lasted at least three years.[65] It follows that a substantial proportion of slave women must have abstained from sexual intercourse during much of their adolescence.

Steckel and Gutman also disagreed about whether there was a relationship between marriage and fecundity. Steckel has suggested that for many adolescent and young adults marriage or the anticipation of marriage precipitated the beginning of sexual intercourse. To provide evidence for this, he shows that first births were correlated with the seasonal pattern of marriages, which were concentrated after the harvest and in the slack period between the end of cultivation and the beginning of harvest.

To support his reasoning further, Steckel has also noted that there was more abstention from sexual intercourse among unmarried adult slave women than Gutman inferred. The proportion of slave women living through their childbearing years without ever bearing a child was higher on large plantations (19 percent) than on small plantations (10 percent), and higher on the cotton farms of Georgia and Louisiana (16 percent) than on the tobacco and wheat farms of Virginia (8 percent). Steckel concludes that such high rates of childlessness could not be attributed to physiological sterility alone and estimates that roughly 10 percent of slave women avoided births throughout those years by either abstaining from sexual intercourse until they reached the end of their childbearing lives or by practicing effective contraception.

Steckel addressed another important issue: the extent to which slave women were monogamous in their sexual relationships. When he analyzed the birth records of 525 pairs of births of slave women, he found that women tended to be linked with only one man. In another sample of 413 slave marriages obtained from Civil War pension files, Steckel found that "there was not a single case of more than one woman applying for benefits from a given man."[66]

Steckel's more recent analyses demonstrate that slave culture differed from one plantation to another and that the degree of the slaveowners' influence on slave practices and beliefs was determined by the size of the plantation. These studies also support the ideas set forth by Gutman, Genovese, Blassingame, and Fogel and Engerman that the black family emerged from slavery with remarkable stability.

Conclusion

Reexamining the impact of slavery on the African-American family, contemporary scholars of slave culture argue that it developed as an adaptation to the slaves' environmental conditions. In addition, all of them recognize at least the indirect influence of whites on this culture. The historians also agree that, regardless of both the idiosyncratic policies of individual slaveowners and the specific plantation culture, most slaves shared some rudiments of an African heritage, placed a priority on relations with kin, accepted various components of Christianity, and sought varying degrees of independence from their masters. In that slaves were not allowed legal marriage and all births during slavery were out of wedlock, what emerged out of this slave culture was a value system that refrained from stigmatizing the offspring of women who gave birth outside of marriage. In addition, two distinct types of family structures emerged from slavery—single parent and two parent families.

What accounts for much of the variance in the different analyses is the failure of some historians to take into account the size of the plantation. Studies have shown that the dual family structure found among African-American families that emerged from slavery was based on the size of the plantation in which those families resided and not the occupational structure on plantations, as Frazier had suggested. On the smaller plantations, slave families were more likely to be separated by sale, and slave women were more likely to have sexual relations with the planters and more likely to become pregnant as teenagers (even though early childbearing patterns, when compared to whites, were found on both large and small plantations); these factors contributed to the much larger proportion of mother-only families. While Frazier argued that single slave mothers were more likely to be field hands, these more recent econometric analyses have demonstrated that single slave mothers were those most likely to have had close contact with the slaveowners who had the smaller plantations. These slaveowners were more intrusive and had a more disruptive influence on the lives of these mother-only slave families.

Gutman, who found so much more stability and uniformity in the slave family than did other historians, based his findings on the records of six plantations with large slaveholdings.[67] He chose these particular plantations because they had exceptional birth registers that permitted him to investigate the intergenerational patterns of marriage among slave families. These types of records were not usually generated on small plantations. Gutman's findings are consistent with the work of other historians who found that these plantations had the least intrusion from whites. In that most slaves were on large rather than small plantations, this factor is the clearest explanation for the stability of the majority of black families following emancipation.

A reexamination of the historical literature on slavery draws attention to the fact that the marriage and family patterns of African-Americans are related to a distinctive set of experiences they have had in this country. These experiences have been created as the cultural expectations of African-American families have interacted with societal institutions, and it is the combination of these factors that has generated changes in family structure over time.

Notes

1. John D'Emilio and Estelle B. Freedman, *Intimate Matters: A History of Sexuality in America* (New York: Harper & Row, 1988): 5–6.

2. I am using the term *culture* as it has been conceptualized by Sidney W. Mintz. Mintz finds in culture "a kind of resource" and in society "a kind of arena," the distinction being "between sets of historically available alternatives or forms on the one hand, and the societal circumstances or settings within which these forms may be employed on the other. . . . Culture is *used*; and any analysis of its use immediately brings into view the arrangements of persons in societal groups for whom cultural forms confirm, reinforce, maintain, change, or deny particular arrangements of status, power, and identity"; "Foreword," in *Afro-American Anthropology: Contemporary Perspectives*, ed. Norman Whitten and John F. Swzed, (New York: Free Press 1970), 1–16.

3. For a historical analysis that traces the underclass to the slave plantations and to a "distinct underclass of slaves," see Orlando Patterson, "Toward a Study of Black America: Notes on the Culture of Racism," *Dissent* 36 (Fall 1989):476–86.

4. Works whose central concern is the role of mother-only families in the families in the persistent poverty found in black ghettos include Ken Auletta, *The Underclass* (NY: Random House), 1982; Isabel Sawhill, "The Underclass: Part 1, an Overview," *Public Interest* (month 1989); William Darity, Jr., and Samuel Myers, Jr., "Changes in Black Family Structure: Implications for Welfare Dependency," *American Economic Review* 73 (Summer, 1983):59–70; Irwin Garfinkel and Sara McLanahan, *Single Mothers and Their Children: A New American Dilemma* (Washington D.C., Urban Institute Press 1986); and Andrew Cherlin, *Marriage, Divorce, Remarriage* (Cambridge, MA: Harvard Univerity Press, 1992).

5. William J. Wilson, *The Truly Disadvantaged: The Inner City, the Underclass, and Public Policy* (Chicago: University of Chicago Press, 1987), 64. In citing Gutman, many scholars, like Wilson, interpreted this finding as evidence that there were no differences between black and white familial patterns. But this is not the case. Not only have historians successfully challenged Gutman's work, but Gutman himself argued that the fertility behaviors of slaves were influenced by the institution of slavery, especially the early childbearing patterns. Gutman also documented higher rates of male-absent households among blacks compared to native-born whites.

6. Historians who have successfully challenged Gutman's scholarship include Mechal Sobel, *The World They Made Together: Black and White Values in 18th-Century Virginia* (Princeton: Princeton University Press, 1987); Cheryl Ann Cody, "There was no 'Absalom' on the Ball Plantation: Slave-Naming Practices in the South Carolina Low Country, 1720–1865," *American Historical Review* 92 (June, 1987):563–596; Phillip Morgan, "Three Planters and Their Slaves: Perspectives in Slavery in Virginia, South Carolina and Jamaica, 1750–

1790," in *Race and Family in the Colonial South*, ed. W. D. Jordan and S. Skemp (Jackson: University of Mississippi Press, 1987).

In the 1981 edition of *Marriage, Divorce, Remarriage*, Andrew Cherlin argued, like many other social scientists during the same period, that "the family patterns of urban blacks differ today from the patterns among whites in large part because of differences in the current experiences of city-born-and-bred blacks and whites. Instead of looking back to slavery or to the rural, postbellum South, we need to look at life in the cities today." In his 1992 edition, he asserted "I now think that was an overstatement that paid too little attention to the historical roots of the recent changes." (170, n. 76.)

7. Samuel Preston, Suet Lim, and S. Phillip Morgan, "African-American Marriage in 1910: Beneath the Surface of Census Data," *Demography* 29 (February 1992):13. Preston and Lim, at the University of Pennsylvania, are conducting a research project that is focusing on widowhood reports to determine if they mask a substantial amount of nonmarriage, separation, or divorce. Some have speculated that taking these widowhood reports at face value would overestimate the effects of mortality on black/white family differences.

8. For a superb review of this literature, see, for example, Brenda E. Stevenson, "Black Family Structure in Colonial and Antebellum Virginia: Amending the Revisionist Perspective," in *The Decline in Marriage among African Americans*, ed. M. Belinda Tucker and Claudia Mitchell-Kernan (New York: Russell Sage Foundation, 1995), 28–56. For further discussion of these revisionist perspectives, see Orlando Patterson, "The Crisis of Gender Relations among African Americans," in *Race, Gender, and Power in America*, ed. Anita Hill and Emma Jordan (New York: Oxford University Press, 1995); especially see pp. 61–65.

9. W. E. B. DuBois, The Philadelphia Negro: A Social History (1899; reprint, New York: Schocken Books, 1981); and *The Negro-American Family* (1909; reprint, Chicago, Il: University of Chicago Press, 1978), 9.

10. Carter G. Woodson, *The African Background Outlines* (Washington, D.C.: Association for the Study of Negro Life and History, 1936).

11. Melville J. Herskovits, *The Myth of the Negro Past* (Boston: Beacon Press, 1941), 169.

12. For scholars who argue that the African heritage did have an impact on the black family, see Sidney Mintz and Richard Price, *An Anthropological Approach to the Afro-American Past* (Philadelphia: Institute for the Study of Human Issues, 1976); Wade Nobles, "Africanity: Its Role in Black Families," *Black Scholar* 5 (June 1974): 10–17; Ron Lesthaeghe, *Reproduction and Social Organization in Sub-Saharan Africa* (Berkeley: University of California Press, 1989); Niara Sudarkasa, "Interpreting the African Heritage in Afro-Amrican Family Organization," in *Black Families*, ed. Harriette McAdoo (Beverly Hills, Calif.: Sage, 1981); see also Robert Farris Thompson, *Flash of the Spirit* (New York: Random House, 1983), which addresses the question of cultural "survivals" of Africa in the United States by establishing African links in language, religion, and folktales.

13. By the 1850s, theories of biological and genetic determinants of racial differences were prevalent. For representative works see George Fitzhugh, *Cannibals All! or, Slaves Without Masters* (1857; reprint, C. Van Woodward, ed., Cambridge, Mass.: Harvard University

Press, Belknap Press, 1960); Henry Hughes, *Treatise on Sociology* (Philadelphia: 1854). These works generally found black people incapable of any stable family life, thus in need of patriarchal masters. For explanations of the distinct sexual mores found among blacks during this period, see, for example, Frederick Hoffman, who, after reviewing data on crime and nonmarital rates among blacks concluded that "neither religion nor education has influenced to any appreciable degree the moral progress of the race"; *Race Traits and Tendencies of the American Negro* (NY: Dix & Edwards, 1896) 236. And James Rhodes observed that not only was licentiousness a natural inclination of the African race, but slave women, due to their "entire lack of chastity [,] had yielded without objection, except in isolated cases, to the passion of their masters"; *History of the United States from the Compromise of 1850* (NY: Harper & Bros, 1893), 318, 332, 335.

14. DuBois, *Negro American Family*, 127–130.

15. DuBois decided to focus on the institution of slavery in that the prevailing belief was the one set forth by Ulrich Bonnel Phillips, who found no evidence to *support the existence* of slave breeding in the antebellum South; *American Negro Slavery* (NY: D. Appleton & Co., 1918) 7.

16. W. E. B. DuBois, *Negro American Family*, 47, 49.

17. E. Franklin Frazier, *The Negro Family in the United States* (reprint; Chicago: University of Chicago Press 1966), 1939; 125. This argument has been more recently challenged by a new generation of scholars studying the American institution of slavery. For a conception of the slave family as matrifocal with sex-stratified roles for both males and females, see Deborah Gray White *Arn't I a Woman?* (:1986), For an argument on the dominance of the male slave, see Robert W. Fogel and Stanley L. Engerman, *Time on the Cross* (Boston: Little, Brown, 1974). Scholars providing evidence on the equality and shared authority and responsibility of male and females slaves include John Blassingame, *The Slave Community: Plantation Life in the Antebellum South* (New York: Oxford University, 1972); Eugene Genovese, *Roll Jordan, Roll: the World the Slaves Made* (New York: Panthcon, 1974); and Jacqueline Jones, *Labor of Love, Labor of Sorrow: Black Women's Work and the Family from Slavery to the Present* (New York: Basic Books, 1985). While Jones agreed with equality concept set forth by Genovese and Blassingame, she further noted that this concept of equality was virtually meaningless in that both male and females slaves were reduced to a state of powerlessness within the institution of slavery.

18. Kenneth M. Stampp, *The Peculiar Institution: Slavery in the Ante-Bellum South* (New York: Knopf, 1956), 340.

19. Ibid., 343–48.

20. Ibid., 327, 329.

21. Stanley M. Elkins, *Slavery: A Problem in American Institutional and Intellectual Life* (Chicago: University of Chicago Press, 1959), 130.

22. Ibid., 239–45. For challenges to Elkins's thesis, see, for example, Roy Simon Bryce-LaPorte, "Slaves as Inmates, Slaves as Man: A Sociological Discussion of Elkins' Thesis," in *Debate Over Slavery:Stanley Elkins and his Critics.* (Urbana: University of Illinois Press, 1971), ed. Ann J. Lane. See also Blassingame, *Slave Community*; Fogel and Engerman, *Time on the Cross*; Frederickson and Lasch, "Resistance to Slavery," in *Civil War History* 13 (1967):

315–29. Robert Fogel notes that "most scholars believed Elkins' view was too extreme, but his critics were divided on the degree of exaggeration"; *Without Consent or Contract: The Rise and Fall of American Slavery* (New York: W. W Norton, 1989), 172.

23. This argument was once again rekindled by David Ellwood, when (1988) he critiqued the debate and characterized the "situation" versus "cultural" arguments on poverty as the "most confused and perplexing intellectual histories of any topic related to the disadvantaged"; *Poor Support: Poverty in the American Family* (New York: Basic Books, 1988), 195.

24. This report also created a furor among academic researchers, who responded by emphasizing the strengths of African-American families. Some social scientists argued that Moynihan failed to take into consideration nonlegal and sometimes nonresident kin relations that were important in nurturing poor children with single parents. Reconsiderations of conceptions of the black family include Carol Stack, *All Our Kin: Strategies for Survival in a Black Community* (New York: Harper & Row, 1974); Robert B. Hill, *The Strengths of Black Families* (New York Emerson Hall, 1971); Joyce Ladner, *Tomorrow's Tomorrow: The Black Women* (New York: Doubleday, 1971); Robert Staples, "The Myth of the Black Matriarchy," *Black Scholar* (February 1970). See also Lee Rainwater and William L. Yancey, *The Moynihan Report and the Politics of Controversy* (Cambridge, Mass.:MIT Press, 1967).

25. For additional sources on the African legacy found among slaves, see, for example, Sidney W. Mintz and Richard Price, *The Birth of African-American Culture: An Anthropological Perspective* (Boston: Beacon Press, 1992) and Herskovitz, *Myth of the Negro Past.* Reconsiderations of the influence of the African legacy on the family formation patterns of African-Americans include Caroline Bledsoe, "Transformation in Sub-Saharan African Marriage and Fertility," *Annals of the American Academy of Political and Social Science* 510 (July, 1990) 115–125; Niara Sudarkasa, "African and Afro-American Family Structure: A Comparison," *Black Scholar* (November–December 1980): 37–60. For an ethnographic analysis of a Mississippi community which concluded an African heritage most influenced the black family, see Demitri B Shimkin, Edith Shimkin, and Dennis Frate, eds., *The Extended Family in Black Societies.* (The Hague: Moton, 1978). Finally, for an examination of the ethnic and cultural aspects of race and family, see Andrew T. Miller, "Social Science, Social Policy, and the Heritage of African-American Families," in *The "Underclass" Debate: Views from History,* Michael Katz, ed. (Princeton: Princeton University Press, 1993) 254–93.

26. Fogel and Engerman, *Time on the Cross;* For critical reviews of *Time on the Cross,* see, for example, John Blassingame, "The Mathematics of Slavery," *Atlantic Monthly,* August 1974, 78–82; Paul A. David and Paul Temin, "Capital Masters, Bourgeois Slaves," *Journal of Interdisciplinary History* 5(Winter 1975) 445–459; Eric Foner, "Review Essay," *Labor History* (Winter 1975); Nathan Glazer, "A New View of Slavery," *Commentary* 52, August 1974, 68–72; Herbert Gutman, "The World Two Cliometricians Made," *Journal of Negro History* 60 (Winter 1975):53–227; Thomas L. Haskell, "Were Slaves More Efficient? Some Doubts About *Time on the Cross,*" *New York Review of Books,* 21 September 19, 1974, 38–42; Roger Ranson, "Was it Really All that Great to be a Slave," *Agricultural History* 48(October, 1974) 578–586; William J. Wilson, "Slavery, Paternalism, and White Hegemony," *American Journal of Sociology* 81(March 1976) 1190–1198; and C. Vann

Woodward, "The Jolly Institution," *New York Review of Books*, 21 May 2, 1974, 3–6. In spite of these criticisms, Robert Fogel went on to win the Nobel Prize for economics in 1993.

27. Fogel and Engerman, *Time on the Cross*, 5.

28. Ibid., 141.

29. Ibid., 84,85.

30. Blassingame, "Mathematics of Slavery," 81.

31. These were the same scholars who had fomented some of the harshest attacks on Fogel and Engerman's methodological approach and some of their findings.

32. Genovese, *Roll, Jordan, Roll*, 452.

33. Ibid., 7.

34. Blassingame, *Slave Community*. In the same year that *Slave Community* was published, another book was published by a less well-known press that also emphasized that white planters mainly sought to control the labor conditions of slaves by interfering sexually with the slaves and the "reproduction" of slave offspring. Slaves could only try to make the best of an institution that destroyed normal family relations. George Rawick, *From Sundown to Sunup* (Westport, Conn.: Greenwood Press, 1972).

35. Neither Elkins's nor Blassingame's typology included females, and the slave family in *Slave Community* is defined in terms of male influence and leadership.

36. Another historian who evaluated the role of religion, consciousness, and black family life during slavery during the 1970s was Lawrence Levine; *Black Culture and Black Consciousness: Afro-American Folk Thought from Slavery to Freedom* (New York: Oxford Univ. Press, 1977).

37. Blassingame, *Slave Community*, 154.

38. Frederick Douglass, *Life and Times of Frederick Douglass* (New York: Crowell-Collier, 1962), 60.

39. See, for example, Adele Logan Alexander, *Ambiguous Lives: Free Women of Color in Rural Georgia, 1789–1879* (Fayetteville: University of Arkansas, 1991) for a portrayal of the lives of women of color who bore children by white males and lived in a realm situated somewhere in the interstices of the legal, social, and economic realms of empowered whites and subjugated blacks.

40. Herbert Gutman, *The New Black Family in Slavery and Freedom 1750–1925* (New York: Vintage, 1976). For an analysis of the specific contributions of Gutman's work see Nathan Irvin Huggins, "Herbert Gutman and Afro-American History," *Labor History* 29 (Summer 1988):323–337.

41. Gutman, *New Black Family*, 75.

42. Specifically, Gutman criticized Genovese's work and asserted, "An adaptive culture does not develop among slaves in *Roll Jordan Roll*. Instead, 'slave culture' itself is made dependent upon the 'paternalistic compromise.' Rather than shaping the relationship between slaves and their owners, the 'culture' is 'caused' by the relationship"; *Black Family*, 316; Genovese, *Roll, Jordan, Roll*, 464.

43. Paul D. Escott, *Slavery Remembered: A Record of Twentieth-Century Slave Narratives* (Chapel Hill: University of North Carolina Press, 1979), 19.

44. Some of the disagreements between Genovese and Gutman have centered on Gen-

ovese's use of concepts such as "elaborate web of paternalistic relations" and "paternalistic ethos," and while Gutman never said it directly, he may have viewed Genovese's use of these concepts as a variation on the themes set forth in Stanley Elkins's work. Even though Gutman and Genovese were closer than Elkins and Genovese in their belief in the slaves' drive to counter the destructive forces of the slavemaster, Gutman strongly disagreed with Genovese's emphasis on the influence of the slavemaster over the slave.

45. Gutman, *Black Family*, 76.

46. For an in-depth analysis of the legal, economic, and cultural factors influencing slave marriage and family in antebellum Virginia, see Brenda E. Stevenson, "Black Family Structure in Colonial and Antebellum Virginia," in *The Decline in Marriage Among African Americans*, ed. M. Belinda Tucker and Claudia Kernan-Mitchell (New York: Russell Sage Foundation, 1995) 28-56.

47. Genovese, *Roll, Jordan, Roll*, 465.

48. For scholarly accounts of the structure and behavior of southern European families, see J. E. Cashin, "The Structure of Antebellum Planter Families: 'The ties that bound us was strong'," *Journal of Southern History* 56 (August, 1990):55–70; Daniel E. Smith, *Inside the Great House: Planter Family Life in Eighteenth Century Chesapeake Society* (Ithaca, N.Y.: Cornell University Press, 1980); Elizabeth Fox-Genovese, *Within the Plantation Household: Black and White Women of the Old South* (Chapel Hill: University of North Carolina Press, 1988); Susan Lesbock, *The Free Women of Petersburg: Status and Culture in a Southern Town, 1784–1860* (New York: Norton, 1984); Bertram Wyatt-Brown, *Southern Honor: Ethics and Behavior in the Old South* (New York: Oxford University Press, 1982); Jean E. Friedman, *The Enclosed Garden: Woman and Community in the Evangelical South, 1830–1900* (Chapel Hill: University of North Carolina Press, 1985).

49. Leon Litwack, *North of Slavery: The Negro in the Free States, 1790–1860* (Chicago: University of Chicago Press, 1961, 243.

50. Gutman, *Black Family*, 79.

51. Drew Gilpin Faust, "Culture, Conflict, and Community: The Meaning of Power on an Ante-bellum Plantation," *Journal of Social History* 14 (Fall 1980): 90, 91.

52. Thomas L. Webber, *Deep Like the Rivers* (New York: Norton, 1978), xxii-xxiii.

53. Genovese, *Roll, Jordan, Roll*, 625.

54. When former slaves were interviewed, for example, 82 percent spoke of the physical presence of their mothers during their childhood years, and only 42 percent remembered having contact with their fathers. About one-third of those who did make mention of the presence of their fathers during childhood noted that these men did not live with the family on the same plantation.C. L. Perdue, T. E. Barden, and R. K. Phillips, eds., *Weevils in the Wheat: Interviews with Virginia ex-Slaves.* (Charlottesville: University Press of Virginia, 1976): 149–151. However, when Ann Patton Malone utilized a historiographic developmental model that purports to predict slave family change and stability, she concluded that "that the dominant type was the simple family; that within the simple family category, the two-parent nuclear family usually prevailed"; *Sweet Chariot: Slave Family and Household Structure in Nineteenth-Century Louisiana* (Chapel Hill: University of North Carolina Press, 1992).

55. Stephen C. Crawford, "Quantified Memory: A Study of the WPA and Fisk University Slave Narrative Collections" (Ph.D. diss., University of Chicago, 1980).

56. Orville V. Burton, *In My Father's House are Many Mansions: Family and Community in Edgefield, South Carolina* (Chapel Hill: University of North Carolina Press, 1985), 184.

57. Richard H. Steckel, "A Peculiar Population," *Journal of Economic History* 46(Sept. 1986):721–41.

58. A gang system provided a powerful instrument for the supervision and control of labor on slave plantations. The distinction between gang systems and other types of slavery is discussed in Orlando Patterson, *Slavery and Social Death: A Comparative Study* (Cambridge: Harvard Univ Press, 1982). For evidence regarding the division of labor on large tobacco plantations, see Alan Kulikoff, *Tobacco and Slaves: The Development of Southern Culture in the Chesapeake, 1680–1800* (Chapel Hill: University of North Carolina Press, 1986). Kulikoff discovered that on large plantations only about half (47 percent) of the slaves lived in nuclear households and on small plantations only about 18 percent did.

59. The issue of the failure to take into adequate account the differences between slave experiences on large and small plantations is not a new one. Kenneth Stampp called attention to the issue of plantation size to historians studying slavery, but many scholars who study slave culture continue to fall victim to this. Throughout *Peculiar Institution* Stampp pointed to the different circumstances and conditions of life for slaves on small and large plantations.

Paul Escott's analysis of former slave narratives found that slaves on plantations with fewer than fifteen slaves reported significantly fewer whippings and less cruelty, more often rated their food as equal to that of their owners, and had a more favorable attitude toward their master than did slaves on larger plantations. These findings point to the rewards associated with the closer fraternization with the slaveholders; *Slavery Remembered*, 19–23.

Genovese notes that at least half of the slaves in the South lived on units with twenty slaves or more; *Roll, Jordan, Roll*, 7. If his figures are accurate, this may explain why the majority of slave families had two-parent households, in that these families were under less pressure on the larger plantation. Gutman (*Black Family*) argues that most slaves in the latter part of the eighteenth century were purchased by whites of lesser means. As a result, most eighteenth-century and first-generation slaves lived on relatively small plantations with fewer than twenty slaves. In that all but one of the plantations in Gutman's sample had 100 slaves or more, what is less clear in Gutman's work is whether or not there was a shift to larger plantations in the nineteenth century.

60. Crawford, *Quantified Memory*, 132.

61. Steckel, Richard. "Miscegenation and the American Slave Schedule," *Journal of Interdisciplinary History* 11(Autumn, 1980): 251–263.

62. B. A. Botkin, ed., *Lay My Burden Down: A Folk History of Slavery* (Chicago: University of Chicago Press, 1945), 54–55.

63. While Gutman (*Black Family*) found slave women's age at first birth to range from 17 to 19, Trussell and Steckel found it to be around 20.6 years, whereas Richard Dunn calculated it at 19.22 on the Mount Airy Virginia Plantation, and Fogel and Engerman (*Time on the Cross*) computed it the highest, at 22.5;

64. Richard H. Steckel, "A Peculiar Population," *Journal of Economic History* 46(Sept

1986):721–41. Also see Steckel, *The Economics of U.S. Slave and Southern White Fertility* (New York: Garland Publishing, 1985).

65. Whereas Steckel found significant variation in the sexual practices on plantations of different sizes and regions, his failure to control for plantation size when analyzing the sexual practices of adolescent slaves weakens his argument.

66. Ibid., 197.

67. All but one of the plantations in Gutman's sample had 100 slaves or more. And the best of the records he examined were from the Good Hope plantation in South Carolina, which toward the end of the slavery era had about 175 slaves. Gutman agrees with the quantitative historians that everyday contact with owners had to be less frequent on larger plantations. He states the "size of the plantation is what matters, not whether their owners viewed themselves as 'capitalists' or 'paternalists' "; *Black Family*, 103. At the same time, he asserts that blacks created their own distinctive African-American culture on the small slave plantation; *Black Family*, 327–60. What is missing from Gutman's analysis is a comparative analysis of the small versus the large plantations.

CHAPTER TWO

SHARECROPPING AND THE RURAL PROLETARIAT

Proportionately, black women and children always worked for wages to a greater extent than even their poor-white counterparts, a fact that had far-reaching implications for age and gender relations within the black community. **Jacqueline Jones, "Southern Diaspora"**

There is a subtle deference on the part of Negro men to their women. This is not the remants of a feudal chivalry . . . but it is the deference of a comrade-ship. **Marion Cuthbert, "Problems Facing Negro Young Women"**

Demographers and econometricians have noted some interesting changes in the fertility patterns of African-Americans since the middle of the nineteenth century. Between 1620 and 1860 growth rates among slave populations in North America were much higher than elsewhere in the New World.[1] But between 1880 to 1940 the birthrates for black women in the United States fell by more than one-half—a decline, according to Engerman, that was much sharper, both absolutely and relatively, than the decline for whites.[2]

Although fertility rates generally correlated with marriage rates for most cohorts in the U. S. population, the correlation did not hold for emancipated slaves, who had not been allowed legal marriages under the system of slavery. One result of this was that social and literary images of the sexually licentious black woman, constructed during slavery, did not fade with emancipation. An article, written by a wealthy southern white woman and published in 1904 in a national magazine, is representative of this kind of racist imagery:

[D]egeneracy is apt to show most in the weaker individuals of any race; so negro women evidence more nearly the popular idea of total depravity than the men do. They are so nearly lacking in virtue that the color of a woman's skin is generally taken (and quite correctly) as a guarantee of her immorality. On the whole, I think they are the greatest menace possible to the moral life of any community where they live. And they are evidently the chief instruments of the degradation of the men of their race. . . . I sometimes read of virtuous negro women, hear of them, but the idea is absolutely inconceivable to me. . . . I cannot image such a creation as a virtuous black woman.[3]

Throughout the country during the late nineteenth century, politically minded black women formed a network of clubs committed to addressing issues of racial injustice; and part of their first national conference held in Boston in July 1985, was devoted to a discussion of how to deal with objectionable images of black women.[4]

Of the many intellectual challenges raised by emancipation, none was more crucial than developing a coherent explanation for the increasing difference between black and white women in the number of births outside of marriage. Perhaps alone among contemporary observers, Phillips Bruce tried to identify a *source* of the difference:

> The number of illegitimate children born to unmarried negresses is becoming greater every year, but this instead of being a lasting stain on their reputation or a stumbling block in the path of their material thrift is an advantage when regarded from a practical point of view. . . . When [these children] are old enough to work, then they constitute a valuable dowry to whoever marries their mothers, such women occupying somewhat the position of widows with considerable property at their command, which they confer absolutely upon their husbands at the hour of marriage.[5]

While he does not explicitly say so, Bruce clearly seems to be referring to the system of sharecropping. A discussion of the evolution of sharecropping and its impact on black family life will demonstrate how inextricably economic, political, and social issues are woven together.

Sharecropping and the Family Ethos

The end of slavery brought significant changes to black family life, for it altered the economic, social, and legal arrangements under which children were conceived, born, and reared. Sharecropping, one of those changes, arose immediately after emancipation and was the dominant institution in the agrarian South for nearly seventy years.

Most southern planters could not reconcile themselves to the fact of emancipation and continued to believe that blacks would never work of their own free will.[6] In response, northern Republicans established the Freedman's Bureau, which sought to provide former slaves the opportunity to be paid wages for their labor

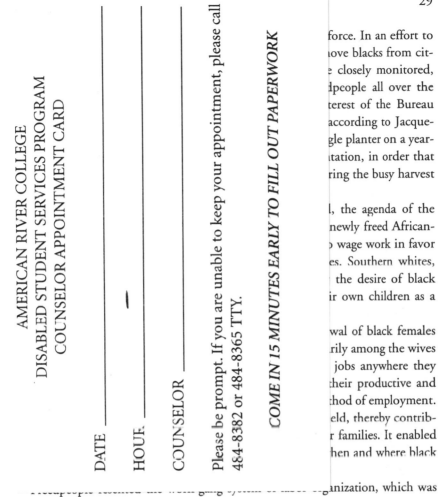

force. In an effort to
...ove blacks from cit-
... closely monitored,
...dpeople all over the
...terest of the Bureau
...according to Jacque-
...gle planter on a year-
...itation, in order that
...ring the busy harvest

..., the agenda of the
...newly freed African-
... wage work in favor
...es. Southern whites,
...the desire of black
...ir own children as a

...wal of black females
...rily among the wives
...jobs anywhere they
...their productive and
...thod of employment.
...eld, thereby contrib-
...r families. It enabled
...hen and where black

...people ...... the work-gang system of labor organization, which was prevalent on plantations after the war, because supervision by an overseer was reminiscent of the master–slave relationship. In addition to the black family's desire for autonomy in their work, three additional factors contributed to the demise of the work-gang system and the evolution of family sharecropping: the gradual decentralization of labor organization; poor work performances by groups; and discord over the distribution of earnings.[10]

The most prevalent arrangement between southern landlords and black farmers was the "fifty-fifty" contract: the profits from the crop were to be divided evenly; but in return for providing a house for the sharecropper's family on a yearly basis, the landlord could deduct from the worker's share of the profits the cost of furnishings and supplies given "on credit" during the year. The rise of debt peonage, enforced by criminal statutes and connecting personal financial credit to crop liens, provided planter-merchants with "a degree of control over their work force far beyond that available to employers elsewhere in the nation."[11] Indeed, whether hired as individual wage earners or as family sharecroppers, most blacks belonged to a rural proletariat without control over either the land or the fruits of their labor. The majority of blacks would remain economically dependent on the same group of people they had served as slaves.

While the prospect of black families gaining control over their own productive labor was proving illusory, the hope that black women would be able to stay at home and care for their own households and children was also dying. The poverty that many black families were already experiencing was exacerbated by the depressions of the 1870s. A report by Boston cotton brokers who inquired into the disastrous cotton crop of 1867–68 concluded that the greatest loss resulted from the decision of "growing numbers of Negro women to devote their time to their homes and children."[12] Under the sharecropping system, the bigger the crop, the more favorable the economic outcome at the end of the year. Because an entire household was under contract, every able-bodied family member was needed to make the year successful, and children became more of an economic asset to their parents. Although black women may have preferred to wash, sew, cook, and care for their children, a heavy premium was clearly placed on their reproductive and agricultural labor. In a long-term perspective, the birth of a child augmented the household's labor supply. And, as Jacqueline Jones put it, "Individualism was a luxury that sharecroppers simply could not afford".[13]

There were also noneconomic reasons for newly freed families to stay together, beyond the fact that large families were needed to maximize agricultural productivity. The worst fear of newly freed slaves was that the postwar economy would force them to take jobs far away from their families. A freedperson's proximity to kinship groups was usually a crucial factor in determining precisely where he or she would settle. Even when black workers moved on at the end of the sharecropping year, they tended to stay within the same county. Kinship relations among blacks had a powerful effect on working and living arrangements, which suggests that feelings of mutual obligation and interdependence, and not simply economic motives, influenced the migratory movements of the black family.[14]

By the end of the nineteenth century, 80 percent of American black families resided in rural areas, primarily in the Cotton Belt. And by 1910 fully nine-tenths of all southern blacks who made a living from the soil worked as tenants, sharecroppers, or contract laborers, and most made barely enough to pay for rent and food.[15] Considering the limited job opportunities in the North and in urban areas in the South during this period, it is not surprising that most freedpeople remained concentrated in rural areas in the Cotton Belt and under the tyranny of southern planters.[16]

Black Male Patriarchal Authority

Although historians have generally agreed that black males and females were rendered equally powerless during slavery, there has been less emphasis on the fact that emancipation was followed by attempts to establish the black man's patriarchal authority within the family. According to Eric Foner, the movement began when black men participated more directly in the struggle for freedom than black women by serving in the Union Army.[17] Peter Kolchin writes that "almost immediately after the end of the war . . . there was a new determination for [black] men to reassert their position as head of the family."[18]

Black male militancy had escalated during the mid–nineteenth century as black males at the proceedings of the National Negro Convention in 1855 declared, "As a people, we have been denied the ownership of our bodies, our wives, home, children, and the products of our own labor." The convention leaders then went on to resolve to "vindicate our manhood, command our respect and claim the attention and admiration of the civilized world."[19]

The Freedman's Bureau soon "vindicated" the black man by designating him as head of the black household and establishing his right to sign contracts for the labor of his entire family. Equally significant, wage scales were set that paid black women less than black men for identical plantation labor.[20] Sometimes the Bureau even allocated less land to families without a male head of household.[21] Furthermore, agents tried to hold husbands responsible for seeing that their wives worked according to contractual guidelines established with the Bureau. For example, one Bureau official reportedly made a black man promise "to work faithfully and keep his wife in subjection" after she refused to work.[22]

The gender division of labor among freedpeople became more clearly defined after emancipation. Due to the larger grouping of kinship clusters at this time, the obligations of black women—for nurturing children and elders and for promoting the general welfare of the community—probably increased.[23] Herbert Gutman has argued that these responsibilities were also probably greater in the African American community than in immigrant and poor white communities, due to social obligations and concern for non-kin.[24] Gutman does not point out that a disproportionate number of other new hardships were falling on black women. One of the new challenges they faced after emancipation was regaining custody of children who were being seized for apprenticeship, without parental consent, by former slaveowners and other predatory whites. Freedman's Bureau officials, who had the power to make arrests when charges were made against former owners, received many letters written by black mothers asking for assistance in getting their children back from them.[25]

Another development during this period was an alarming increase in wife-beating in the African-American community. Black women were also having difficulty accepting the increasingly patriarchal quality of black family life. Many of the same women who wrote complaints about abuses of their children also mentioned family disputes. The Freedman's Bureau received hundreds of complaints by black women of battery, adultery, and nonpayment of child support. And some women went so far as to object to their husband's signing labor contracts for them.[26]

These reports to the Freedman's Bureau were not the first accounts of this nature made by black women to white authorities. Ann Patton Malone conducted a detailed study of planters' records during slavery and found frequent reports of domestic violence involving slave men against their wives. She attributed this violence to an "overwhelming sense of powerlessness and impotence which threatened the man's concept of his manhood and fatherhood."[27] Black women were clearly ambivalent about making such reports to the white authorities, for they understood that this information could be used to justify all sorts of terrorism, including lynching, against black men. Black women's hesitancy to report their husbands was clearly reflected in an article in the Mobile *Daily Register* which noted that when the guilty men were arrested, the women "usually begged the mayor to let their husbands off." Not surprisingly, the *Register* misinterpreted this ambivalence on the part of the black wife: "[T]he negro women seem to labor under the impression that their husbands have a perfect right to beat them on every occasion."[28]

What brought about the promulgation of patriarchal values in the postbellum black community? First, political developments brought new gender distinctions. After 1867 black men could hold office, serve on juries, vote, and take leadership positions in the Republican party; black women could do none of these things. In addition, only black men could serve as delegates to black political conventions.[29] Black men had internalized the values of their white oppressors and their "manhood and freedom were tied to personal power," which included power over their spouses, as James Horton convincingly argues:

> All women were expected to defer to men, but for black women deference was a racial imperative. Slavery and racism sought the emasculation of black men. Black people sought to counter such effect. Part of the responsibility of black men was to "act like a man," and part of the responsibility of black women was to encourage and support the manhood of our men . . . never intimidate him with her knowledge or common sense, let him feel stable and dominant."[30]

Second, the Christian religion played a pervasive role. E. Franklin Frazier has recognized that institutions such as the black church "sought to affirm the man's interest and authority in the family."[31] Frances Butler Leigh, after a visit to the Sea

Islands of Georgia, remarked that "the good old law of female submission to the husband's will on all points held good." She writes of seeing a black woman who had been expelled from her church "sitting on the church steps, rocking herself backwards and forwards in great distress." On asking why, Leigh learned that the woman had "refused to obey her husband in a small matter." When Leigh intervened on her behalf, the church required the offending woman to make a "public apology before the whole congregation" before readmitting her.[32] Perhaps Orville Burton comes closest to summarizing the church's influence when he writes:

> The Bible delivered a powerful patriarchal message to the agrarian former slave population. Old Testament theology, as preached and practiced, focused on a father figure and implanted patriarchal values. Preachers and deacons, leaders charged with the welfare of their fellow worshipers as well as their spiritual guidance, were always men.[33]

In 1937, John Dollard conducted detailed ethnographic studies of a southern town that was comprised of working- and middle-class blacks. His observations suggest that, particularly within the private sphere of the family, there were "different conceptions of [parental] roles" that were based on class:

> In the life histories of the middle-class group the father plays a considerable role and the mother does not seem to play a disproportionately important one. The father seems to appear regularly as disciplinarian and as one who stresses restrictive aspects of the culture. It is very likely that families whose children emerge into middle class have already a tradition and discipline which is superior to the mine run of lower-class Negroes, and further, that the family form tends to approximate the white patriarchal type.[34]

These observations enhance our understanding of the source of much of the tension in the sharecropper household. Dollard's finding that the patriarchal family structure was more likely to exist in middle-class black families suggests that there was more resistance among the wives in the lower-class households to the subordinate role they were granted after slavery. The wives in lower-income households probably had more egalitarian working relationships with their husbands in that they were working side by side, and were therefore more likely to challenge their patriarchal authority.

The Postbellum Marriage Quandary

In the immediate aftermath of slavery, laws required the registration of marriages among former slaves, and failure to comply rendered offenders liable for penalties as adulterers. Ministers who performed these marriages sent the certificates to the

Freedman's Bureau. Although it might seem that the institution of slavery would have weakened black family ties and the sense of family obligation, some whites were "astonished by the eagerness with which former slaves legalized their marriage bonds."[35]

Some of the first documented sociological insights into African-American family patterns at the turn of the century came from W. E. B. DuBois. He studied the black residents of a town he called Farmville, midway between Petersburg, Virginia, and the North Carolina line, an archetypal point of departure for the coming Great Migration to the North. He conducted an in-depth ethnographic study of its one to two thousand black residents, in that he lived among them, participated in their social life, and visited with them in their homes. He commented that "the moral tone of the Negroes has room for great betterment" and wrote that whenever "a low inherited standard of sexual morals is coincident with an [unfavorable] economic situation . . . the inevitable result is prostitution and illegitimacy."[36] He also noted that postponement of marriage was common, "largely for economic reasons." DuBois would go on to conduct four more Bureau of Labor Statistics studies, covering five Black Belt counties in Georgia and one in Alabama.[37]

Some of the most definitive data on the differences between the family formation patterns of blacks and whites during Reconstruction are provided by Orville Burton's 1985 analysis of 1880 federal census data on Edgefield County, South Carolina. Of the unmarried women who headed households there in 1880, only 14 white women had children at home, whereas 166 black women did. A majority of unmarried black and white female heads of households with children had more than one child, and black women predominated in this group. Only one white woman with an out-of-wedlock child lived with her parents, compared to nearly one-third of the black women. And whereas white unmarried women gave their children their own surnames, Burton found that the pattern of names among children of some unmarried black women suggested that the children were given their father's surname. Burton writes, "Perhaps this showed that the black community, which was denied legal marriage before emancipation, acknowledged a certain legitimacy to these unions. Certainly this evidence underscores the patriarchal orientation of the Afro-American community." In spite these higher rates of mother-only families, when compared with the whites in Edgefield County, Burton found that blacks preferred the traditional male-headed family with a husband-wife team. He added, however, "there are indications even in the patriarchal Edgefield Afro-American society that black women had more autonomy than white women did in theirs."[38]

Charles S. Johnson, an African-American scholar trained at the University of Chicago, provided one of the first in-depth analyses of the family formation patterns of blacks living in the South. He studied a homogeneous group of 612 black families living in rural Alabama who had adjusted "both physically and mentally to the tradition of cotton cultivation."[39] When he looked at the patterns of child-bearing outside of marriage, he found that 122 women in 114 families had 181 children out of wedlock. All but 3 of these 114 families included an unmarried mother. Thirty-three of these 122 women were daughters living at home with their parents.

What Johnson discovered was a pattern of marital relations without the legal formalities, which would naturally contribute to a very high rate of out-of-wedlock births. Noting that these families were very poor, he cited the actual cost of the divorce procedure as one reason why many couples separated informally. He added that divorce was considered unnecessary unless one party objected to the separation. Apparently the courts were lenient toward this omission, "so long as the practice affects no one but Negroes."[40]

Ruth Reed presented findings that supported Johnson's observations. She found that blacks did not resort to the courts to resolve domestic problems. For example, she found that of the fifty-two divorce suits that had been filed in the county of Gainesville, Georgia, only four were brought by blacks. She summarized her findings as follows: "Many negroes seem unconscious of the fact that a divorce is necessary before entering into marriage again after a separation. And such marriages are entered into freely without fear of interference from the white man's court."[41]

Johnson also found that, compared to whites, blacks had earlier marriages, higher fertility rates, and larger families. He attributed these differences to three factors: (1) lower social class, with home ownership and education as key defining elements; (2) the persistence of the old belief that the social status of a Negro slave woman was to an important degree "based upon her breeding power"; and (3) the new incentive for the black tenant farmer to "reckon his children as a personal asset" or as a necessity in order to make his farm profitable. These early childbearing patterns Johnson that discusses are confirmed in Figure 2.1, which charts the mean fertility of blacks and whites from the time when records were first kept.

Johnson suggested several reasons why in these rural communities early marriages were not encouraged in the event of an unplanned teenage pregnancy. Because the family was the most efficient unit for raising cotton and food crops, and would be weakened if a young person married and left home, marriage was postponed; alternatively, when young couples did marry, they were often expected to live in and become part of the parents' household. Johnson wrote:

> The active passions of youth and late adolescence are present but without the usual formal social constraints. Social behavior rooted in this situation, even when its consequences are understood, is lightly censured or excused entirely. . . . When pregnancy follows, pressure is not strong enough to com-

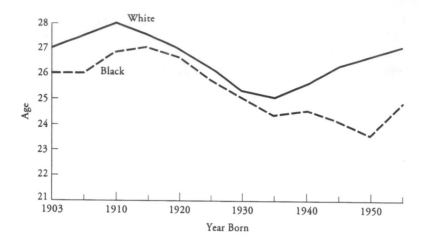

FIGURE 2.1   Mean age at fertility of white and black cohorts born 1903–1956. (From M. D. R. Evans, "American Fertility Patterns: A Comparison of White and Non-White Cohorts Born 1903–56," *Population and Development Review* 12, no. 2 [June 1986])

pel the father to either marry the mother or support the child. The girl does not lose her status, perceptibly, nor are her chances for marrying seriously threatened. . . . There is, in a sense, no such thing as illegitimacy in this community.[42]

However, when children "result from the deliberate philandering of young men," those men *"are universally condemned."* [43]

Johnson found bifurcated sexual behaviors based on class among southern blacks, and these findings are reported in his study of youth in the Black Belt before the Second World War. He found that among "elite" blacks, even young men accepted rigid standards of chastity. Parents kept close rein on their daughters, as the testimony of one North Carolina girl demonstrated: "Yes, I have a boy friend. He call on me and takes me to socials. Sometimes mama lets me go to movies with him in the afternoon, but if he goes with me at night pappa and mama go to."[44]

Finally, in describing the values toward marriage held in this community, Johnson wrote:

Married life imposes certain obligations which are, in the feeling of this element of the community, more binding than necessary or practical. It gives license to mistreatment; it imposes the risk of unprofitable husbands; and it places an impossible tax upon freedom in the form of a divorce.[45]

Although Johnson did not describe how widespread these ideas on marriage were among the population he surveyed, some 1900 census data analyzed by Gutman offers an alternate perspective on the role of marriage:

[A] significant number everywhere but especially in rural places reported the birth of a child either prior to marriage or during the first year of marriage. Such evidence indicated the prevalence of prenuptial intercourse, childbirth out of wedlock, and bridal pregnancy. But the small number of single women aged thirty and older shows that marriage usually followed either pregnancy or the birth of a child.[46]

How do we reconcile the discrepancy between the accounts of Gutman and Johnson regarding the marriage rates among blacks during this early period? In spite of Johnson's statements about the propensity of blacks not to marry, fewer than 6 percent of the 612 couples that he studied had not married. However, 105 of his respondents were widowed, whereas only 2 were divorced. The differences in the marriage rates between black women and white women are reported in the census data from 1890 to 1920. According to these reports, black women had higher marriage rates than white women. The percentage of currently married white women was higher, however, because more black women reported that they were widowed.[47]

The public use sample of 1910 census data was rereleased in the early 1990s, and when a team of demographers examined the newly released data, they found that these early marital status reports were seriously flawed.[48] Figure 2.2 reflects the revised figures. Too many widows were reported, according to these demographers, a discrepancy that suggests a propensity to legitimate a birth outside of marriage. They found that by age fifty, 94.5 percent of the black women had married, just as 94 percent of Johnson's sample had married.

When the figures on female headship of families from 1910 to 1980 were recently examined, however, the analysts concluded that African-American women were more likely than white women not to coreside with a spouse, if ever married.[49] This may be where the discrepancy lies. While black women may have married at higher or equal rates to those of white women, when these marriages were disrupted, black women were less likely to dissolve them legally—a point on which scholars agree. This analysis is consistent with Johnson's, which reflected disproportionately large estimates of widowhood, very low divorce rates, and incredibly high numbers of reported marriages. This begins to explain how high rates of female headship, reported marriages, and nonmarital birthrates could exist simultaneously among African-Americans.

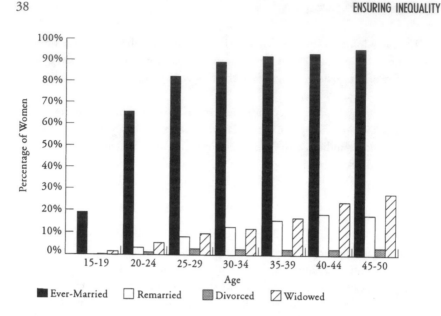

FIGURE 2.2   Features of the marital status of the African-American female population in the 1910 public use sample. (From Samuel Preston, Suet Lim, and Phillip Morgan, "African-American Marriage in 1910: Beneath the Surface of Census Date," *Demography* [February 1992])

African-Americans' Changing Migration Patterns

In spite of the fact that sharecropping reinforced the family ethos and contributed to the proximity of extended family members, by 1920 scholars began to observe that many black women were raising children without a spouse present; they found that only about 75 percent of black mothers were married and living with spouses.[50] The percentages of nonmarital births in U.S. cities with populations over 100,000 were reported by the Children's Bureau. These data on birthrates come from some of the first statistical reports that controlled for the marital status and race of the mother. Only two cities, Baltimore and Washington, D.C., reported the race of the mother. The annual average percentages for births outside of marriage for the years 1910 through 1914 in Baltimore was 3.8 for whites and 23.3 for blacks. For Washington, D.C. these figures were 2.1 for whites and 20.9 for blacks.[51]

Census data on the gender of the person heading the household were not available until 1930. The figures in Figure 2.3 tend to support scholars who have asserted that rural farms had the smallest proportion of female-headed families when compared to rural towns and to urban areas.[52] The differences in family structure that were beginning to emerge between rural and urban blacks were

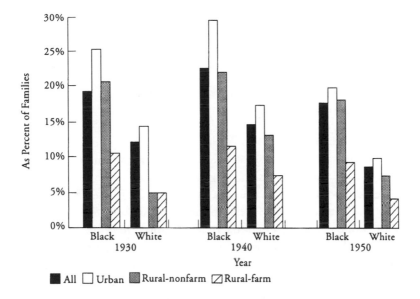

FIGURE 2.3   Mother-only families, 1930–1950. Figures for blacks include all nonwhites. (From the decennial census)

created by the changing migratory patterns of males and females: Black men were moving to agricultural areas to find work, whereas black women were moving to urban areas, where more domestic service opportunities were available.[53] The unbalanced gender ratios are also crucial to understanding the higher proportion of black households headed by single mothers, especially in urban areas.

Kelly Miller, a Howard University professor, writing in 1910 about the patterns of movement among southern blacks, observed: "Negro women rush to the city in disproportionate numbers, because in the country there is little demand for such services as they can render. They cannot remain at the hard, bone-breaking labor of the farm." Kelly went on to discuss the plight of black men on the farm and commented, "the compensation of rural workers is so meager that the male alone cannot earn a reasonable livelihood for the whole family." In Kelly's view, the black men then follow the women into the cities but when the black man arrives he "has no fixed industrial status . . . and loiters around the ragged edge of industry, and is confined to the more onerous and less attractive mode of toil." Kelly goes on to say that the black women, on the other hand, "find an unlimited field of employment in the domestic and household industries."[54]

David Katzman, in his book *Seven Days a Week,* concurs with Kelly, stating that from 1870 to 1910, the number of female domestic servants rose from 960,000 to 1,830,000. Katzman attributes the proliferation of domestic jobs to the "expansion of the urban-based middle-class, a result of the rapid industrialization and accompanying urbanization," and goes on to say that nearly all observers of the time agreed that "the number of domestics was limited not by the demand, but by the inadequacy of the supply."[55]

The Impetus for Northern Migration

After the brief period of migration following emancipation, freedpeople were rooted in the South, trapped in debt peonage, with very little motivation to explore opportunities in the North. Most historians agree that the outbreak of war in 1914, by restricting the flow of European immigrants, contributed to the critical labor shortage among industrial employers in the northern United States.[56] This shortage became worse with the mobilization of the American armed forces in 1917. Two economists, Roger Ransom and Richard Sutch, posit that "it required a series of shocks from without" during the wartime shortages of World War I to reawaken the dormant migratory impulse in southern blacks.[57] The new availability of jobs in the North provided the "pull" for the first wave of immigration by southern blacks. The hope for more economic possibilities created by the war was reflected in the *Chicago Defender*'s statement: "The opportunity we have longed for is here. . . . The war has given us a place upon which to stand."[58]

The "push" was provided by economic changes that were simultaneously occurring in the rural South. The flooding of the Mississippi River in 1912 and 1913 was followed first by drought and then by rainstorms in 1915. The credit market was tightened, and planters had difficulty obtaining the capital to recover from these disasters. The cotton economy was further destabilized by the spread of the boll weevil and by continuing soil exhaustion in older cotton-growing regions. There was also the systematic exclusion of blacks from the Southern textile industry, where virtually all of the factory jobs went to poor whites until the mid-1960s.[59] In this climate, acts of barbarism were aimed directly at blacks (for example, "whitecapping," in which whites from nonplantation districts literally drove blacks from their land.[60]

Labor economists debated whether the labor market changes alone were a sufficient impetus for such a mass movement. Carter G. Woodson argued that if blacks had been treated fairly "as men," they might have stayed in the South in spite of the availability of jobs in the North.[61] Two years later, when DuBois compared the two regions of the country, he wrote that "the North is no paradise, but the South is at best a system of caste and insult and at worst a Hell."[62] Thomas J. Woofter likewise presented evidence that the conditions in the South were a factor contributing to the northern migration when he reported that the black tenants allowed even a token amount of self-sufficiency by the plantation owners were most likely to linger on the plantations and refrain from moving to the North.[63] When St. Clair Drake and Horace Cayton wrote their seminal book in the mid-1940s, having critically reread studies on the migration, they concluded that the "basic impetus" had been and still remained economic.[64] Paula Giddings, while conceding the relevance of a failing southern economy, asserts that the strongest concern of black women migrants seemed to be the protection of their families.[65]

James Grossman summarized the meaning of these developments when he wrote:

> Movement became as central to southern black life as it has been to the American experience in general, emerging as a major theme in black music. . . . White efforts at social control, motivated in part by the refusal of blacks to remain satisfied with their "place," only fueled black dissatisfaction and stimulated the migratory impulse.[66]

One of the major ways in which white Southerners maintained social control was by regulating the system of public welfare. When John Hope Franklin investigated public welfare in the South during the Reconstruction era, he found that "even in the makeshift programs of the early postwar years, public welfare efforts all too frequently addressed themselves exclusively to the needs of the whites."[67] John Dollard, who also found during his fieldwork that Southern whites resisted giving federal relief to blacks, explained it this way:

> The reason appears to be that such relief would take the pressure off the Negro families to seek employment on the farms or in the white households, and there is fear that the standard of relief offered would compete too favorably with the local living standards of the Negroes.[68]

Mary Larabee wrote that field supervisors of the local welfare department could exhibit an "intense desire" not to interfere with "local labor conditions" and therefore often agreed with advisory boards of citizens who saw "no reason why the employable Negro mother should not continue her usually sketchy seasonal labor or indefinite domestic service rather than receive a public assistance grant."[69]

The "few cases" of public assistance that Larabee found in the Federal Emergency Relief Administration (FERA) report were probably those of black tenant farmers who were receiving benefits through the efforts of the planters for whom they worked.[70] The Freedman's Bureau initially sanctioned a contract system that bound black workers to a single planter for an entire year, even though sharecropping work was seasonal; many planters therefore sought to lessen financial responsibilities by getting relief from welfare agencies for some of their workers.[71] One way of doing this was to "split" black households: the planter would provide compensation only to the able-bodied workers in the family, leaving the young, the ill, and the elderly eligible for federal relief. The complicity of FERA's state administrators in such arrangements contributed to the black family's obligatory dependence on the state.[72]

The observations of Mary Larabee were supported by Hylan Lewis as late as the mid-1950s, when he studied black families in a small, rural southern town. He found that about 19 percent of the schoolchildren were born to unmarried mothers, 20 percent of the black mothers in the community were single, and many were on a "bare subsistence level." Although some of the black residents of this community were collecting social security, only three cases during the study were recipients of "charity and philanthropy." These cases included a nonnative of the community who was involved in a serious accident; an "ill and destitute" female resident; and the wife of a feebleminded tenant who lived in a remote spote on the edge of town and died of malnutrition.[73]

Conclusion

Sharecropping, which began immediately after the Emancipation Proclamation, quickly became the dominant institution in the agrarian South and left a deep imprint on black family life. Although sharecropping reconstituted the black family as a unit, it also created new strains and challenges, such as those resulting from the efforts of the Freedman's Bureau to encourage a patriarchal authority within the black family, rather than working with the egalitarian relations that had existed under slavery.

Sharecropping created a rural black proletariat, which, according to some social scientists, experienced more social isolation than groups of blacks residing in urban areas. This isolation helped perpetuate a distinctive set of marriage and family characteristics, which included high fertility rates, more births outside of marriage, and high rates of marriage dissolution. This finding is puzzling in view of statistics showing a higher proportion of married couples on tenant farms than in urban areas during this period.

Many historians have conceded that tenant farming fostered stronger family ties than slavery. But most failed to note that the policies of the Freedman's Bureau policies discriminated against women who tried to run farms without husbands, and that many complaints were made against husbands for abusing the authority recently conferred on them by the Bureau. In reality, the policies of the Freedman's Bureau were a mixed blessing for black families, and may have indirectly contributed to the demise of two-parent families.

These questionable Bureau policies were buttressed by changing migration patterns among blacks and by the different opportunities for work in urban areas: Whereas many domestic service jobs were opening up for black women, black men found it difficult, or impossible, to find jobs. For black women who were single or married but unable to live amicably with husbands on a tenant farm, urban areas were the land of opportunity. This is the clearest explanation for why mother-only families were more prevalent in urban areas.

Despite the high marriage rates that were reported during this period, child-bearing outside of marriage was still prevalent in black communities, both rural and urban. In the rural areas, marriages of adolescents were discouraged because the economic unit of the tenant-farm family would be disrupted when a young person left home. These family formation patterns were further strengthened by norms that emphasized the institution of marriage but refrained from stigmatizing black women who gave birth without getting married.

Referring to black family formation found in the Deep South during the 1930s, Robert E. Park, in his foreward to Charles Johnson's *Shadow of the Plantation*, wrote:

> But customs persist and preserve their external forms after they have lost their original meaning and functions. Institutions are imposed upon people to whose traditions, instincts, and actual needs they are quite foreign, or have not yet been fully assimilated. Fashions change, and with the change institutions, though they persist, are looked upon with profoundly changed attitudes.[74]

Norms that emerged during slavery were further reinforced by the sharecropping system. Since women who produced many children were highly prized, and every able-bodied family member was needed to make sharecropping a successful economic venture, children were valued as a commodity. Children were also valued for the emotional needs they met. When Hortense Powdermaker interviewed blacks in a small town in Mississippi during the 1930s, she found the black women "more buoyant and hopeful" than the black men in her sample. She offered this explanation:

> The general optimism of the women relates to their identification with their children both as cause and effect. The children carry them ahead into a future where more may be possible; and the future seems more promising, more important, more worth struggling for, because of the children.[75]

In short, economic institutions in the South valued both the laboring and the childbearing capacities of black women, and it was in the context of these institutions that distinctively black patterns of family formation were sustained.

The efforts of the Freedman's Bureau served to protect the interests of Southern planters. Those planters and state officials created a system of dependency for black families who were sharecroppers, in which they had neither full employment nor continuous assistance from the state. Racial oppression and the collapse of the southern economic empire were the catalyzing forces for blacks to migrate to the urban North in search of a better life. In this new economic climate, however, the system of obligatory dependence created in the South for black sharecropping families, coupled with distinct family formation patterns, would become a major liability as poor black families tried to adjust to life in major urban centers. And finally, the gravity of the transition to the urban North would further weaken two-parent black families already beleaguered by slavery and sharecropping.

Notes

1. Richard Sutch, "The Breeding of Slaves for Sale and the Westward Expansion of Slavery." in *Race and Slavery in the Western Hemisphere; Quantitative Studies*, ed. Stanley L. Engerman and Eugene D. Genovese (Princeton: Princeton University Press, 1975). Sutch has attributed these growth differentials to the influence of the slave-breeding practices of planters. He also asserts that the planters' practices "fostered polygamy and promiscuity among slaves" (198). In Stanley L. Engerman's opening chapter he challenges Sutch's analysis and argues that these issues were far more complicated than Sutch realized; *Race and Slavery*. See also Robert W. Fogel and Stanley L. Engerman, "Recent Findings in the Study of Slave Demography and Family Structure," *Sociology and Social Research* 63 (April 1979): 566–89.

2. Stanley L. Engerman, "Black Fertility and Family Structure in the U.S., 1880–1940," *Journal of Family History* 2 (June 1977):117–38; For the analyses of other scholars who have evaluated these changes, see Herman Lantz and Llewelyn Hendrix, "Black Fertility and the Black Family in the Nineteenth Century: A Re-examination of the Past," *Journal of Family History* 3 (Fall 1978):251–61; Jack Erickson Eblen, "New Estimates of the Vital Rates of the U.S. Black Population during the Nineteenth Century," *Demography* 11 (May 1974):301–319; Phillips Cutright and Edward Shorter contend that the decline was the result of the poor health of black women as a group; "Effects of Health on Completed Fertility of Nonwhite and White U.S. Women Born between 1867 and 1935," *Journal of Social History* 13 (Winter 1979): 191–217.

3. Quoted in Bettina Aptheker, *Woman's Legacy: Essays on Race, Sex, and Class in American History* (Amherst: University of Massachusetts Press, 1982), 62.

4. The catalyst for the black women's clubs to address these issues came from a letter that had been received by J. W. Jacks, a white male editor of a Missouri newspaper. He forwarded the letter to Josephine S. Pierre Ruffin, editor of *The Women's Era*, the first magazine in the United States to be owned, published and managed exclusively by black women. This letter, by a white man, attacked the virtue of black women, and the evidence had been supplied by other black women. Mrs. Ruffin circulated the letter widely to prominent black women and to the heads of other women's clubs around the country calling for a conference to discuss this and other social concerns of black women. The following year the National Association of Colored Women (NACW) was officially launched from this

conference, organization predating both the National Urban League and the NAACP. For a detailed account of the activities of the organization see "Black Feminism versus Peasant Values" in *The Golden Age of Black Nationalism*, ed. Wilson J. Moses (Hamden, Conn.: Archon, 1978), 103–31.

5. Phillip A. Bruce, *The Plantation Negro as a Freeman* (New York:G. P. Putnam, 1889), 19–20.

6. For discussion of the Reconstruction and the emergence of federal policies for the newly freed slaves, see Barbara J. Fields, "Ideology and Race in American History," in *Region, Race, and Reconstruction: Essays in Honor of C. Vann Woodward*, ed. J. Morgan Kousser and James M. McPherson (New York: Oxford University Press, 1982). For a synthesis that gives equal time to the protagonists in the Reconstruction drama, see Eric Foner, *Reconstruction: America's Unfinished Revolution 1863–1877* (New York: Harper & Row, 1988). The Republican Party's southern economic program is highlighted by Louis S. Gerteis, *From Contraband to Freeman: Federal Policy Toward Southern Blacks, 1861–65* (Westport, Conn.: Greenwood Press, 1973).

7. Jacqueline Jones, "Southern Diaspora: Origins of the Northern 'Underclass,' in *The "Underclass" Debate: Views from History*, ed. Michael B. Katz (Princeton: Princeton University Press, 1993), 33–34.

8. Other scholars likewise reported that black women were no longer working in the fields"; To review the findings of a survey conducted in 1868 on the labor and economic conditions in the South, see, for example, Francis W. Loring and C. F. Atkinson, *Cotton Culture and the South Considered with Reference to Emigration*, (Boston: Williams, 1869); Jonathan M. Wiener, "Class Structure and Economic Development in the American South, 1865–1955," *American Historical Review* 84 (October 1979):970–92.

9. For discussion of the wage labor contributions of black women and children, see Claudia Goldin, "Female Labor Force Participation: The Origin of Black and White Differences, 1870–1880, *Journal of Economic History* 37 (March 1977), 91–96; to understand how emancipation altered control over their labor, see Janet Herman, *The Pursuit of a Dream* (New York: Oxford University Press 1981).

10. Gerald D. Jaynes, *Branches without Roots: Genesis of the Black Working Class in the American South, 1862–1882.* (New York: Oxford University Press, 1986), 59.

11. Harold D. Woodman, "Post-Civil War Southern Agriculture and the Law," *Agricultural History* 53 (January 1979):33. For more on planters' arrangements with black farmers see Joseph D. Reid, Jr., "White Land, Black Labor, and Agricultural Stagnation: The Causes and Effects of Sharecropping in the Postbellum South," *Explorations in Economic History* 16(January 1979):31–55; Jay R. Mandle, *The Roots of Black Poverty: The Southern Plantation Economy After the Civil War* (Durham, N.C.:Duke University Press, 1978).

12. Herbert Gutman, *The Black Family in Slavery and Freedom 1750–1925* (New York: Vintage, 1976), 167.

13. Jacqueline Jones, *Labor of Love, Labor of Sorrow: Black Women's Work and the Family from Slavery to the Present* (New York: Basic Books, 1985), 102.

14. Gutman presented 1880 data from 14,345 southern rural and urban households,

which disclosed that "nine in ten blacks lived in households that had at their core two or more members of a black nuclear family"; *The Black Family*, 443.

15. Jones, *Labor of Love*, 80.

16. For a discussion of the economic and social forces that kept freedpeople in the South during this period, see Roger L. Ransom and Richard Sutch, *One Kind of Freedom: The Economic Consequences of Emancipation* (Cambridge: Cambridge University Press, 1977); Jonathan Weiner, *Social Origins of the New South: Alabama, 1860–1885* (Baton Rouge: Louisiana State University Press, 1978).

17. Foner, *Reconstruction*, 87–88.

18. Peter Kolchin, *First Freedom: The Response of Alabama Blacks to Emancipation and Reconstruction* (Westport, Conn.: Greenwood Press, 1972), 62. Black male leaders like Alexander Crummell and Martin Delaney sought to move the race forward by advocating for patriarchal authority. See Wilson Jeremiah Moses, *Alexander Crummell: A Study of Civilization and Discontent* (New York: Oxford University Press, 1989), 218–20.

19. Howard Bell, ed., *Proceedings of the National Negro Convention, 1830–1864* (New York: Arno Press, 1969), 33.

20. Examinations of the Freedman's Bureau's treatment of black women include Foner, *Reconstruction*, 87–88 and Orville Burton, *In My Father's House Are Many Mansions: Family and Community in Edgefield, South Carolina* (Chapel Hill: University of North Carolina Press, 1985), 231; Jones, *Labor of Love*, 62–63.

21. In spite of the Bureau policies' bias against black women, one observer found "scores of coloured women in the South working and managing plantations of from 20 to 100 acres. They and their boys and girls doing all the labour, and marketing in the fall from ten to fifty bales of cotton"; Frances Ellen Harper, "Colored Women of America," *Englishman's Review*, January 15, 1878, 12–13.

22. Jones, *Labor of Love*, 62.

23. For an important sociological study about extended kin obligations among African-Americans, see Theodore Rosengarten, *All God's Dangers: The Life of Nate Shaw* (New York: Knopf, 1974). A rural Alabama cotton farmer and the son of former slaves, Shaw was illiterate when interviewed in his eighty-fifth year.

24. Gutman, *The Black Family*, 224–29.

25. See Gutman for detailed accounts of the former slaves' concerns throughout the South about the abuses of former slaveowners in the apprenticeship of black children in the immediate aftermath of emancipation; *The Black Family*, 402–412.

26. Reconsiderations of the dissidence of black women during this period include Noralee Frankel, "Workers, Wives, and Mothers: Black Women in Mississippi, 1860–1870" (Ph.D. diss., George Washington University, 1983); Barry A. Crouch and Larry Madaras, "Reconstructing Black Families: Perspectives from the Texas Freedman's Bureau Records," *Prologue* 18 (Summer 1986):109–21.

27. Ann Patton Malone, *Sweet Chariot* (Chapel Hill: University of North Carolina Press, 1992), 229.

28. Quoted in Kolchin, *First Freedom*. For Frances Ellen Harper's account of the spou-

sal abuse she found when she toured the South, see William Still, *The Underground Railroad: A Record* (Philadelphia: People's Publishing, 1879), 773.

29. For a discussion of how political developments further reinforced black male patriarchal authority, see James O. Horton, "Freedom's Yoke: Gender Conventions among Antebellum Free Blacks," *Feminist Studies* 12 (Spring 1986):51–76.

30. Horton, "Freedom's Yoke," 70.

31. E. Franklin Frazier, *The Negro Family in the United States* (Chicago: University of Chicago Press, 1939), 102.

32. Quoted in Gutman, *The Black Family*, 73.

33. Burton, *In My Father's House*, 255.

34. John Dollard, *Caste and Class in a Southern Town, Caste and Class in a Southern Town* (Garden City, N.Y.: Doubleday Anchor, 1949), 450–51.

35. Foner, *Reconstruction*, 84. The eagerness of blacks to marry is related to their enthusiasm to find the whereabouts of family members who had been separated from them during slavery and its aftermath. For example, Betty M. Kuyk analyzed the *Richmond Planet*, Virginia's largest black newspaper, and found that thirty-five years after the end of the Civil War, requests were so frequent concerning lost or missing relatives that the paper established a regular column in which it printed the letters, entitled "Do You Know Them?"; "Seeking Family Relationships," *Negro History Bulletin* 42 (July 1979): April-May-June.

36. W.E.B. DuBois, "The Negroes of Farmville, Virginia: A Social Study," *Bulletin of the Department of Labor* 14(January 1898): 17, 28–30.

37. W.E.B. DuBois, "The Negroes in the Black Belt: Some Social Sketches"[1899]; "The Negro Landholder of Georgia"[1901]; "The Negro Farmer"[1906] in *Contributions by W.E.B. DuBois in Government Publications and Proceedings* ed. Herbert Aptheker (Millwood, N.Y.: Kraus-Thomson, 1980). The monograph "The Negroes of Lowndes County, Alabama," was destroyed by bureau officials.

38. Burton, *In My Father's House*, 292–93.

39. Charles S. Johnson, *Shadow of the Plantation* (Chicago: University of Chicago Press, 1934), 7.

40. Ibid., 49.

41. Ruth Reed, "The Negro Women of Gainesville, Georgia," Phelps-Stokes Fellowship Studies, No. 6, *Bulletin of the University of Georgia* 22 (December 1921): 38.

42. *Johnson, Shadow of the Plantation*, 49.; Johnson's observations regarding the early childbearing in these communities are supported by the data analyzed in M.D.R. Evans, "American Fertility Comparisons of White and Non-white Co-horts Born 1903–56, *Population and Development Review* 2, 12 (June 1986). Evans reports the mean fertility age of whites and nonwhites (primarily black) and documents the lower age of fertility for blacks when compared to whites. In the earlier cohorts (1903–18), the mean age was about one year later for whites. In the 1925–41 cohort, the differences declined to about half a year and then stabilized; later, the differences grew steadily. (I discuss the reasons for the increases in black adolescent fertility later.) These data are presented in Figure 2.1.

43. Johnson, *Shadow of the Plantation*, 67. (My italics.)

44. Charles S. Johnson, *Growing Up in the Black Belt: Negro Youth in the Rural South* (1941, reprint; New York: Schocken 1967), 226, 231.

45. Johnson, *Shadow of the Plantation*, 83.

46. Gutman, *The Black Family*, 449.

47. W.E.B. DuBois determined in *The Philadelphia Negro: A Social Study* (1889; reprint, New York: Schocken, 1967) that the mortality rate among Philadelphia's black males was "fierce" and that half of the African-American women with children in the 1880s were widows.

48. Samuel H. Preston, Suet Lim, and S. Philip Morgan, "African American Marriage in 1910: Beneath the Surface of Census Data," *Demography* 29 (February 1992): 1–15.

49. Philip Morgan and Ellen A. Kramarow, "Stability and Change in Female Headship: The United States 1910–1980," (unpublished paper, April 1992).

50. For reexaminations of the marriage patterns of blacks during this period, see T. J. Woofter, *Negro Migration: Changes in Rural Organizations and Population in the Cotton Belt*, (1920; reprint, New York: AMS Press, (1971). Studying 742 African American mothers in Athens, Georgia, Woofer expressed concern that "large numbers" of black mothers, without spouses, were rearing children. He found that 73 percent were living with a husband. See also Reed, "Negro Women of Gainesville," 7–61. Reed's findings showed that 75.1 percent of black women were married and living with husbands. Johnson also found that 75 percent of the families he studied had a male as head of the household; *Shadow of the Plantation*, 51.

51. Department of Labor, Children's Bureau, "Illegitimacy as a Child-Welfare Problem," pt. 1 Bureau Publication no. 66 Washington, D.C.: Government Printing office, 1920); 25.

52. The communities in Georgia that were studied by T. J. Woofter and Ruth Reed were similar, in that the blacks who were gainfully employed were more likely to rely on some type of domestic service than on tenant farming. The exception is Johnson's sample, which was drawn from a community of tenant farmers; the rates of single-parent families in his population exceeded the averages reflected in the census data. Another explanation for the higher rates of single parents in Johnson's sample is that is that by the 1930s, tenant farming was on the decline, and if figures on family structure had been recorded earlier, a larger proportion of the families may have reported a male as head of the household.

53. W.E.B. DuBois, *The Negro American Family* (Chicago: University of Chicago Press, 1978[1909]); T. J. Woofter, *The Negro Problem in the Cities* (New York: Doubleday, Doran, 1928).

54. Kelly Miller, *Race Adjustment: Essays on the Negro in America*, (New York: Neale, 1910), 173.

55. David Katzman, *Seven Days a Week* (New York: Oxford University Press, 1978), 46–47.

56. For further discussion of relationship between white immigrants and black migration, see Brinley Thomas, *Migration and Urban Development: A Reappraisal of British and American Long Cycles*, (London: England, 1972).

57. Roger L. Ransom and Richard Sutch, *One Kind of Freedom: The Economic Consequences of Emancipation* (Cambridge,: Cambridge University Press, 1977), 196.

58. Quoted in James Grossman, *Land of Hope* (Chicago: University of Chicago Press, 1989):14.

59. For an excellent analysis of the labor practices in the Southern textile industry, see Allen H. Stokes, Jr., "Black and White Labor for the Development of the Southern Textile Industry, 1800–1920 (Ph.D. diss., University of Southern Carolina, 1977).

60. For an excellent description of the practice of "whitecapping," see Nell Irvin Painter, *Exodusters: Black Migration to Kansas after Reconstruction* (New York: Knopf, 1977).

61. Carter G. Woodson, *A Century of Negro Migration* (Washington, D.C.: The Assn for the Study of Negro Life and History 1918), 69.

62. W. E. B. DuBois, "Brothers Come North," *Crisis* 19 (January 1920): 106.

63. The findings from the 1917 survey are reported in Woofter, *Negro Migration.*

64. St. Clair Drake and Horace R. Cayton, *Black Metropolis: A Study of Negro Life in a Northern City* (New York: Harcourt, Brace, 1945), 99–100.

65. Paula Giddings, *When and Where I Enter: The Impact of Black Women on Race and Sex in America,* (New York: Morrow, 1984), 71.

66. James Grossman, *Land of Hope: Chicago, Black Southerners, and the Great Migration,* (Chicago: University of Chicago Press, 1989), 28.

67. John Hope Franklin, "Public Welfare in the South During the Reconstruction Era, 1865–80," *Social Service Review* 44 (December 1970): 390.

68. Dollard, *Caste and Class,* 125.

69. Mary Larabee, "Unmarried Parenthood under the Social Security Act," in *Proceedings of the National Conference on Social Work, 1939* (Chicago: Roger S. Hall, 1940), 449.

70. These data dispute a journalistic account of the black migration set forth by Nicholas Lemann when he quotes an informant who states that "most people on welfare here [in Chicago], they went on welfare there [in Mississippi]. . . . They have been mentally programmed that Mister Charlie's going to take care of them"; "The Origins of the Underclass, Pt. I," *Atlantic Monthly* 257 (June 1986): 35, 41, 47.

71. Many black families moved from one plantation to another in spite of these restrictions. See Peter Gottlieb for a report from a Mississippi landowner on the hectic movement of black families from one plantation to another, *Making Their Own Way* (Urbana: University of Illinois Press), 22–23. Gottlieb argues that these patterns reflect that they were cultivating a dozen or more different plots of land for different landlords.

72. For the results of FERA surveys on planter–tenant relations, see Harold C. Hoffsomer, "Landlord–Tenant Relations and Relief in Alabama," Federal Emergency Relief Administration Confidential Research Bulletin 2738 (Washington, July 10, 1934); A. R. Mangus, "The Rural Negro on Relief," Federal Emergency Relief Administration Research Bulletin 6950 (Washington, D.C.: 1935).

73. Hylan Lewis, *Blackways of Kent* (Chapel Hill: University of North Carolina, 1955), 122–124.

74. Robert E. Park, foreword to Johnson, *Shadow of the Plantation,* xiii.

75. Hortense Powdermaker, *After Freedom* (New York: Viking, 1939):367

CHAPTER THREE

THE AFRICAN-AMERICAN FAMILY IN THE MATERNALISTIC ERA

The number of Negro cases [on public welfare] is few due to the unanimous feeling on the part of the staff and board that there are more work opportunities for Negro women and to the intense desire not to interfere with local labor conditions. That attitude that "they have always gotten along," and that "all they'll do is have more children" is definite.

A southern field supervisor, quoted in Mary Larabee, "Unmarried Parenthood under the Social Security Act"

The 1890s marked the beginning of a new period in the history of social welfare dubbed the Maternalistic Era.[1] The failure of private and public relief efforts was clearly exposed by the depression of 1893, and the decade witnessed exponential growth in urban areas, an influx of new immigrants, agitation from a militant labor movement, and mounting criticism of institutional care for children. Most reformers rejected large institutions as a way of caring for children, and believed that children should be taken from their families simply on account of poverty. Michael Katz argues that the child-saving campaign shifted to an emphasis on family preservation and rested on a new psychology that encouraged an "enhanced role for government and a reordered set of relations between families and the state."[2]

Public welfare as we know it emerged with the passage of the Social Security Act in 1935. While the women reformers from the Children's Bureau managed to quietly nationalize the Mothers' Pension concept, the programs for female workers, mothers, and children that proliferated in the United States during the early 1900s were made possible by both black and white female activism. This first generation of female activists professionalized their objectives, bureaucratized their techniques, and organized their reform networks.[3] By these means they built a set of interlocking organizations that strengthened their influence on the enactment and implementation of social programs for families and children.[4]

Black Women's Activism for Social Provisions

The black women who worked to eradicate poverty and illiteracy in their communities understood that they could not easily separate the issues of impoverishment from those of racial inequality. They understood, in the words of Deborah White, that "the race problem . . . inherently included the problem of poverty."[5] The education of the black masses was generally viewed as the key to "uplifting" the black race. And the importance of the untiring efforts of black women in the struggle for racial equality was emphasized. In 1892 Anna Julian Cooper wrote in *A Voice of the South* that black women were "the fundamental agency under God in the regeneration . . . of the race, as well as the groundwork and starting point of its progress upward".[6] Mary Church Terrell, in a speech at a Charity Organization Society meeting in 1910, declared: "If anyone should ask me what special phase of the colored American's development makes me most hopeful of his ultimate triumph over present obstacles, I should answer unhesitatingly, it is the magnificent work the women are doing to regenerate and elevate the race."[7]

During the late nineteenth century, a club movement emerged among women of both races, fueled by a sense that progress in the world could accelerate if women expanded their role. Chicago alone reported forty-one black women's clubs by the year 1913 with a total of twelve hundred members. However, as Paula Giddings notes, while reform and aid to the poor was high on the agenda of both white and black clubs, the efforts of the black women had a different emphasis, because they understood that "their fate was bound with that of the masses."[8] Leaders of black women's clubs participated in the founding of such organizations as the NAACP, the National Urban League, and various social service agencies to assist black victims of an oppressive society.[9]

Some of the earliest of these social service activities were documented by Frances Ellen Harper in an article entitled "Colored Women of America," published in England in 1878. She mentions a Kansas Relief Organization, which provided funds for black migrants. Citing an article in *Freedom's Journal* that claimed that there were ten times as many white women as black women in poverty in New York City, she identifies the black-run Mother Society of New York as largely responsible for this difference. She also cites rumors that a black woman by the name of Mary Ellen Pleasant financed John Brown's raid at Harpers Ferry and underwrote the building of New York's African Methodist Episcopal Church even though she was a Catholic.[10]

Black women also began to challenge the male view that women belonged in the home with children. One such statement illustrates the prevailing attitudes during this period: "The race needs wives who stay at home, being supported by their husbands, and then they can spend time in the training of their children."[11] The economic reality was that few black men could earn a "family wage," so black women had to work outside as well as inside the home. As Mary Church Terrell put it, black women "had two heavy loads to carry through an unfriendly world, the burden of race as well as that of sex."[12] An alternative to the black male view of woman's place was offered by Selena Sloan Butler, an educator and a Spelman graduate:

> It is argued by most people that women's specific and only mission is that of maternity. . . . Since so much is expected of her, is it not right that she should be given opportunity for development in the highest and broadest sense, that her physical, mental, and *moral* nature may be prepared to fill the highest and noblest calling allotted her?[13]

These views were not only challenged by women; DuBois likewise challenged the prevailing beliefs on women in *Darkwater*, published in 1920. In his essay "The Damnation of Women," DuBois declared that "the uplift of women is, next to the problem of the colorline and the peace movement, our greatest modern cause."[14] He advanced the following solution: "The future woman must have a life work and economic independence. She must have knowledge. She must have the right to motherhood at her own discretion."[15] Observing the exponential increases in the numbers of working women (between 1910 and 1920 the number of women in the work force doubled), he continued: "We cannot imprison women again in a home or require them all on pain of death to be nurses and housekeepers."[16] Having attained an independence from men under slavery, DuBois concluded, black women were in a position to give leadership to the whole struggle for women's emancipation.

Although black women reformers agreed with DuBois that black women could not be "imprisoned" in their homes, at the same time Linda Gordon has noted that they understood "slavery had undermined the bases of maternalism—home and family ties, the sanctity of marriage, and the instincts of motherhood."[17] Rather than trying to balance their activism in the public sphere with home and children, many educated black women opted to have no children.[18] These women viewed maternalistic reform as the highest priority, which included an emphasis on work with children.

The aspirations, zeal, and commitment shown by the leaders of the black women's groups took shape within the broader climate of the black community as a whole. Black colleges, especially black women's colleges, instilled in their female students a sense of social responsibility, a belief that their education and training should not only be used for personal advancement but also to "uplift" the race, and most of them had outreach programs to provide education and social services for the masses of black people. But while the philanthropic efforts of the black community were noteworthy, they were not sufficient to overcome the longstanding adversity faced by the black family as the result of slavery, sharecropping, and the prolonged neglect of the federal government.

The Emergence of Mothers' Pensions Programs

In 1911, Illinois and Missouri led the states in efforts to aid poor children in their own homes by establishing the Mothers' Pensions programs. In deciding which poor mothers would be eligible for aid, state legislators and social agencies could consult the Conference on the Care of Dependent Children, commonly known as the First White House Conference, convened by Theodore Roosevelt in 1909. The conference proceedings announced agreement on this goal:

> Children of parents of *worthy character*, suffering from temporary misfortune, and children of reasonably efficient and *deserving mothers* who are without the support of the normal breadwinner should, as a rule, be kept with their parents, such aid being given as may be necessary to maintain *suitable homes* for the rearing of children.[19]

The principle that financial assistance to children was to be given to children in their own homes only if they had parents with a "worthy character" was adopted by the Mothers' Pensions programs, and later served to deny or restrict benefits to many poor black unmarried mothers. Although persons in the nascent profession of social work were taking the lead in developing child welfare policies, ideological tensions that existed within the fledgling profession generally prevented the advancement of social policies that would support poor mothers.[20] (The one notable exception was the Sheppard-Towner Act of 1921, to be discussed later.)

For example, in 1912—one year after Illinois and Missouri had initiated their widows—Frederic Almy, a leader in the Charity Organization Society read a paper to the National Conference of Charities and Corrections "Public Pensions to Widows. Experiences and Observations Oppose Such a Law." When Almy finished his presentation, COS leader, opened the discussion with these remarks:

> illegitimacy would, undoubtedly, have the effect of these crimes upon society. It is a great deal more worthiness of such mothers than of the widow, ous for the state to attempt relief on any large

Folks was supported by Mary Richmond, another leader in the COS, who protested the idea of pensions for widows and said that "so far from being a forward step, 'funds to parents' is a backward one".[22] Although the private charity leaders such as Richmond and Almy were outspoken, they were in the minority at this 1912 NCCC meeting.

The leaders of the COS were opposed by a broad coalition of progressive re-formers who argued that private charity and emergency public relief were no longer capable of sustaining the growing numbers of poor single mothers and their chil-dren. This coalition was comprised of federated women's associations such as the General Federation of Women's Clubs and the National Congress of Mothers. While these groups valued working-class support, their membership were mostly middle-aged, middle-class, poorly educated married white women.[23] Mark Leff, in his analysis of the Mothers' Pension movement in the Progressive Era, has main-tained that social workers in the private charities were opposed to the public pro-vision of relief because they wished to retain control of their traditional turf—the provision of in-home services for individuals and families. Some administrators of these Mothers' Pensions programs also advocated strict behavioral guidelines for mothers who wanted to qualify for funds; it is not clear whether they were influ-enced by COS leaders, or came to these ideas on their own.[24]

Although the COS, a group advocating private charity, had no control over publicly funded Mothers' Pensions programs, it left an indelible mark on mater-nalistic reform policy in general: the idea that support to single mothers was a gift to the "deserving" and that the state was obliged to supervise single mothers, mend dissolved marriages, and restore the dependency of wives on husbands whenever possible. For example, Florence Kelley, an activist from the Hull House and a divorced mother, supported the family wage as the appropriate goal of reform legislation. Despite her European socialist education, she did not believe that as-sistance to single mothers should be a matter of entitlement. She praised the "Amer-ican tradition that men support their families [and] wives throughout life," and lamented the movement that made the man no longer the breadwinner.[25] She also argued against the provision of child care for mothers who worked, except in cases of temporary emergency; she believed the social cost of mothers working outside the home was too high.[26] The real-world consequences of these attitudes would negative for poor single mothers, who were disproportionately African-America

Presentations made at the NCCC in 1909 reflected the ideas set forth by leaders of the COS and clearly had an impact on the eligibility criteria adopted the Mothers' Pensions programs: The only families who were eligible in all were those whose fathers had been permanently eliminated by death, lon imprisonment, or incurable insanity. Such "suitability" guidelines written manner, which avoided the more perplexing questions of how to deal w supporting fathers and unmarried mothers, had the effect of excluding many blacks from receiving benefits. Winifred Bell, citing one of the few studies conducted in 1934 on the Mothers' Pensions cases, states that 82 percent of the caseloads across the country dealt with widows, and that 96 percent of the mothers were white, 3 percent black, and 1 percent of other racial extractions.[27] (Christopher Howard, challenging Bell's claims, has asserted that the proportion of black families receiving mothers' pensions was roughly equal to the proportion of blacks in the total population in most northern and western states. His argument would have been strengthened if he had presented evidence to substantiate his assertion.[28]

Two primary factors contributed to the underrepresentation of black families in the Mothers' Pensions programs. First, the citizenry were reluctant to vote in favor of funding any public welfare programs for poor families, and the Mothers' Pensions programs in particular were never adequately funded. Second, there was resistance among social workers to giving public benefits to unmarried mothers; and since black mothers were overrepresented in that category, it would follow that they would be denied benefits more often than white mothers.[29] (The disparities between black and white mothers who were unmarried are reflected in Table 3.1, which gives percentages of out-of-wedlock births for both black and white women from 1929 to 1939.)

Social workers who denied public benefits to unmarried mothers were protected by the "suitable homes" guidelines. And their attitude was widely shared. As Gunnar Myrdal remarked, "According to popular belief in the South, few Negro low income families have homes which could be called 'suitable' for any purpose."[30] Most state welfare programs systematically excluded unmarried mothers, and the guidelines they used would set the precedent for the Aid to Dependent Children (ADC) title of the Social Security Act of 1935, which would become the federal government's second major program of public assistance for families in poverty.[31]

The Sheppard-Towner Maternity and Infant Act

This country's first federal program for social welfare was the Sheppard-Towner Maternity and Infant Act of 1921, which provided matching federal funds for maternal and infant health education. Julia Lathrop became the first woman to head a federal agency when she was appointed head of the Children's Bureau when it was established in 1912.[32] In the years when she was working on the legislative proposal for Sheppard-Towner, she made two deliberate judgments that were critically important for rural and nonwhite mothers. First, she decided to emphasize outreach to rural areas, where she perceived an enormous demand, rather than simply keep the focus on established programs. Anticipating the problems she would have getting her legislation through Congress, she established a national

Table 3.1   Number and Percentage of Live Births to Single Parent White and
Black Mothers in the United States, 1929–1938*

	White			Black		
		Single Parent Births			Single Parent Births	
Year	Total	Number	Percent	Total	Number	Percent
1929	1,566,075	27,280	1.77	231,010	33,141	14.35
1930	1,588,597	29,490	1.86	241,467	34,077	14.11
1931	1,518,513	30,137	1.98	237,923	35,815	15.05
1932	1,472,655	31,422	2.13	243,088	39,161	16.11
1933	1,399,690	30,308	2.17	235,094	39,338	16.73
1934	1,462,837	31,284	2.14	247,234	40,226	16.27
1935	1,461,196	31,749	2.17	238,862	39,625	16.59
1936	1,456,761	30,069	2.06	234,873	38,770	16.51
1937	1,487,811	30,543	2.05	246,093	41,042	16.68
1938	1,551,262	31,882	2.06	250,053	42,374	16.95
1939	1,526,398	31,114	2.040	251,840	43,570	17.30

*Exclusive of California, Massachusetts, and New York, which do not require a report
as to legitimacy, and South Dakota and Texas, which were not included in the
registration area during the entire eleven-year period.
SOURCE: Department of Labor, Children's Bureau, based on data from Census
Bureau, National Archives, RG 102, Box 173.

political network—consisting of local groups, federated women's associations, and
legislators—which helped muster the support she needed in congressional districts
that were not urban-industrial.[33] Second, she decided that it was strategically important that her legislation not be characterized as "charity." She believed that the
Sheppard-Towner programs, like the public schools, should be open to all American citizens and not just to the poor; motherhood, she claimed, was a venerated
service and children the nation's greatest assets. For these reasons, the Sheppard-
Towner Act was able to bypass the thorny issue of the mother's "suitability."

The effects of the Sheppard-Towner Act have been given mixed reviews. On
the positive side, public historian Richard Meckel states that the extension of state
and local maternal and infant health education reached "non-whites who had been
virtually ignored up to this time."[34] He makes the point that among the southern
states that fully utilized Sheppard-Towner matching funds were states like Alabama
and Georgia, which had not enacted mothers' pensions or protective labor laws.
On the negative side, Robin Muncy has noted that while the Act created career
opportunities for professional women, it threatened the autonomy of other women,
specifically those "mothers whose homes were 'invaded' by Lathrop's troops." Some
women "resisted and resented the intrusions," and this resistance was found par-

ticularly in communities of African-American, Native American, and foreign-born women. Specifically, she cites a study that found that the implementation of the Sheppard-Towner Act exposed them to the race and class identities that divided American women and "empowered some at the expense of others."[35]

African-American Mothers as the Undeserving Poor

With the passage of the Social Security Act in 1935, the federal government was for the first time responsible for public welfare. The Act did not initially include federal assistance for children in poor families. However, based on a report written by Katherine Lenroot and Martha M. Elliot of the Children's Bureau with the help of Grace Abbott, the Mothers' Pension plan was incorporated into the final Social Security bill as part of Title IV, the ADC program.[36] Under this program, eligible mothers were viewed as caregivers for their children, so that the benefits provided could be considered as going to the child and not the caregiver. Not until 1950 did the Social Security Act authorized any federal financing for benefits directed specifically to the mother.

The women reformers from the Children's Bureau managed to quietly nationalize the Mothers' Pensions concept, and the institutional structure that was created has worked against poor mothers. Two mutually exclusive categories emerged from the Social Security Act: social insurance and public assistance. Social insurance benefits were entitlements drawn from funds that workers had paid into, whereas public assistance was means-tested and stigmatized the recipient as poor. Analyzing this new institutional structure, McLanahan and Garfinkel note that widows were the only single mothers who were provided sufficient public benefits to allow them to invest in full-time child care without "paying the penalty of stigma and poverty."[37]

To secure the maximum federal funds available through ADC, most states needed to broaden the eligibility conditions written into their Mothers' Pensions statutes. Consequently, after 1935, many small communities that had offered benefits only to selected widows were suddenly involved in a federal–state effort to extend benefits to a broader group of families. Women with physical disabilities and mothers with dependent children were the primary recipients of ADC. A Woman's Bureau study entitled "Unattached Women on Relief in Chicago, 1937," found that compared to white women in the same situation, black women were more likely to be migrants from the South, younger, and physically handicapped. Jones does not discuss why the black women should have been younger than the white women; presumably that fact reflects well-documented earlier childbearing patterns among black women. According to the authors of the paper, the disabilities found among black women were due to the fact that black women had worked their whole lives as domestic servants and were no longer able to do so.[38]

One case illustrates this point. A fifty-three-year-old black widow had migrated to Chicago and supported herself and her children for forty years by doing domestic work. When she lost the last of her domestic work in 1932, she attempted to get assistance from her adult sons. One unmarried son never contributed to her support, and another son and his wife contributed minimally over the next several years. She moved in with another son and could not sustain a relationship with him or his wife; she left his home in despair and applied for welfare. From 1932 to 1937, in spite of problems with her health, she was able to get by on a combination of work relief jobs and direct welfare payments.[39]

In a paper presented to the National Conference of Social Work, Mary Larabee reported that during fiscal year 1937 only 3.5 percent of all children covered by the ADC program were living with their unmarried mothers. She noted that in five of the reporting states no children of unmarried mothers had been accepted, and in eleven other states less than fifty children had unmarried mothers. In reporting these facts, she stated that the "suitable home" philosophy was chiefly responsible for the exclusion of unmarried mothers and the "disproportionate exclusion of Negro and other nonwhite children."[40]

When Gunnar Myrdal discussed public assistance, he found that while there were "higher relief rates for Negroes, it was usually more difficult for them to get relief than it was for whites with similar needs."[41] He agreed with Larabee that the special eligibility requirements contained in most state laws concerning the "suitability" of the home may have had something to do with it. "Such regulations," he wrote, "may easily lend themselves to rather arbitrary interpretations whereby, in particular, many Negro families can be cut off from any chance of receiving this kind of assistance."[42]

In one of the few such studies conducted during the 1930s, Newell D. Eason evaluated the attitudes and experiences of black clients receiving ADC assistance, all of whom had recently come to Los Angeles from the rural areas in the South. The opening statement in the study, entitled "Attitudes of Negro Families on Relief," indicated that "Negroes are on relief in almost twice as great a proportion to their numbers in the population as are whites."[43] Eason placed the responsibility for blacks going on welfare on their employers, who "undermined the Negroes ambition [as workers] by replacing them in their jobs with white workers. . . . The Negro is then literally forced on relief."[44] Continuing, he stated that once a black person lost his or her job and went on welfare, the individual developed a negative attitude toward work:

In only a few cases were there found Negroes trying to help themselves by gardening, taking in washing, etc. In no instance were any found occupying their time by making any little novelties to sell or trying to learn a new trade to follow on their own account. They were on the whole averse to any suggestion of self-help.[45]

Eason then addressed the impact of welfare on the parent-child relationship:

There seems to be a weakening of the tie between parents and children due to the fact that the children seek the things they want from the social workers rather than the parents. . . . Parental authority as a result appears to be on the wane.[46]

When Drake and Cayton examine welfare during the depression years, they only discuss it against the backdrop of the options available to unmarried black mothers. They describe the "adjustment" that poor mothers made to "illegitimate" children as follows: 1. In two-parent families, the daughter could live with her parents and contribute to the support of the family. 2. In single-parent families, the daughter could work while the grandmother cared for the child. 3. The mother could set up an independent household and depend on "relief" for support. 4. She could "find a boyfriend to support herself and [her] child." They further state that "occasionally" a woman with an "illegitimate" child is even "fortunate enough to find a boy friend who may marry her."[47] In the writings of Drake and Cayton, welfare is only mentioned within the context of unmarried motherhood, however; they do not evaluate its impact on widows or divorced mothers who had worked as domestics for most of their adult lives.

Frazier was one of the few social scientists during this period to identify the beneficial aspects of welfare. In a paper entitled "Some Effects of the Depression on the Negro in Northern Cities," written during the same time frame, he summarized a study that found that infant mortality had declined in black neighborhoods where the number of welfare cases had been highest, and he remarked: "The mother on relief remains at home and is thus able to take greater precautions in regard to her own health during pregnancy, and devote more care to her child after its birth."[48]

A Tale of Six Cities

African-Americans suffered terribly during the Great Depression in both the North and the South. Blacks who were concentrated in the South were hit hard by the crisis in agriculture; those in the North, who worked primarily in domestic service and less skilled industrial positions, were hit by massive and persistent unemployment. When Richard Sterner summarized the data from the Department of Labor and the U. S. Public Health Service published in 1935–36, he found that while

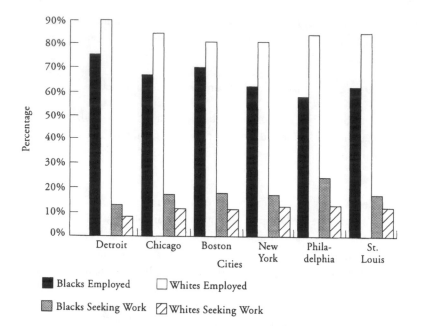

FIGURE 3.1   Percentage of households falling into various categories of employment, husband-wife families by city, 1935–1936. (From National Archives, Federal Security Agency, Social Security Board, "Statistics of Family Composition in Selected Areas of the U.S.," Bureau Memo 45)

66.9 percent of the white families had over $1,000 a year to spend, only 31.8 percent of the black families had even this much. In other words, two out of three black families were living on less than $85 a month.[49]

Blacks had experienced an expansion of their ranks in nothern industries during the 1920s. The depression offered the opportunity, however, to bring black employment down. According to Lizabeth Cohen, for example, between 1930 and 1940 the proportion of blacks in the low-skilled meat industry in Chicago dropped from 31 percent to 20 percent. By the end of 1932, 40 to 50 percent of Chicago's black work force was unemployed.[50] Data collected from 1934 to 1935 by yet another government department, the Federal Security Agency, are presented in Figure 3.1. This figure shows the percentages of blacks and whites who were employed and who were seeking work. The highest percentages of employed blacks were in Detroit and Boston, with rates of 75 and 62 percent; the lowest rate was 50.7 in Philadelphia. Perhaps more interesting, the difference between black and white employment rates in Boston

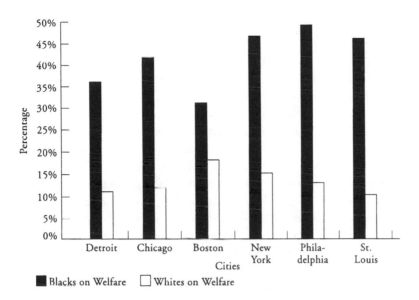

FIGURE 3.2   Percentage of single-parent households on welfare, by city, 1935–1936. (From National Archives, Federal Security Agency, Social Security Board, "Statistics of Family Composition in Selected Areas of the U.S.," Bureau Memo 45)

was only about 5 percentage points, whereas in Philadelphia it was 20 points. The high figure for Detroit probably reflects a relatively stronger industrial economy based on automobile manufacturing. These figures suggest that wage employment was still the major source of income for most blacks. (The explanation for Boston is different and will be discussed later.)

The weakness of the economy during the 1930s is most clearly reflected in the proportion of families receiving welfare (Figure 3.2), which, though high for both blacks and whites, was significantly higher for blacks. In St. Louis, Philadelphia, and New York, the proportion of black father-absent families on welfare was close to 50 percent, whereas that figure never exceeded 20 percent for white father-absent families.

These alarming figures suggest that despite the ingenuity used by social welfare administrators to deny public assistance to black mothers and children, by the mid-1930s "relief rivaled domestic service and agriculture as a source of income for black Americans."[51] Although blacks were overrepresented on the welfare rolls, in 1934 the average person on welfare was a white household head, thirty-eight years of age, with an elementary school education and ten years of work experience in an occupation. According to these figures, only about 17 percent of the welfare population represented "broken families or alone persons," and female heads of household were only about 14 percent of the total.[52]

Of all the groups during the Depression, however, black men had the highest unemployment rates; and black women did little better.[53] Indeed, the high unemployment in agriculture and domestic service, in which black women were concentrated, provides one explanation as to why black single-parent families had a much higher utilization of welfare than white single-parent families. Census data from this period also show a drop in black women's labor force participation, from 42 percent of black women in 1930 to 37.8 percent ten years later.[54]

Why were the disparities on all indexes between blacks and whites substantially smaller in Boston than in other cities? Elizabeth Pleck, who studied poverty and race in Boston from 1865 to 1900, points toward an answer. She found that the blacks in Boston were disproportionately "urban, mulatto, literate, and from the Upper South." Blacks from the Upper South, in her view, had the characteristics of the South's free blacks. "The logical conclusion is that most black Southerners in Boston had been free even before the Civil War."[55] If the black elite in Boston had managed to escape the devastating effects of slavery and sharecropping on the black family, this fact could explain the small disparities between blacks and whites in Boston during the 1930s.

To sum up, this analysis of black families in six cities during the 1930s shows that where employment rates were highest, the numbers of welfare cases were the lowest. In other words, it appears that when given job opportunities, blacks opted for participation in the labor force rather than welfare assistance. Overall, however, it seems clear that the Great Depression and its aftermath took an added toll on the black family.

Richard Polenberg confirmed this statement when he evaluated the 1940 census data and found that there were 12,866,000 blacks and they lagged behind whites on all of the major indicators. Whereas one out of three white males held white-collar positions, only one out of twenty black males were so employed. Among white women who worked, one out of ten was employed as a domestic; that figure for black women was six out of ten. Twice as many blacks as whites farmed, but a much smaller proportion worked their own land. Data on housing, health, and education revealed a similar pattern. Four times as many blacks as whites lived in houses with more than two persons per room, but only half as many lived in houses with two rooms per person. The black mortality was nearly twice that of whites. In Washington, D.C., the infant mortality rate among whites was 37 per 1,000 infants; among blacks, 71. Blacks could expect to live on average twelve years less than whites. Among blacks over the age of twenty-five, one in ten had not completed a single year of school, while one in a hundred was a college graduate.[56]

FDR's Legacy to African-American Families

President Franklin D. Roosevelt enjoyed popularity among African-Americans; the historian Nancy Weiss indicates that he is largely responsible for getting blacks to shift their commitment to the Democratic Party. At the same time, however, he left an ambiguous legacy for African-Americans. Although they were indebted to him for the assistance they received from the emergency and relief and work programs of the New Deal, very little was done for them in more permanently established social programs.[57]

Race became interwined with social policy when two bifurcated categories emerged from the Social Security Act: social insurance and public assistance. Social insurance benefits were entitlements drawn from funds that workers had paid into, whereas public assistance was means-tested and stigmatized the recipient as poor. Because of the distinction that was made between deserving and undeserving mothers in the Social Security policies, black women, who had always worked in greater proportions than white women, would, over time, be overrepresented in what would become Aid to Families with Dependent Children (AFDC). With this overrepresentation, AFDC would predictably become our nation's most visible and controversial program. Ann Orloff argues that this failure to create uniformity "reflected the inability of Roosevelt administration officials to overcome the deep resistance of Congress and some congressional constituencies to reform."[58]

New Deal agricultural policies, for example, especially those of the Agricultural Adjustment Administration (AAA), hurt southern black sharecroppers by forcing land out of production and shrinking black employment in the South. By providing incentives to landowners to replace sharecroppers with day workers, the AAA helped to transform southern family farming into a wage labor system; but agricultural workers were omitted in the New Deal wage and hour regulations. Planters were supposed to share their federal crop subsidies with their displaced tenants, but very few did so.[59] The greatest inequity, however, was that job opportunities in expanding sectors of the economy were not open to the newly displaced southern black workers.[60] The architects of the New Deal failed to institutionalize any federal commitment to full employment planning.

Another New Deal policy that disproportionately hurt black Americans was the exclusion of certain occupational groups from the Old Age Insurance and Unemployment Insurance programs. Among the major groups excluded were agricultural laborers, private domestic servants, and workers in nonprofit institutions. By excluding agricultural and domestic workers, the Social Security Act left two-thirds of employed blacks with no protection for old age or unemployment. Jerry Cates has maintained that from the Act's inception and until the 1950s, if the black elderly received anything, they were much more likely to receive Old Age

Assistance—an "unearned," means-tested benefit. Whites, in contrast, were more likely to receive Old Age Insurance, an "earned" social insurance benefit.[61] In addition, the Old Age Insurance and Unemployment Insurance policies both contained structural gender biases.[62]

Jill Quadagno has discussed the different treatment of blacks and whites by administrators of New Deal programs in the South. She argues that "cash grants to blacks were monitored" by local relief authorities in the South "so as not to undermine prevailing wage rates and to intrude as little as possible into the planter–tenant relationship."[63] Authorities in the South worried that even meager public welfare grants to temporarily unemployed blacks would have an impact on their availability to work in the fields; accordingly, they often excluded blacks altogether or suspended assistance payments during the harvest period when planters needed field hands. Even when welfare grants were given to blacks, southern states were allowed to pay them less than whites by using different criteria for determining need. According to Quadagno, it was not until the 1950s that southern states became willing to give more liberal federally subsidized grants to needy blacks.

Another assault on poor black families came in the 1939 amendments to the Social Security Act, whereby the "deserving" widows and the children of deceased wage-earners became entitled to a dependents' allowance and were thereby transferred from the ADC program to the Social Security system. This had the effect of focusing the ADC program, or what is now known as "welfare," mostly on abandoned wives, never-married mothers, or widows of nonworking husbands. Over time, the recipients of these benefits would become disproportionately African-American mothers and their children.

Finally, the Social Security Act failed to prohibit racial discrimination in housing and lending policies, and the Federal Housing Authority redlined black neighborhoods and refused to insure mortgages—a policy that contributed to the racial segregation and social isolation of poor blacks currently found in American housing.[64]

Furthermore, FDR refused to endorse an antilynching law because he was afraid of losing Southern support. From 1933 to 1935 lynch mobs murdered sixty-three blacks while southern sheriffs and deputies looked the other way. In 1937 a mob in Duck Hill, Mississippi, took two blacks from jail and set them on fire with blowtorches and then hanged them. The House passed several measures from 1937 to 1940 that would have made lynching illegal. Each measure expired in the Senate, however, because of forceful and consolidated opposition from southern Democrats. Roosevelt, realizing the bill's divisive potential, resigned himself to its defeat and never took a public stand.[65]

In the final analysis, the New Deal had some oppressive effects on African-Americans. It gave them a small program designed for widows with children, which would disproportionately sustain millions of black women and children and eventually become a political liability for the Democratic Party. And it left urban areas with racial discrimination in job opportunities and housing, and this level of inequality would be one of the major catalysts for the changing family structure among African-Americans. Mimi Abramovitz has written:

> For fifty years the gender bias structured into the [New Deal] programs has enforced the economic dependence of women on men, regulated women's labor force participation, assured women's role in maintaining and reproducing the labor force, and in general, upheld patriarchal social arrangements.[66]

Because the number of black households headed by women had their sharpest increase during the 1930s, these gender- and race-biased New Deal programs had their most devastating impact on black mother-only families.

Conclusion

A struggle between contending social forces shaped public benefits for mother-only families during the 1930s. The welfare policies that emerged from this struggle buttressed patriarchal social relations between the state and poor mother-only families. The state increased its power over the black family as the unemployment rates for black males soared. White mothers were more likely to escape the state's influence because they were more likely to marry a man with economic resources and to accede to his wishes. As numerous commentators on marriage and the family have noted, marriage was the most important economic decision a woman could make—her survival and comfort depended on her choices.[67]

The inability of many black mothers to qualify for public assistance under "unsuitable homes" policies (designed to ensure that recipients were morally fit to raise children) and the generally meager size of welfare grants forced black women into the marginal labor market, where they had access to jobs undesired by white women. The black woman's heavy responsibilities in the home and workplace continued to be a major factor in the neglect of her children. This neglect, which was documented by social scientists who studied the black family during this period, contributed to higher rates of delinquency among black adolescents.

New Deal policies increased the vulnerability of poor black families by not offering assistance to agricultural workers and domestic servants. New Deal agricultural policies impoverished rural black families in the South by changing the sharecropping system to a wage labor system. Besides undermining the black family as an economic unit, the erosion of the sharecropping system encouraged even more blacks to migrate northward, leaving behind supportive networks of kin relations and communal institutions. Finally, the industrial North would not be the "promised land" because New Deal policies failed to prohibit racial discrimination in housing and mortgage lending, thereby contributing to the growth of racially segregated urban ghettos and all the social ills they have come to epitomize.

Notes

1. The polity-centered theory set forth in this book has been applied to understanding the genesis of social insurance programs in the American welfare state. It is also useful when applied to the emergence of provisions for poor families. See Ann Orloff and Theda Skocpol, "Why Not Equal Protection: Explaining the Politics of Public Social Spending in Britain, 1900–1911, and the United States, 1880–1920," *American Sociological Review* 49 (1984): 741–42. For a more in-depth analysis see Theda Skocpol, *Protecting Soldiers and Mothers: The Political Origins of Social Policy in the United States* (Cambridge, Mass.: Harvard University Press, 1992); Ann Orloff, *The Politics of Pensions: A Comparative Analysis of Britain, Canada, and the United States, 1880–1940* (Madison: University of Wisconsin Press, 1993). For an alternative explanatory perspective, the corporate liberal theory, see G. William Domhoff, "Corporate Liberal Theory and the Social Security Act," *Politics and Society* 15(1986–87):297–330; J. Craig Jenkins and Barbara G. Brents, "Social Protest, Hegemonic Competition, and Social Reform: A Political Struggle Interpretation of the Origins of the American Welfare State," *American Sociological Review* 54(December 1989):891–909. For one of the most comprehensive analyses of the emergence of federal welfare policy regarding single mothers and the competing visions of how to provide aid during of this period see Linda Gordon, *Pitied but not Entitled: Single Mothers and the History of Welfare 1890–1935* (New York: The Free Press, 1994).

2. Michael Katz, *In the Shadow of the Poorhouse* (New York: Basic Books, 1986); 113.

3. For a detailed investigation into the development and characteristics of the female dominion over child welfare, see Robin Muncy, *Creating a Female Dominion in American Reform 1890–1935* (New York: Oxford University Press, 1991).

4. For an in-depth look at American female reform activities during the Progressive Era, see Lynn Gordon, *Gender and Higher Education in the Progressive Era* (New Haven: Yale University Press, 1990); Carol Smith-Rosenberg, *Disorderly Conduct: Visions of Gender in Victorian America* (New York: Knopf, 1985); Dorothy Sterling, ed., *We Are Your Sisters: Black Women in the Nineteenth Century,* (New York: Norton, 1984); Estelle B. Freedman, *Their Sisters' Keepers: Women's Prison Reform in America, 1830–1930* (Ann Arbor: University of Michigan Press, 1981); Martha Vicinus, *Independent Women: Work and Community for Single Women, 1850–1920* (Chicago: University of Chicago Press, 1985).

5. Quoted in Linda Gordon, "Black and White Visions of Welfare: Women's Welfare Activism, 1890–1945," *Journal of American History* 78 (September, 1991), 580. For a clearer understanding of the multiple commitments of black female reformers, see Cheryl Townsend Gilkes, "Building in Many Places: Multiple Commitments and Ideologies in Black Women's Community Work," in *Women and the Politics of Empowerment,* ed. Ann Bookman and Sandra Morgen (Philadelphia: Temple University Press, 1988).

6. Anna Julian Cooper, *A Voice of the South* (Xenia, Ohio: Aldine, 1892), 28.

7. Mary Church Terrell, "Club Work of Colored Women," *Southern Workman*, August 1901, 435.

8. Paula Giddings, *When and Where I Enter: The Impact of Black Women on Race and Sex in America* (New York: Morrow, 1984), 97.

9. For further delineation of the comprehensive nature of the services provided by the black women's clubs in Illinois, see Elizabeth Lindsay Davis, *The Story of the Illinois Federation of Colored Women's Clubs* (Chicago: n.p., 1922); for more information on the national movement see Elizabeth Lindsay Davis, *Lifting as They Climb* (Washington, D.C.: National Association of Colored Women, 1933).

10. Frances Ellen Harper, "Colored Women of America," *Englishwoman's Review*, January 15, 1878, 10.

11. Quoted in Giles B. Jackson and D. Webster Davis, *The Industrial History of the Negro Race of the United States*, Richmond, Va.: Negro Educational Association, 1911), 93.

12. Mary Church Terrell, "Being a Colored Woman in the United States," Unpublished paper, box 3, folder 53, Mary Church Terrell Papers, Howard University Library.

13. Quoted in Cynthia Neverdon-Morton, *Afro-American Women of the South and the Advancement of the Race, 1895–1925* (Knoxville: University of Tennessee Press, 1989), 3.

14. W.E.B. DuBois, *Darkwater: Voices from Within the Veil* (1920; reprint, New York: Schocken Books, 1969) *1969*), 181.

15. Ibid., 164–65.

16. Ibid., 181.

17. Gordon, *Pitied but not Entitled*, 126.

18. Landon Jones, *Great Expectations: America and the Baby Boom Generation* (New York: Cowand, McCann, & Geoghegan, 1980), 32.

19. The White House Conference, *Proceedings of the Conference on the Care of Dependent Children* (Washington, D.C., 1909), 1. (My italics.) 84th Cong., 2d sess., S. Doc. 721.

20. For an analysis of the tensions that existed within the social work profession at the turn of the century, see Donna Franklin, "Mary Richmond and Jane Addams: From Moral Certainty to Rational Inquiry in Social Work Practice," *Social Service Review* 60 (December 1986): 505–525; Roy Lubove, *The Professional Altruist; The Emergence of Social Work as a Career, 1880–1930* (Cambridge, Mass.: Harvard University Press, 1965).

21. *Proceedings of the National Conference of Charities and Corrections, 1912.* (Chicago: Hall, 1913), 486–87.

22. Ibid., 492.

23. For example, Mary Bogue, an administrator in the Mothers' Assistance Fund in Pennsylvania, presented a paper to the National Conference of Social Work in 1918 on the problems in the administration of these programs, insisting that further objective criteria were needed to identify "suitable homes" and "fit" mothers. In her view, it was improbable that such homes or mothers would be found except where the father was "permanently eliminated"; "Problems in the Administration of Mothers' Aid," *Proceedings of the National Conference of Social Work, 1918* (Chicago: Roger S. Hall,) 350.

24. Mark Leff, "Consensus for Reform: Mothers' Pension Movement in the Progressive Era," *Social Service Review* 47 (September, 1973): 408.

25. Florence Kelley, "Minimum-Wage Laws," *Journal of Political Economy* 20 (December 1912): 1003.

26. Florence Kelley, "The Family and the Woman's Wage," *Proceedings of the National Conference of Charities and Corrections, 1909* (Chicago:), 118:-21. "A friend of mine has conceived the monstrous idea of having a night nursery to which women so employed might send their children. And this idea was seriously described in so modern a publication as Charities and the Commons . . . without a word of editorial denunciation."

27. Kelley was ambivalent on other issues that had an impact on African-Americans as well. She had an honorary position on the board of NAACP's journal *The Crisis* and considered resigning when the publication called for social, economic, and political equality between the races. According to DuBois she would later concede that this was a "plain and temperate statement of a perfectly obvious truth." He eulogized her when she died in 1932. Herbert Aptheker, ed., "DuBois on Florence Kelley," *Social Work* 11 (October, 1966), 100.

28. Winifred Bell, *Aid to Dependent Children* (New York: Columbia University Press, 1965), 9. Bell presented data from the only systematic study of the racial composition of Mothers' Pensions caseloads conducted in 1931, of 46,597 families. About half of the black families lived in two states: Ohio and Pennsylvania. She also presents information from local caseloads, indicating that in Marion County, Indiana, for example, the population was 11 percent black, and no blacks received grants. One black family was chosen in Lake County, Indiana, where 10 percent of the population was black. On the other hand, in Westchester County, New York, where blacks constituted 4 percent of the population, black families were 3 percent of the caseload. In Toledo, Cleveland, Pittsburgh, and Philadelphia, on the other hand, black families represented a larger share of the caseload than of the population. What seems clear is that some local public welfare offices were more vigilant than others in conducting adequate investigations in order to determine the fitness of the mothers.

29. Christopher Howard, "Sowing the Seeds of "Welfare": The Transformation of Mothers' Pensions, 1900–1940," *Journal of Policy History* 4(1992), 201.

30. For an illustration of the way in which unmarried women were handled by a Mother's Aid Department, see Sophonisba Breckinridge, *Family Welfare Work in a Metropolitan Community, Selected Case Records* (Chicago: University of Chicago Press, 1924), sect. 6. This section highlights the fact that "one of the essential bases for a grant is verification of marriage" (634).

31. Gunnar Myrdal, *An American Dilemma* (1944; reprint, New York: McGraw-Hill 1964), 360.

32. Some of these mother-only families were denied benefits because, although the private and urban public charities had assumed primary responsibility for the poor up to this point, they lacked both the financial resources as well as the organizational capability to ease the economic crisis. For some historical accounts that focus on the role of private rather than public charities in reducing the poverty of families, see, for example, Paul Boyer, *Urban Masses and Moral Order in America 1820–1920* (Cambridge, Mass.: Harvard University

Press, 1978); John O'Grady, *Catholic Charities in the United States: History and Problems* (Washington, D.C.: National Conference of Catholic Charities, 1930); Kathleen D. Mc-Carthy, *Noblesse Oblige: Charity and Cultural Philanthropy in Chicago, 1849–1929* (Chicago: University of Chicago Press, 1982); Frank Dekker Watson, *The Charity Organization Movement in the United States: A Study in American Philanthropy* (New York: Macmillan, 1922).

33. For an analysis of how women reformers were able to convince President Taft to appoint Julia Lathrop, see Nancy Weiss, "Save the Children: A History of the Children's Bureau, 1903–1918" (Ph.D. diss., University of California at Los Angeles, 1974), 59–69.

34. Richard Meckel, *Save the Babies: American Public Health Reform Prevention of Infant Mortality 1850–1929* (Baltimore: Johns Hopkins University Press, 1990), 212.

35. Robin Muncy, *Creating a Female Dominion in American Reform 1890–1935* (New York: Oxford University Press, 1991), 94.

36. Ibid., 150–152.

37. Sara McLanahan and Irwin Garfinkel, "Single Mothers, the Underclass, and Social Policy," *Annals of the American Academy of Political and Social Science* 501(January 1989): 96.

38. Harriet A. Byrne and Cecile Hillyer, "Unattached Women on Relief in Chicago, 1937," Department of Labor, Women's Bureau Bulletin 158 (Washington, D.C., 1938).

39. This story is summarized by Lois Rita Helmbood, "Beyond the Family Economy: Black and White Working-Class Women during the Great Depression," *Feminist Studies* 13(Fall 1987): 631.

40. Mary Larabee, "Unmarried Parenthood Under the Social Security Act," *Proceedings of the National Conference on Social Work, 1939* (Chicago: Hall Printing Co., 1940), 447–49.

41. Myrdal, *American Dilemma*, 356.

42. Ibid., 360.

43. Newell D. Eason, "Attitudes of Negro Families on Relief: Toward Work, toward Home, toward Life," *Opportunity* 12 (December 1935): 367.

44. Ibid., 367.

45. Ibid., 368.

46. Ibid., 368.

47. St. Clair Drake and Horace Cayton, *The Black Metropolis* (New York: Harcourt, Brace and Co.), 590, 593.

48. E. Franklin Frazier, "Some Effects of the Depression on the Negro in Northern Cities," *Science and Society* 2 (Fall 1938): 495–96.

49. Richard Sterner, *The Negro's Share* (New York: Harper, 1944), 000.

50. Lizabeth Cohen, *Making A New Deal: Industrial Workers in Chicago, 1919–1939* (Cambridge: Cambridge University Press, 1990): 242.

51. Jacqueline Jones, *Labor of Love, Labor of Sorrow, Black Women's Work and the Family from Slavery to the Present* (New York: Basic Books, 1985), 223.

52. These figures are taken from Gladys L. Palmer and Katharine D. Wood, *Urban*

Workers on Relief, Works Progress Administration, Research Monograph 4, pt. 1 (Washington, D.C., 1936), xxiii–xiv.

53. For an analysis of the unemployment rates among blacks during this period, see Katz, *Shadow of the Poorhouse,* ch. 8; Jones, *Labor of Love,* ch. 6.

54. Department of Commerce, Census Bureau, Sixteenth Census (1940), vol. 3, *The Labor Force* (Washington, D.C.: Government Printing Office, 1945), pt. 1.

55. Elizabeth Pleck, *Black Migration and Poverty, Boston 1865–1900* (New York: Academic Press, 1979), 53.

56. Richard Polenberg, *One Nation Divisible: Class, Race, and Ethnicity in the United States Since 1938* (New York: Viking Press, 1985; ,), 24–25.

57. Nancy Weiss, *Farewell to the Party of Lincoln: Black Politics in the Age of FDR* (Princeton: Princeton University Press, 1983). For a perspective on blacks' response to New Deal emergency and relief programs, see Harvard Sitkoff, *A New Deal for Blacks: The Emergence of Civil Rights as a National Issue,* vol. 2, *The Depression Decade* (New York: Oxford University Press, 1978), ch. 3.

58. Ann Shola Orloff, *The Politics of Pensions: A Comparative Analysis of Britain, Canada, and the United States, 1880–1940* (Madison: University of Wisconsin Press, 1993), 298.

59. For an examination of how New Deal price supports for agriculture pushed the black masses off the land, see Doug McAdam, *Political Process and the Development of Black Insurgency, 1930–1970* (Chicago: University of Chicago Press, 1982), 73–82.

60. For documentation of job discrimination against blacks during the 1930s and 1940s, see Richard L. Rowan, *The Negro in the Steel Industry,* Racial Policies of American Industry Series, Report no. 3 (Philadelphia: Wharton School of Finance and Commerce, University of Pennsylvania, 1968); Walter A. Fogel, *The Negro in the Meat Industry,* Racial Policies in American Industry Series, Report no. 12 (Philadephia: Wharton School of Finance and Commerce, University of Pennsylvania, 1970); Edward Greer, "Racism and U.S. Steel, 1906–1974," *Radical America* 10 (September–October 1976): 45.

61. Jerry Cates, *Insuring Inequality: Administrative Leadership in Social Security 1935–54* (Ann Arbor: University of Michigan Press, 1983).

62. For an in-depth analysis of the structural gender inequities in the New Deal Programs, see Susan Ware, *Beyond Suffrage: Women in the New Deal* (Cambridge, Mass.: Harvard University Press, 1981); Jane Humphries, "Women: Scapegoats and Safety Valves in the Great Depression," *Review of Radical Political Economics* 8 (Spring 1976): 98–121.

63. Jill Quadagno, *The Transformation of Old Age Security* (Chicago: University of Chicago Press, 1988), 246.

64. For more in-depth analyses of how New Deal programs reinforced racial segregation, see Christopher Wye, "New Deal and the Negro Community: Toward a Broader Conceptualization," *Journal of American History* 59 (December 1972) 621–639; E. Franklin Frazier, "The Impact of Urban Civilization upon Negro Family Life," *American Sociological Review* 2 (October 1937):; Arnold R. Hirsch, *Making the Second Ghetto: Race and Housing in Chicago, 1940–1960* (Cambridge: Cambridge University Press, 1983).

65. Robert W. Dubay, "Mississippi and the Proposed Federal Anti-Lynching Bills of 1937–1938," *The Southern Quarterly* (October 1968): 73–87.

66. Mimi Abramovitz, *Regulating the Lives of Women: Social Welfare Policy from Colonial Times to the Present* (Boston: South End Press, 1988), 235.

67. For a clearer understanding of the role that marriage played in a nineteenth-century Southern town, see Suzanne Lebsock, *The Free Women of Petersburg: Status and Culture in a Southern Town, 1784–1860* (New York: Norton, 1984); for a more comprehensive legal analysis of marriage and the family, see Frances E. Olson, "The Family and the Market: a Study of Ideology and Legal Reform," *Harvard Law Review* 96 (May 1983): 1521–33.

CHAPTER FOUR

THE ARDUOUS TRANSITION TO THE INDUSTRIAL NORTH

When Martin Luther King, Jr., decided to take the southern movement north into Chicago, some thought he was pressing his luck.

Henry Hampton and Steve Fayer, Voices of Freedom

The migration to the industrial North not only reshaped African-American history but also left its reverberative imprint on black family life. Asa Briggs has maintained that "to understand how people respond to industrial change it is important to examine what kind of people they were at the beginning of the process."[1] For African-Americans, the understanding begins at the pivotal juncture known as the Great Migration.[2]

Feminist writers have argued that the rise of industrial capitalism and the concurrent separation of home and work not only restructured the labor market but simultaneously strained gender relations within the family system.[3] While this analysis enhances our understanding of what has happened to the black family, it is not sufficient to explain the destabilization of the two-parent family system among African-Americans. I will argue that in trying to refashion their family economies by seeking better opportunities in the North, black families paradoxically weakened a family structure that was already breaking down, and set the stage for the exponential increase in black mother-only families that was "discovered" by social scientists after World War II.

Black Southerners and the Great Migration

For decades prior to the Great Migration, which August Meier has called "after Emancipation . . . the great watershed in American Negro history," the population

Table 4.1   Percentages of Blacks Living in Urban and Rural Areas, 1890–1920

Year	United States		South		North and West	
	Urban	Rural	Urban	Rural	Urban	Rural
1890	20	80	15	85	62	38
1900	23	77	17	88	70	30
1910	27	73	21	79	77	23
1920	34	66	25	75	84	16

SOURCE: Reynolds Failey, *The Growth of the Black Population* (Chicago: Markham Publishing Co., 1971), p. 50.

concentration among southern blacks had been continously shifting.[4] Some blacks left the agrarian areas for cities or small towns, while others simply moved about as seasonal laborers.[5]

Beginning early in the twentieth century, social scientists and inquisitive reformers gathered much data on the northern migration and on black life in "novel" urban environments.[6] What captured their attention was the rapid transition blacks were making from the rural to urban areas. The demographic redistribution of the black population from rural to urban areas from 1910 to 1920 is shown in Table 4.1. Although the changes were minuscule prior to 1910, several major metropolitan areas experienced major black population increases at the same time that southeastern Europeans were also arriving. Even though these migratory movements were relatively small when compared to later periods, these pioneers developed linkages and mechanisms of support that would serve very important functions for the migrants who would follow.[7]

Under the system of tenantry in the southern agricultural economy, the black family had worked as a unit, but in the industrial economy of the North new challenges threatened the black family's unity. One aspect of the migratory process, often overlooked, was the financial losses that were incurred by black migrants in the course of their move to the North. In many southern towns, whites attempted to impede the migration of blacks by refusing to buy property from them. At least one-fourth of the fifty Mississippi migrants interviewed in Chicago by Charles Johnson in 1917 either had been unable to sell their property or had disposed of it at a substantial loss.[8] Rather than remain in the South, many families endured heavy financial losses when they were unable to sell property and personal possessions that could not be easily carried on a train or bus. Other families handled these problems by having one member go North and send for the others later. These separations rarely increased family cohesiveness.[9]

In an effort to offset the economic uncertainties they faced as the result of the northern migration, black families pursued strategies that increased the responsibilities of both young and old family members. According to Mark Stern, one of the most effective economic strategies for the poor was child labor.[10] There was a proliferation of cottage industries in black households, and many families also took in boarders. For example, a 1917 survey conducted in Pittsburgh found that four-fifths of the black migrant families with three or more rooms kept boarders in their homes.[11] While these increased duties for black women and children may have ameliorated a family's economic instability somewhat, they raised an already high level of marital and family strain.

The pressure on black wives and mothers to supplement household production with wage labor also escalated. The shortage of domestic servants in the North throughout the early part of the twentieth century made it much easier for black women, but not black men, to find work by migrating. One early observer noted that black women were finding "an unlimited field of employment in the domestic and household industries."[12]

As black women moved North in search of better work opportunities, the separated members of black families experienced a sense of loss and feelings of despair and social isolation. A study conducted in 1913 compared the experiences of blacks in the South with their lives in their new urban environment in Harlem. (Of the thirty-five interviewed, however, only ten were women.) In the South, the respondents had belonged to a church, which had housed communal social events and was the center of their social life. In the North the church was less important to them. Social visiting had also been an important part of their world in the South: thirty-three of the thirty-five had spent at least one evening a week visiting friends, listening to music, singing, or chatting with friends and relatives. In the North, they said visiting as a social custom was much reduced and they had fewer friends. They were also more suspicious of their environment, and this included their neighbors. For example, in the South they had responded to a doorbell with "come in"; in the North, their response was likely to be "who's there?"[13] In short, blacks exchanged the intimacy of small-town and rural community life for the detached and impersonal social relations of the city.

Domestic Service and Its Repercussions in the North

In his 1913 study of Athens, Georgia, T. J. Woofter concluded that "the broadest and most intimate point of contact between the races in the South is through domestic service, and the attitude of the servant to the housewife, and the housewife to the servant, had much to do with the attitude of the races in general."[14] Because white domestics were rare in the South, domestic service was an integral part of the system of racial subordination. And in the South the wages of household servants were so low that even working-class white housewives could afford to hire black domestics. In Northern states, by contrast, domestics were rarely found in the homes of working-class whites.

Howard Rabinowitz, in a study of race relations in the South between 1865 and 1890, analyzed newspaper commentaries in southern cities and found that the incompetence of domestic servants was a common theme in white newspapers. For example, the *Macon Journal* concluded that "it is the experience, we believe, of every housekeeper in Macon that colored servants are hard to obtain, and in nine out of ten [cases], worthless." In these newspaper commentaries, black domestics were characterized as docile and childish, stereotypes that were then used to justify white subjugation and exploitation of blacks.[15] These attitudes and patterns of behavior were deeply embedded not only in the cities but in the larger southern social structure, and they set a standard that both whites and blacks found very difficult to change.

Black women who were able to move northward in search of a better life were confronted with a new set of problems. One way of finding work in the North was through employment agencies, many of which sent black women, untutored in the ways of city life, to work in houses of prostitution. Frances Kellor, the director of the Inter-Municipal Committee on Household Research in New York, noted that "Negro women who are led into immoral habits, vice, and laziness, have in too many instances received their initiative from questionable employment agencies."[16]

Jane Edna Hunter's autobiography, *A Nickle and a Prayer,* gives a firsthand account of this phenomenon.[17] Born in 1882 on a plantation in South Carolina, Hunter was trained as a nurse in Charleston and then at Hampton Institute. She arrived in Cleveland in 1905 with very little money. In an attempt to find lodging she mistakenly approached a bordello and gained immediate insight into the conditions that a black woman alone had to face. She wrote that at home on the plantation she was well aware that some girls had been seduced, but she was totally unaware of what she refers to as the "wholesale organized traffic in black flesh." When she goes to a dance hall she is likewise appalled to find that the first floor of the hall is "the resort of bad women," and that this entire section of the town was filled with unlawful business establishments.

Although she was a well-trained nurse, Hunter had to work as a domestic servant until she finally secured a position in a doctor's office. In an effort to help other black women migrants avoid the hardships and miseries she had observed, she established the Working Girls' Home Association, which later became the Phillis Wheatley Association. In describing the goals of this organization, which trained black women for domestic service, Hunter wrote: "The most important factor in successful domestic service is happy human relations between the lady of the house and the maid. . . . The girl who is fairly well-trained and well-disposed will become interested in the life of the family that she services, and will be devoted to its happiness."[18]

Northern Domestic Service and Its Impact on Family Life

During the timme Jane Hunter was preparing black women to work as domestics and to become interested in the life of the families they served, the demographic shift, some historians have documented, was taking a large toll on black families.[19] One of the early observers of urban economic conditions among blacks during this period was Mary Ovington, a close friend of W. E. B. DuBois.[20] She wrote that among women in the "laboring classes" in New York City at the turn of the century, seven times as many blacks as whites were engaged in what she called "self-supporting" work. She also noted that 90 percent of the black women workers were in "domestic and personal service."[21]

In *The Philadelphia Negro*, W. E. B. DuBois surveyed the black domestics of Philadelphia and likewise found that 84.3 percent of all black women were working as either servants or laundresses. Isabel Eaton, in a report published in DuBois's book, wrote that within the black servant group in Philadelphia, nearly 73 percent had been born in the Southern Atlantic seaboard states, the District of Columbia, Maryland, or Virginia. Roughly the same migratory patterns could be found in cities throughout the North.[22]

Ovington's observations suggest that the lives of black and white women differed in several important repects. For example, she found that black women entered the paid labor force at about the age of fifteen and could not afford to retire from it after marriage, which "only entails new financial burdens." She also observed that although the wife is usually ready to be both a friend and helpmate, should the husband "turn out a bad bargain, she has no fear of leaving him, since her marital relations are not welded by economic dependence."[23]

Ovington then noted that the labor force participation of black women in New York was having an impact on their children: "Truancy is not uncommon in colored neighborhoods. . . . [A child] remains on the street when he should be in school, or arrives late with ill prepared lessons. . . . You see [children] in the late afternoon sitting on the tenement stairs."[24] She presents statistics from the records of the Children's Court of New York showing that of the black children arrested, the highest percentage were picked up because their behavior suggested "improper guardianship."[25]

In evaluating the economic adjustment that black migrants from the South were making in Chicago, Irene Graham analyzed unpublished 1920 census data. She found that "practically all Negro adult males are gainfully occupied" but adds that "to be occupied, according to the census, does not by any means signify regular employment." She also found a large proportion of black mothers were not only employed but engaged in the "most menial and lowest paid work."[26] Some analysts have even argued that compared to black women, black men held more jobs, received higher pay, and occupied many higher-level positions.[27] Graham summarizes the impact of the black woman's employment on her family as follows:

> Family life in the urban Negro group apparently cannot be maintained without sources of income supplementary to the earnings of the chief wage earner. But these supplementary methods of support are undertaken at a heavy cost, because of the large proportion of wives and mothers who would naturally be the homemakers but who must go to work outside of the home.[28]

A rigorous analysis of gender gaps in earnings and occupations conducted by the economist Claudia Goldin confirmed Kelly's observation that the occupational shifts made by black women during this period were from farm labor to private household work. Using 1940 Public Use Sample tapes, she found that in both 1890 and 1930, fully 90 percent of all black women who worked for wages were employed in only two sectors, personal service and agriculture; that as late as 1940, fully 60 percent of all employed black women were servants in private households; and that in 1940 black females earned only *two-thirds* as much as comparable service workers. She states that the "ratio of black to white female earnings must have decreased from 1890 to 1940, an inference that is consistent with the formidable restrictions on black women's employment during this period." In discussing women's economic progress and the ambiguity of the benefits that they have gained in the workplace, Goldin argues that remedies should be directed toward the "division of labor in the home" and "the role of the state in enforcing the contractual obligations of fathers."[29]

Black Women and Double Duty

When Irene Graham analyzed the "division of labor in the black home," she found:

> [The] wife must rise early to make her husband's coffee before he starts for work, leaving out something for the children to eat before school . . . then hurrying off for perhaps an hour's travel or more in order to reach her own work; [then] coming home at night to an unswept house, beds unmade, and another hastily prepared meal cooked and eaten. . . . If many of [these women] manage to preserve something of a normal, happy home atmosphere, it is nothing short of miraculous."[30]

The more fortunate wives had adolescent daughters who could help with child care and housekeeping. And because the most effective family strategy for impoverished black families was child labor, many of these daughters had to take jobs outside the home to augment the family's household income. The overall picture of black family home life during this period is a one of disorganization. Jacqueline Jones adds, "it is important to note that there is little evidence to suggest that unemployed black husbands took care of cleaning, cooking, or child care while their wives were at work."[31]

It seems clear that most black women who worked long hours as domestics for white families suffered a great deal of stress and internal conflict. What is often overlooked is the fact that many of them were on duty around the clock and were allowed to go home only on weekends. It was the fortunate domestics who were able to find "day" work and go home to their families in the evening.[32]

Such pressures contributed to fertility rates so low among urban black women that they were not self-reproducing. Initially, Clyde Kismer found that the fertility of black women in New York was lower than that of white women of similar and higher occupational status in several urban communities.[33] However, when Frazier analyzed these fertility patterns among black women in Chicago and New York, he found that the women with the lowest fertility rates were migrants from the South and lived in the poorest neighborhoods.[34] When demographers reexamined the fertility patterns of blacks and factored in the migratory transitions during this period, they likewise found that demographic shifts seemed to have had a sharper effect on blacks than on whites.[35]

The Black Male, Industrial Work, and Marital Strains

Black men who migrated to the industrial North found even fewer job opportunities than black women. Employers were inclined to hire them only for jobs considered too physically demanding and poorly paid for whites. For example, one observer of the South Works of U.S. Steel in Chicago found only blacks and Mexicans on the "relining gang," a team that worked in terrible dust and heat to clean out old bricks from caved-in furnaces and replace them with new ones. In the packinghouses of Chicago, "workers breathed foul air, endured extreme temperatures, and toiled under dirty skylights or unshaded electric light bulbs." And although black migrants had been slaughtering farm animals before coming north, the work in these factories was distinctly different.[36]

One of hardest transitions for the black migrant was the adapting to industrial time. The new work was not only more rapid and continuous in its tempo, but it required systematic attendance. Southern agricultural labor, on the other hand, had depended not on the clock but on the sun, the cyclical nature of the crops and the harvesting season. Patterns of agricultural labor focused on the tasks that had to be completed, and less attention was given to regulating the time spent by workers. The flexibility that southern workers were accustomed to in tenant farming disappeared in the closely supervised and regulated conditions of industrial work.[37]

The working conditions in the North contributed to a high level of uncertainty in the lives of wage-earning black men, in turn reinforcing instability in their marital relations. St. Clair Drake and Horace Cayton observed in the 1940s that "roving masses of Negro men" were "an important factor . . . in preventing the formation of stable, conventional family units" among lower-class blacks.[38] The economic instability among black men increased their reliance on black women, who found it much easier to get work as domestic servants in white households.[39] As domestics, black women had a great deal of control over the resources of the white household, and could rely on custom to take leftover food and discarded clothing home to their families. This custom, described by Southerners as "service pan," was viewed as part of the contractual agreement with white employers, because wages were so low that many black families depended on the extra food and clothing to supplement the meager household income. When Benjamin Locke looked at this practice in Harlem, he noted that lower-class blacks had "better and more abundant food than is eaten, perhaps, by any other race of people of the same economic status."[40] In the city of Norfolk, Virginia, the chief of police declared that the custom of women domestics bringing home food was the direct cause of the "great excess of idleness and viciousness among Negro men, who would "soon prefer stealing to working."[41]

When Drake and Cayton analyzed the economic reliance of black men on black women, they come to a very different conclusion. They argued that although the black man was in a weak financial position vis-à-vis the black woman, he was in a dominant position otherwise. Like all women, they stated, poor black women have "affectional and sexual needs," but because they have limited options for securing husbands they have to "take love on male terms." Black men, on the other hand, can take advantage of this situation and exchange erotic courtship for monetary benefits. They note that although such men may be looked upon with envy by their friends, it is generally considered "unfair" to "live on a woman."[42]

There were several reasons why black women working as domestics assumed dominating control in the black household. First, they were employed indoors and worked in good and bad weather, whereas black men worked largely out of doors and were discharged in unfavorable weather. In addition, the colder climates during the winter months in the North were a new experience for black male migrants from the south. One writer during this period found that a "cessation of labor for two weeks or a month often means that outside charity must help or that crime must be resorted to, in order to make up the deficit."[43]

Second, a black domestic also had greater access to the influence of her white male employer, who could help her family members by finding jobs, providing bail money, and so forth. The wife's access to this white power further eroded the authority of the husband within the household.

Although domestic tensions were intensified by the black father's resentment of

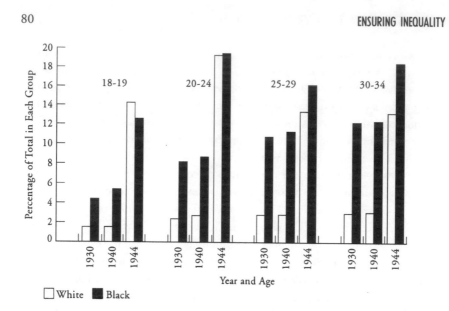

FIGURE 4.1   A comparison of husband absenteeism between married black and white women 18 to 34 years old in the years 1930, 1940, and 1944. (From J. D. Durand, *The Labor Force in the United States 1890–1960* [New York: Gordon and Breach, 1968], table B-1)

unstable employment and poor working conditions, it was his diminished authority within the family that contributed most to domestic conflicts. Some black men sought to regain some of their autonomy and self-worth by abandoning their families. In the 1930s Frazier maintained that "family desertion has been one of the inevitable consequences of the urbanization of the Negro population. . . . It appears from available sources of information that desertions are more frequent in Negro families than in families of other racial groups."[44] Data presented in a book written much earlier by Joanna Colcord support Frazier's contention. Summarizing the findings from a study of 480 deserters conducted by the New York COS in 1916 and 1917, Colcord found that whereas blacks were 5.6 percent of the population in that city, 11.2 percent of the deserters were black. Of the racial and ethnic groups included in the study, blacks had the highest proportion of deserters. Another investigation of desertions conducted in Chicago between 1909 and 1915 found that blacks constituted 21.1 percent of all of the desertion cases.[45]

When John Durand compared husband absenteeism between blacks and whites in the years 1930, 1940, and 1944 he likewise found the rates much higher for black husbands (Figure 4.1). For example, in the age cohorts 25–29 and 30–34 during the years 1930 and 1940, husband absences averaged 10 and 12 percent respectively for blacks, whereas for whites these figures were typically at 3 percent.

And although these figures escalated for both groups in 1944 due to the war efforts, in the age cohorts 25–34 these figures were still considerably higher for blacks. It seems clear that the multifaceted mechanisms of urbanization were catalysts in the disintegration of the black two-parent family.

The Balkanization of the Black Community

Chapter 3 documented the way in which the black community responded to poverty at the turn of the century. There was an increase in the activism among black women agaist poverty in their communities. As the northward migration of blacks proliferated, however, these earlier responses were transformed. With the growth of a new black middle class, tensions escalated between the new black "elite" and the black poor, who were primarily migrants from the rural South.

Much of this tension was fueled by the advocates of conservative racial reform. One of the most visible of these was William Henry Baldwin, Jr., a wealthy white Yankee businessman who had gained a reputation as a social reformer and civic leader. As a trusted friend of Booker T. Washington, Baldwin was also a leading northern patron of southern education. The idea for the Industrial Condition of Negroes in New York (which shortly became the National Urban League) had also originated with him.[46] He advised blacks to stay in the South and participate in that region's industrial development, because the northern cities promised only "slums, a high death rate, vice and exploitation, and hostility from organized labor."[47]

Whenever whites could find a black leader opposed to northern migration, they published his views or rushed him to the speaker's platform.[48] Fred R. Moore, one of the black founding members of the National Negro Business League and a close associate of Booker T. Washington, was one of those black leaders that whites could count on. As the publisher and editor of the New York newspaper *Age* and one of the board members of the new National Urban League (founded in 1911), he had a ready-made forum for his views.

Concerned that the black community was not doing enough to alleviate the suffering of the black migrants from the south, Ida Wells-Barnett founded the Negro Fellowship League in 1910 in Chicago. Its objective was to assist black immigrants from the South who were "uneducated, unemployed, and living in . . . undesirable neighborhoods." Mrs. Wells-Barnett was disappointed by the lack of support she received from the more affluent blacks. Although they respected her commitment and hard work, they were unwilling to go into impoverished neighborhoods and work with the blacks who lived there.[49] And they feared that a continual influx of poor migrants would jeopardize their tenuous relationships with local whites.

The kind of attention given to the issue of black migrants by the black middle class is most evident in the founding in 1911 of the National Urban League, which would become the dominant black social service agency after World War I. The National Urban League's social welfare programs were initially geared toward the "employable" migrant, and its services included "orienting them to the city and finding suitable housing."[50] Although the National Urban League shared important common ground with the settlement movement, the settlements were much more active in advancing reform efforts. According to Nancy Weiss:

> The Urban League was generally preoccupied with adjusting Negro migrants to urban life as it existed. While settlement workers were among the leaders pressing for progressive legislation reforms, the Urban League tried to change private practices rather than the laws.[51]

In New York City, for example, black migrants were frequently referred to as a "hoodlum element," "vagrants," and "criminals in search of the sporting life." In 1905 an editorial in a local black weekly claimed that "many of the worthless people of the race are making their way northward." This hostility toward southern migrants intensified the pride of native black New Yorkers and led to the founding of the Sons of New York. Similar reactions were found in Milwaukee, where one black newspaper editor referred to black migrants as a "floating, shiftless, and depraved element."[52]

The tension between the southern migrants and the northern born blacks was likewise demonstrated in Boston when a white newspaperman reported in the *Sunday Herald* that he had witnessed three different voodoo ceremonies, which were conducted by a priest from New Orleans and attended by black migrants from the West Indies, Virginia, and Maryland. Embarrassed black leaders initially charged the newspaper with misrepresentation and denied that the voodoo ceremonies had taken place. The National League of Boston, a black civil rights organization, was later forced to admit that voodoo did exist within the black community, but it tried to minimize its influence.[53]

The split between the black elite and the black poor appeared most clearly in the "hypersegregation" found in black residential neighborhoods in urban areas during this period.[54] Restrictive covenants in real estate contracts not only enforced residential racial segregation but also limited the expansion of black neighborhoods. Edith Abbott, in a study of black housing in Chicago between 1908 and 1935, found that 80 percent of black families headed by unskilled laborers spent one-fifth or more of their monthly income on rent, whereas only 30 percent of white families in the same occupational classification spent that much. According to Florette Henri, between 1900 and 1920 the exploitation of blacks in the realm of housing prevailed in every major city except Washington, D.C.[55]

In a 1937 paper, Frazier documented the "spatial organization" among blacks residing in northern urban areas. Within neighborhoods where blacks resided, he found that various elements had become segregated according to their "economic and cultural organization."[56] He divided the black communities in Chicago and Harlem into concentric zones and found that the poorest families lived in the center and the more affluent in the "peripheral" zones; more specifically, single, unattached, separated, divorced, and widowed blacks lived in the center and married couples with children lived in the outer zones. In Chicago, he also found that the juvenile delinquency rate declined from 42.8 percent in the center to 1.4 percent in the outermost zone.[57]

Drake and Cayton found there were "ecological patterns" emerging among Chicago blacks, who were sorting themselves into community areas that might be designated as lower-class and middle-class. They found that there were five black community areas: One was entirely "lower-class," two were completely "middle-class," and the other two were mixed. The comparisons he made between the five communities yielded social data on such items as families on relief, out-of-wedlock births, education, death rates, and infant mortality rates. Whereas the out-of-wedlock birthrate for blacks in the lower-income neighborhoods was 126.5 per thousand, it was 36.8 per thousand in middle-income neighborhoods. And while the infant mortality rate was predictably higher in the lower-income black neighborhoods, the birthrate for middle-income blacks was substantiantially higher, probably yet another indicator of their better health status.[58] In summarizing a study that found that infant mortality had declined in black neighborhoods where the number of welfare cases had been highest, Frazier remarked: "The mother on relief remains at home and is thus able to take greater precautions in regard to her own health during pregnancy, and devote more care to her child after its birth."[59]

A "Moral Panic" in the North

The growing stratification within the black community nationally was further intensified by the increases in black arrests in northern cities. For example, between August 1916 and August 1917, the number of blacks in Chicago jails increased from 9 percent to 57 percent, while the number of white prisoners fell by more than 50 percent. Alarmed by these figures, the Committee on Urban Conditions among Negroes concluded that "the large number is due to the large Negro migration from the South."[60]

The disproportionate number of black arrests was another indicator of the hostility that faced newly arrived migrants from the South. Most of the those arrested for vagrancy were newly arrived migrants simply looking for a place to stay. Many were arrested for such minor offenses as gambling or being inebriated and disorderly in their conduct. The black community in the North was clear on one thing: any impropriety on the part of the black migrant reflected on the entire race and was reported more frequently than to the white press.[61]

The reaction of the black middle class to the problems of the northern migration could be described as a *moral panic*. A moral panic has been defined as "an official reaction to a person, group of persons or series of events that is out of all proportion to the actual threat offered, when 'experts' . . . perceive the threat in all but identical terms, and appear to talk 'with one voice' of rates, diagnoses, prognoses, and solutions."[62]

In 1915 Booker T. Washington gave a speech to blacks in New York under the auspices of the National Urban League. He was presented as one of the "socially accredited experts" with solutions to the problems that were emerging as the result of the changing migration patterns.[63] In his speech, he echoed the admonitions of middle-class blacks to the migrant newcomers: "Get into your professions, take advantage of your night schools, labor is honorable, idleness is disgraceful." He closed with his strongest admonition: "If you have a strong, vigorous, healthy body, do not ruin it by frequenting drinking places, gambling establishments, and dance halls."[64]

In a book written by William H. Jones in 1927, ostensibly drafted to study recreation and amusement among blacks in Washington, D.C., we find the same strong moral tones. Jones condemned the dancing he saw in nightclubs as nothing more than "sexual pantomime." He viewed this kind of recreation as primarily responsible for encouraging quick intimacy and leading the young "on the downward path to crime"; he urged the "more advanced groups of Negroes" to mobilize a campaign of social disapproval against "vulgar, sexually suggestive modern dances." Finally, Jones implored the black middle class to discipline the black working class by implementing "mechanisms of control whereby forces which tend to disintegrate and demoralize the higher forms of culture may be excluded or annihilated."[65]

Jane Hunter also saw the recreational activities of blacks in areas of "commercialized vice" as a major challenge facing the black community. Rather than blame the blacks, however, she attacked corrupt city politicians and organized crime, noting that vice was concentrated in the "heart of the newly created Negro slum district[s]." But echoing Jones, she described the atmosphere found in these vice districts as one of "unrestrained animality, the jungle faintly veneered with civilized trappings." Like other members of the black middle class, she worried that the interracial cooperation she had built up in the Phillis Wheatley Association for "worthy purposes" could be undermined by the meeting of "blacks and whites in night clubs."[66]

In analyzing descriptions of black women migrants written during this period,

Hazel Carby finds "fears of a rampant and uncontrolled female sexuality . . . fears of the assertion of an independent black female desire that has been unleashed through migration." She adds that the goal of Hunter and other reformers during this period was the "transformation of the behavior of migrant working-class black women to conform to the middle-class norms of acceptable sexual behavior." She concludes that the appeal to the "mobilization of social disapproval appears to be as much about generating a black middle-class ideology of solidarity and coexistence as about challenging threats to the social mores of that group."[67]

This conclusion was anticipated by Drake and Cayton in the 1940s. In describing the attitudes of the black middle class in Chicago toward the newly arrived black migrants from the rural south, they wrote: "[T]he whole orientation of the Negro upper class thus becomes one of trying to speed up the processes by which the lower class can be transformed from a poverty-stricken group, isolated from the general stream of American life, into a counterpart of middle-class America."[68]

The Emergence of "Underclass" Family Patterns

Outside the South, according to Stanley Engerman, black families headed by women increased by 33 percent in the 1930s, making it the "most important decade for the increase in female-headed and one-parent present households." This fact, he argues, "raises important questions about the relative roles of the northward movement of the 1920s and the economic impact of the depression of the 1930s."[69]

Many analyses made during this period blame the urban black culture for the deterioration of the black family. For example, when Drake and Cayton observed in Chicago that greater numbers of children were being born to families without fathers in the household, they described the single mothers as members of the lower class "who had been in the city less than five years." In their view, such "accidents" happened only "rarely to girls of other social classes, or even to lower-class girls wise to the ways of the city."[70]

E. Franklin Frazier went further than most in defining the specific impact that city life was having on black migrants from the South:

> If these families have managed to preserve their integrity until they reach the northern city, poverty, ignorance, and color force them to seek homes in deteriorated slum areas from which practically all institutional life [has] disappeared. Hence, at the same time that these simple rural families are losing their internal cohesion, they are being freed from the controlling force of public opinion and communal institutions.[71]

Gunnar Myrdal noted that there was an "extremely high rate of illegitimacy among Negroes" during this period. While he did not endeavor to trace the etiology of the higher rates among blacks, he asserted that the "unwed mother tends, although there are many exceptions, to have looser morals and lower standards, and in this respect does not provide the proper milieu for her child. It would be better both for society in general and for the mother if she had no child."[72]

Frazier discussed the changing rates of nonmarital pregnancies and was one of the first observers during this period to note that these mothers were "comparatively young." Of the group of 300 unmarried mothers he studied in Chicago (circa 1930), 50 were under the age of seventeen, and 165 (55 percent) were under twenty. In the group he studied in New York City, 56 percent were under twenty years old. And while he viewed the lack of parental supervision as a contributing factor, he noted that a daughter's pattern was often "similar to that of her mother."[73]

Frazier then describes a person who is "typical of such women" to illustrate his point. She comes to the city from a rural community in Maryland, with no formal education. She marries when she is thirteen, but is deserted three years later when her husband migrates to Florida to find work. She never obtains a divorce from her first husband and begins living with another man, with whom she has three children. When this man deserts her, she begin living with another man by whom she also has children. When this third man deserts her she applies for welfare, reporting herself as having been married to all three men. But when the social worker finds no record of her marriages, she acknowledges the deception and tells the truth.[74]

Drake and Cayton also discuss single black mothers and present a case they characterize as "extreme"—a woman who has migrated from South Carolina, has never married, and has five children by different men. Whereas Frazier's case was taken from the welfare case records, Drake and Cayton interviewed this woman, who described her situation as follows: "None of my five children are whole sisters and brothers. . . . I'm living with a boyfriend now. He wants to marry, but I don't want to be bothered . . . If he can't help me or pay me, I can't use him. I can find love anywhere."[75]

Frazier summarized his analysis of births to single black mothers by stating that the problem was confined almost entirely to "naive and ignorant peasant folk who are newcomers to the city," adding that "during the course of their migration to the city, family ties are broken, and the restraints which once held in check immoral sexual conduct lose their force."[76] Drake and Cayton also claim that most single mothers are newcomers to the city and conclude that "the lower class, unlike the middle and the upper, not only tolerate illegitimacy, but actually seem almost indifferent toward it."[77] What seems clear is that the complex processes of urbanization were not only contributing to the proliferation of the mother-only family among African-Americans, but to a new urban "underclass.".[78]

Conclusion

The Great Migration represented a shift in the experience of African-Americans in the United States and launched them into the industrial sector of the economy. Under the system of tenant farming in the southern agricultural economy, the black family had worked as a unit and had the support of communal institutions. The transition to an industrial economy presented formidable challenges to the black family and further weakened an already beleagured family structure.

The serious shortage of domestic servants throughout the latter part of the nineteenth century in the North allowed black women a great deal of geographic mobility and served as the impetus for the northward movement. This created problems for the black family for two primary reasons: First, black men could not find as many employment opportunities in the urban North, and marital and family ties were attenuated as the result of these changing migratory patterns. Second, black women were at risk for all types of exploitation as they moved out of the protected rural environments and into the corrupt "vice" industries found in urban areas. For example, some of the employment agencies used by black women in the North were actually fronts for prostitution rings.

One of the greatest challenges that black migrants faced in the urban North, however, was the loss of communal and familial institutions they had come to rely on in the South. For example, the black migrants in the North who were surveyed in 1913 indicated that they were experiencing a sense of isolation because they had lost several important elements of their Southern life: the church as the center of social life; the custom of visiting in the homes of friends and neighbors; and the intimacy, familiarity, and sustenance found in small-town community life.

With the transition to urban communities, southern recreational and social customs wre replaced with the amusements offered by the movie theatres, night clubs, dance halls, and gambling establishments that were in the so called Negro slum districts. Some social commentators during this period expressed concern that this "commercialized vice" was leading young people into early sexual intimacy and pushing the black community "on the downward path" to demoralization, disintegration, and crime.

Class relations within the black community were strained, as the black "elite" blamed the growth of these activities on the newly arrived immigrants. And although black leaders in the North feared that these activities would jeopardize their tenuous relationships with the white establishment, they did not advance reform efforts to curtail even some of the unlawful aspects of these enterprises. The National Urban League, for example, focused its efforts instead on "adjusting Negro migrants to urban life as it existed."[79]

In an effort to offset the uncertainty that black families faced as the result of the northern migration, family strategies were devised that increased further the responsibilities of all family members, but especially those of women. Black women were driven into the labor force, where they were confined to domestic service by virtue of their exclusion from factory work and clerical jobs. The restrictions on black women's employment were reflected in the decrease in the ratio of black female earnings to white female earnings from 1890 to 1940; according to Claudia Goldin, black women earned only two-thirds as much as comparable workers by 1940.

Observers during this period found that black family life was chaotic largely because of the long and irregular hours that black mothers spent working in the homes of white families. Their prolonged absences were said to have an impact on children in several ways: There was a documented increase in truancy in black neighborhoods in the North; those children who did attend school often arrived with their lessons unprepared; and there was a surge in the arrests of black children for petty crimes, which were most often described as the result of "improper guardianship."

The black man, too, found it difficult to adjust to conditions of work in the North. Employers would hire black males only when they thought the work unsuitable for whites, and so they worked at the most oppressive, strenuous, and low-paying jobs. Unlike agricultural labor, industrial work was rapid and continuous in tempo and required systematic attendance. Black workers lost the flexibility they had when they worked on tenant farms and were not as closely supervised. In short, more arduous working conditions in the North increased the level of uncertainty in the lives of wage-earning black men.

As domestics, black women in the North had more control over household resources, and black men became more reliant on them. Marital conflicts were intensified by the black father's resentments of the conditions of his work as well as its instability. But it was the diminished male authority within the black family that contributed most to domestic conflicts and finally to family desertion. Social scientists during this period found that desertion by fathers was more frequent among black families than among families of any other racial or ethnic group.

Observers also noted that blacks were sorting themselves into neighborhoods according to income and social class, with single, unattached, separated, or divorced mothers residing in the poorest areas. Predictably, social scientists found that residents in the poorest areas had the highest welfare utilization, infant mortality rates, and births to single mothers, and the lowest levels of education. In southern towns, blacks from the various class strata had lived side by side. The effects of concentrated poverty and what we now call "hypersegregation" were emerging for the first time in black neighborhoods.

The economic impact of the Great Depression, coupled with the demographic shift of blacks to urban areas, is reflected most clearly in the fact that the 1930s was the decade of the greatest increase in mother-only black families. The response to weakened marital ties among poor African-Americans was a family pattern characterized by strong ties between mothers and children, and marginalized relationships with the biological fathers. With black fathers' increasing desertion of their families, the most economically disadvantaged single black mothers became more reliant on assistance from welfare. And although these families represented a minority of the black poor during this period, these nascent family patterns would contribute not only to the proliferation of single black mothers but to a new urban "underclass" after World War II.

Notes

1. Asa Briggs, review of *Making of the English Working Class*, by E. P. Thompson, *Labor History* 6 (Spring-Fall, 1965):84–91.

2. The term *Great Migration* has most often been used to denote the movement of blacks to the North during the First World War. Gilbert Osofsky describes the black migration to the North as a black population shift which began at the turn of the century and is continuing today (he wrote this in 1963); *Harlem: The Making of a Ghetto: Negro New York, 1890–1930* (1963; reprint, New York: Harper & Row, 1971). Most scholars agree, however, that the first great wave of migration occurred between 1910 and 1930, when approximately 1.5 million blacks left the South.

3. For an analysis of how the rise of the industrial family ethic shaped black and white family strategies, see Mimi Abramovitz, *Regulating the Lives of Women: Social Welfare Policy from Colonial Times to the Present*, (Boston: South End Press, 1988); Kathryn M. Neckerman, "The Emergence of "Underclass" Family Patterns, 1900–1940," in *The "Underclass" Debate: Views from History*, ed. Michael B. Katz (Princeton: Princeton University Press, 1993), 194–219. For a clear historical and theoretical presentation of the women's movements and a good synopsis of current research on gender and family, see Linda J. Nicholson, *Gender and History: The Limits of Social Theory in the Age of the Family* (New York: Columbia University Press, 1986).

4. August Meier, *Negro Thought in America, 1880–1915* (1963; reprint, Ann Arbor: University of Michigan Press 1988), 170.

5. For one of the earliest delineations of some of the "human" factors in the changing migration patterns of southern blacks, see Rupert B. Vance, *Human Factors in Cotton Culture: A Study in the Social Geography of the American South* (Chapel Hill: University of North Carolina Press 1929).

6. Among the important works, to name just a few: Irene Graham, "The Negro Family in the Northern City," *Opportunity* 8 (February 1930):48–51; Mary Ovington, *Half A Man* (1911; reprint, New York: Hill and Wang, 1969); Louise Kennedy, *The Negro Peasant Turns Cityward* (New York: Columbia University Press, 1930); Emmett Scott, *Negro Migration During the War* (New York: Oxford University Press, 1920); George E. Haynes, *The Negro*

at Work in New York City (:New York, Columbia University Studies in History, Economics, and Law, 1912); V. D. Johnston, "Negro Migration to Northern Cities," *Opportunity* 1 (1923): 235–38; Thomas J. Woofter, *Negro Migration: Changes in Rural Organizations and Population of the Cotton Belt* (1920; reprint, New York: AMS: Press, 1971); Claude V. Kiser, *Sea Island to City: A Study of St. Helena Islanders in Harlem and Other Urban Centers* (New York: Columbia University Press, 1932).

7. For more on how these linkages and mechanisms of support facilitated the exodus of blacks from the Cotton Belt to the city of Chicago, see James Grossman, *Land of Hope: Chicago, Black Southerners, and the Great Migration* (Chicago: University of Chicago Press, 1989).

8. In Grossman, *Land of Hope*, 105.

9. For an analysis of the impact of the northern migration on the black family, see Peter Gottlieb, *Making Their Own Way: Southern Blacks' Migration to Pittsburgh, 1916–1930* (Urbana: University of Illinois Press, 1987); Joanne J. Meyerowitz, "Holding Their Own: Working Women apart from Family in Chicago, 1880–1930," (Ph.D. diss., Stanford University, 1983); Elizabeth R. Bethel, *Promised Land: A Century of Life in a Negro Community* (Philadelphia: Temple University Press, 1981).

10. For an analysis of the role of child labor in family strategies of the poor in Erie County, New York, see Mark Stern, *Society and Family Strategy, Erie County, New York 1850–1920* (Albany: State University of New York Press, 1987), 41.

11. Abraham Epstein, *The Negro Migrant in Pittsburgh* (Pittsburgh: University of Pittsburgh Press, 1918), 15.

12. Kelly Miller, *Race Adjustment: Essays on the Negro in America* (New York: Neale, 1910), 173.

13. Benjamin H. Locke, "The Community Life of a Harlem Group of Negroes" (M.A. thesis, Columbia University, 1913), 1–2, 6–10, 22–32.

14. T. J. Woofter, Jr., "The Negroes of Athens, Georgia," Phelps-Stokes Fellowship Studies no. 1, *Bulletin of the University of Georgia* 14 (December 1913), 43.

15. Howard N. Rabinowitz, *Race Relations in the Urban South 1865–1890* (New York: Oxford University Press, 1978); see also Woofter, "Negroes of Athens, Georgia," 59–61.

16. Frances A. Kellor, "Southern Colored Girls in the North: The Problem of Their Protection," *Charities* (March 18, 1945): 581–585.

17. Jane Edna Hunter, *A Nickle and a Prayer* (Cleveland: Elli Kani, 1940).

18. Ibid., 162–66.

19. David Katzman, *Before the Ghetto: Black Detroit in the Nineteenth Century* (Urbana: University of Illinois Press, 1973); Osofsky, *Harlem: The Making of a Ghetto*; Kenneth L. Kusmer, *A Ghetto Takes Shape: Black Cleveland, 1870–1930* (Urbana: University of Illinois Press, 1976); Allen Spear, *Black Chicago: The Making of a Negro Ghetto, 1890–1920* (Chicago: University of Chicago Press, 1967).

20. W.E.B. DuBois once said of her writings on black economic conditions, "She knows more than anyone I know"; quoted in David L. Lewis, *W. E. B. DuBois: Biography of a Race* (New York: Holt, 1993), 348.

21. Ovington, *Half a Man*, 56, 57, 149; Ovington's figures were derived from census

data. David M. Katzman found that in 1920 the percentage of black women in domestic service occupations exceeded 60 percent in Chicago, 70 percent in New York City, and 80 percent in Philadelphia, and the percentages had increased by 1930; *Seven Days a Week: Women and Domestic Service in Industrializing America* (Urbana: University of Illinois Press, 1978) 219–22.

22. Isabel Eaton, "Special Report on Negro Domestic Service in the Seventh Ward, Philadelphia," in W.E.B. DuBois, *The Philadelphia Negro: A Social Study* (1899; reprint, New York: Schocken, 1967), 414.

23. Ovington, 140,141. Thomas J. Woofter agrees with Ovington's analysis of why black mothers work in disproportionate ratios to white mothers, finding that "sometimes it is hard for men to find employment and wages are low"; *The Negro Problem in the Cities* (New York: Doubleday, Doran, 1928), 192.

24. Ovington, *Half a Man*, 60–62.

25. Ibid., 67. Ovington's figures were taken from the Children's Court Records in New York for the years 1904, 1905, 1906. Another study conducted on truancy in Chicago during the same period confirmed Ovington's findings: Gertrude H. Britton, *An Intensive Study of the Causes of Truancy in Eight Public Schools in Chicago* (Chicago: Hollister, 1906).

26. Irene J. Graham, "Family Support and Dependency among Chicago Negroes: A Study of Unpublished Census Data," *Social Service Review* 3(December, 1929): 541–542.

27. Sharon Harley, examining gender, work, and domestic roles in the black community from 1880 to 1930, found that black men worked in disproportionately higher numbers, received higher pay, and occupied many of the top-level positions, when compared to black women. She presents census data and findings from other studies that evaluated the wage structure of domestic and personal service workers, which indicated that black male elevator operators and day workers earned more per hour than female workers; "For the Good of Family and Race: Gender, Work, and Domestic Roles in the Black Community, 1880–1930," *Signs: Journal of Women in Culture and Society* 15 (Winter 1990):336–49. For other perspectives on black women's precarious hold on employment during this period, see Marion Cuthbert, "Problems Facing Negro Young Women," *Opportunity* 14 (February 1936): 47–49; Elizabeth Ross Haynes, "Negroes in Domestic Service in the United States," *Journal of Negro History* 8 (October 1923):384–442.

28. Graham, "Family Support and Dependency among Chicago Negroes:" A Study of Unpublished Census Data," *Social Service Review* 3(December 1929): 562.

29. Claudia Goldin, *Understanding the Gender Gap* (New York: Oxford University Press, 1990), 213, 249.

30. Graham, "Family Support and Dependency among Chicago Negroes," 556.

31. *Black Women's Work and the Family from Slavery to the Present* (New York: Basic Books, 1985), Jacqueline Jones, *Labor of Love, Labor of Sorrow*, 128.

32. For an understanding of the advantages and disadvantages of the live-out system for the black domestic and her family, see *Seven Days a Week*, 198–99, 272–73.

33. Clyde Kismer "Fertility of Harlem Negros," *Milbank Memorial Fund Quarterly* 13(July 1935).

34. For an analysis of the decline in the fertility of black women during this period, see E. Franklin Frazier, "The Impact of Urban Civilization upon Negro Family Life," *American Sociological Review* 2 (October 1937):609–618; Frazier documents neighborhood effects on these fertility rates. Other studies conducted during the 1930s also documented these fertility trends among blacks; see, for example, Warren S. Thompson and Pascal K. Whelpton, *Population Trends in the United States, Estimate of Future Population of U.S. 1940–2000*. (Washington, D.C., Government Printing Office 1943)—they observed that blacks in large cities, including Chicago and New York, "were not maintaining their numbers on a permanent basis in either 1920 or 1928" (280); St. Clair Drake and Horace Cayton found significant fertility differentials between middle- and lower-income blacks; *The Black Metropolis*, 659–60.

35. Hope T. Eldridge and Dorothy S. Thomas, *Population Redistribution and Economic Growth, United States, 1870–1950*, vol. 3, *Demographic Analyses and Interrelations* (Philadelphia: American Philosophical Society, 1964); Reynolds Farley, "Fertility among Urban Blacks," *Milbank Memorial Fund Quarterly* 48 (1970):183–214; William E. Vickery, "The Economics of the Negro Migration: 1900–1960," (Ph.D. diss., University of Chicago, 1969); Avery M. Guest and Stewart Tolnay, "Urban Industrial Structure and Fertility: The Case of Large American Cities," *Journal of Interdisciplinary History* 13 (Winter 1983): 387–409.

36. For descriptions of industrial working conditions for blacks in the North, see, for example, Lizabeth Cohen, *Making A New Deal: Industrial Workers in Chicago, 1919–1939* (New York: Cambridge University Press, 1990). For a depiction of conditions in the slaughtering and meatpacking industries, see Catherine E. Lewis, "Trade Union Policies in Regard to the Negro Worker in the Slaughtering and Meatpacking Industry in Chicago" (M.A. thesis, University of Chicago, 1945), 73–74; For further discussion and description of the low level jobs of blacks in Chicago, see Dempsey J. Travis, *An Autobiography of Black Chicago* (Chicago: Urban Research Institute, 1981). For a depiction of conditions in the slaughtering and meatpacking industries see Alma Herbst, *The Negro in the Slaughtering and Meat-Packing Industry in Chicago* (Boston: Houghton Mifflin, 1932). For an analysis of the half-century since the First World War when rural Southern Spanish-speaking white and black workers first encountered the factory and the machine, see Robert Coles, *South Goes North* (Boston: Little, Brown 1971); Grossman, *Land of Hope*, 188–92.

37. For a discussion of the tempo of cotton cultivation, see Vance, *Human Factors*. For evidence that highlights the difference between agricultural "task orientation" and industrial "time orientation" see E. Thompson, "Time, Work-Discipline, and Industrial Capitalism," *Past and Present* 38 (December 1967): 60.

38. Drake and Cayton, *Black Metropolis*, 583.

39. When DuBois found unemployment among black males in the community of Farmsville circa 1897, he noted that "one of the principal reasons for idleness is irregular employment." He goes on to say that if a man is of "ordinary caliber he easily lapses into the habit of working part of the year and loafing the rest." When comparing the black men to the black women, he found that "[the women] are on the whole more faithful and are beocming better educated than the men, and they are capable of doing far better work than

they have a chance to do" *On Sociology and the Black Community*, ed. Dan S. Green and Edwin D. Driver (Chicago: University of Chicago Press, 1978), 180–81.

40. Benjamin H. Locke, "Community Life of a Harlem Group," 32.

41. The "Norfolk problem" was also mentioned by Helen Pendleton of the COS, who agreed that it was also common in Baltimore; "Negro Dependence in Baltimore," *Charities* 15 (October 7, 1905): 52.

42. Drake and Cayton, *Black Metropolis*, 583–84, 587.

43. Richard R. Wright, Jr., *The Negro in Pennsylvania: a Study of Economic History* (New York: Arno Press, 1969), 160.

44. E. Franklin Frazier, *The Negro Family in the United States*, 1939; reprint, rev. and abr. (Chicago: University of Chicago Press, 1966), 245.

45. Joanna Colcord, *Broken Homes* (New York: Russell Sage Foundation, 1912), 44–45; Earl E. Eubank, *A Study of Family Desertion* (Chicago: The Dept of Public Welfare, 1916; reprint, Boston: Houghton Mifflin, 1966). 15–16.

46. According to Gunnar Myrdal, the primary task of this organization was to find jobs for blacks, by impressing upon employers the idea that black labor was "efficient and satisfactory"; for a more comprehensive discussion, see *An American Dilemma: The Negro Problem and Modern Democracy* (New York: Harper & Row, 1944).

47. Nancy Weiss argues that Baldwin's concerns "foreshadowed tenets later central to the National Urban League"; *The National Urban League, 1910–1940* (New York: Oxford University Press, 1974), 36–37.

48. Grossman, *Land of Hope*, 56.

49. Quoted in *Crusade for Justice, the Autobiography of Ida B. Wells*, ed. Alfreda M. Duster (Chicago: University of Chicago Press, 1970), xxv.

50. Philip Jackson, "Black Charity in Progressive Era Chicago," *Social Service Review* 52 (September 1978): 413; For a more comprehensive perspective on the Urban League, Nancy Weiss, *National Urban League*; Arvarh E. Strickland, *History of the Chicago Urban League* (Urbana: University of Illinois Press, 1966).

51. Nancy Weiss, *Farewell to the Party of Lincoln: Black Politics in the Age of FDR* (Princeton: Princeton University Press, 1983), 87–88.

52. Quoted in Osofsky, *Harlem: The Making of a Ghetto*, 21; Seth M. Scheiner, *Negro Mecca: A History of the Negro in New York City, 1865–1920* (New York: New York University Press, 1965), 117; *Black Milwaukee: The Making of an Industrial Proletariat, 1915–1945* ed. Joe Trotter, Jr. (Urbana: University of Illinois Press, 1985), pp. 30–31.

53. Elizabeth Pleck, *Black Migration and Poverty, Boston 1865–1900* (New York: Academic Press, 1979) 77–78.

54. For some of the most detailed analyses of segregation in Chicago during this period, see Thomas Philpot, *The Slum and the Ghetto: Neighborhood Deterioration and Middle-Class Reform, Chicago 1880–1930* (New York: Oxford University Press, 1978). Philpot argues that "there was probably no southern city in which blacks were so segregated as they were in Chicago" (210).

55. Edith Abbott, *The Tenements of Chicago 1908–1935* (Chicago: University of Chicago Press, 1936), 124. It should also be noted that excessive rents were charged to poor

blacks in Philadelphia; these accounts were documented by Richard R. Wright, Jr.; *Negro in Pennsylvania* 161–161; Florette Henri, *Black Migration: Movement North 1900–1920* (Garden City, N.Y.: Anchor Doubleday, 1975), 103.

56. E. Franklin Frazier, "Impact of Urban Civilization upon Negro Family Life," 609–18.

57. Ibid., 617.

58. Drake and Cayton, *Black Metropolis*, 659.

59. E. Franklin Frazier, "Some Effects of the Depression on the Negro in Northern Cities," *Science and Society* 2 (Fall 1938): 495–96. For yet another analysis of these infant mortality rates, see Herbert L. Bryan, "Birth Rates and Death Rates in Relation to Dependency in Selected Health Areas in Harlem" (M.A. thesis, Columbia University, 1936).

60. Chicago Commission on Race Relations, The Committee on Urban Conditions among Negroes, *The Negro in Chicago* (Chicago: University of Chicago Press, 1920), 330.

61. For a clearer understanding of the vagrancy charges against the migrants, see Henri, *Black Migration*, 119. For more information on the different treatment of blacks in the criminal justice system, see William Tuttle, *Race Riot* (New York: Atheneum, 1974), 22.

62. For an exhaustive discussion of a moral panic, see Stuart Hall, Charles Critcher, Tony Jefferson, John Clarke, and Brian Roberts, *Policing the Crisis: Mugging, the Stage, and Law and Order* (New York: Homes & Meier 1978), 16.

63. According to Booker T. Washington's conservative philosophy, "a program of self-help and solidarity, limited political activity, economic and moral virtues, and both industrial and higher education would be thoroughly realistic, whereas an appeal to the moral sense of the nation would avail little"; quoted in August Meier, *Negro Thought in America, 1880–1915* (Ann Arbor: University of Michigan Press 1966), 215.

64. Quoted in Weiss, *National Urban League*, 63.

65. William H. Jones, *Recreation and Amusement among Negroes in Washington, D.C.: A Sociological Analysis of the Negro in an Urban Environment* (Washington, D.C.: Negro Universities Press 1927), pp. 121–23. Jones acknowledged his debt to Robert E. Park in *Race and Culture* (Glencoe, IL: Free Press 1950) argued that there was a "cycle of events" in the relations of the races wherein "eventual assimilation is apparently progressive and irreversible" (150). At one point Jones characterizes the hilarity in the cabarets as "jungle laughter" and warned that there were not "adequate bulwarks against the encroachment of such behavior forms upon the life of the more advanced groups of Negroes" (122). What Jones seems to be presenting is an ambiguous argument for the assimilation of blacks into American/European culture and an appeal to the black middle class for assistance in this endeavor.

66. Hunter, *Nickle and a Prayer*, 132–33. Katrina Hazzard Gordon also describes the rise of recreational and amusement enterprise in the black community and links it to prostitution and gambling that helped to deliver the black vote to corrupt white politicians; *Jookin': The Rise of Social Dance Formations in African American Culture* (Philadelphia: Temple Univ Press 1990) For another analysis of the political climate in northern cities during the period from 1900 to 1930, see Ira Katznelson, *Black Men, White Cities* (Chicago: University of Chicago Press, 1973).

67. Hazel Carby, "Policing the Black Woman's Body in an Urban Context," *Critical Inquiry* 18 (Summer 1992): 746–47, 751.

68. Drake and Cayton, *Black Metropolis*, 563.

69. Stanley L. Engerman, "Black Fertility and Family Structure in the U.S., 1880–1940," *Journal of Family History* 1–2 (June 1977): 134.

70. Drake and Cayton, *Black Metropolis*, 590.

71. Frazier, *Negro Family*, 340.

72. Myrdal, *American Dilemma*, 178.

73. Frazier, *Negro Family*, 260–62.

74. Ibid., 266–67.

75. Drake and Cayton, *Black Metropolis*, 592.

76. Frazier, *Negro Family*, 267.

77. Drake and Cayton, *Black Metropolis*, 1945, 590, 593.

78. Some authors pointed to the differences between the urban and rural experience for blacks even early in the postbellum period and argued that urban problems, low incomes, and high male mortality, in particular, led to a greater frequency of black single-mother families. Given that most blacks were then still residing in the rural regions of the country and had not started to migrate northward, the twentieth century has received more attention. See Frank Furstenberg, Jr., Theodore Hershberg, and John Modell, "The Origins of the Female-Headed Black Family: The Impact of the Urban Experience," in *Philadelphia: Work, Space, Family, and Group Experience in the Nineteenth Century,* ed. Theodore Hershberg (New York: Oxford University Press, 1981).

79. Nancy Weiss, *National Urban League, 1910–1940* (New York: Oxford University Press, 1974), p. 38.

PART II

CHAPTER FIVE

WORLD WAR II AND ITS AFTERMATH

So comprehensive and fundamental are the changes brought by war, and so closely is the family interrelated with larger society, that there is perhaps no aspect of family life unaffected by war.

Ernest Burgess, "The Effect of War on the American Family"

World War II had a profound effect on American society. For the United States, it lasted twice as long as World War I, brought over fourteen million men and women into the armed forces, and added another ten million to the labor force. Family life, considered as an institution, began a period of significant change. As Arthur Marwick has argued, war always tests existing institutions, and sometimes leads to their transformation or collapse.[1] The severe strain World War II placed on African-American families involved two major challenges: the consequences of wartime disruption, and an exodus from the South that was twice as large as the one that occurred between 1910 and 1930. During the 1940s, 1.5 million blacks left the South. By the end of the decade, the proportion of blacks in urban areas would finally exceed those in rural areas—a shift that had been made by whites some thirty years before.[2]

Wartime Migration and Urban Discontent

During the war more than fifteen million Americans, whites as well as blacks, migrated in search of better job opportunities in urban areas where the industrial economy was growing. Whereas blacks had migrated to the North during the 1930s to escape economic, social, and political oppression in the South, their migration in the 1940s—like that of millions of whites—was spurred by the revival of the nation's economy. For blacks, however, an additional combination of factors contributed to their patterns of northward migration, and their numbers in many northern cities grew to such an extent that in 1940 "new migrants outnumbered the original Negro dwellers eight to one."[3] As Gunnar Myrdal predicted in 1944, there was "bound to be a redefinition of the Negro's status in America" as a result of this war.[4]

One major factor in the northward movement of blacks was the decline in opportunities for agricultural workers caused largely by problems of soil depletion. As white tenant farmers migrated to urban areas in the South, competition between blacks and whites arose where none had existed before. In earlier decades, black workers had occupied a clearly defined niche in the labor market in southern cities: They held the jobs that white men did not want. When young whites moved in from the rural areas and started taking these jobs, blacks were at a distinct disadvantage in competing for them.

The displaced black workers of the South represented an ideal labor pool for the North, with its burgeoning economic activity. For northern industries, the black migrants of this second wave of were more than willing to take bottom-level jobs at low wages, which were nonetheless higher than those they had previously received.[5] They fit Karl Marx's description of wage workers who did not own property: those who "bear the burdens of society without enjoying its advantages, are excluded from society and forced into the most resolute opposition to all other classes."[6]

The Roots of Racial Unrest

Although blacks were migrating in greater numbers to the North, with its promise of unprecedented opportunity, the same sort of Jim Crow laws that separated the races in the South were still on the books in many states in the North.[7] Government offices and military establishments were segregated, as were most public and private facilities, such as hotels, restaurants, railroad and bus stations, libraries, parks, and museums. When blacks sought legal redress, they found that the aim of Supreme Court decisions was to require more equality within separation, not to end the separation.[8]

The issue of equality versus separation was most clearly illustrated in the case of Arthur Mitchell of Chicago, the only African-American to serve in Congress during the 1940s. Mitchell sued after he was forced to move from his Pullman berth into a day coach when the train on which he was traveling crossed into Arkansas. The Supreme Court ruled that he should have been provided with all-black Pullman accommodations just as comfortable as those he had been forced to leave, but not that his rights had been violated when he was separated from the white passengers on the train. The Court said that the issue was "not a question of segregation but of equality of treatment." Mitchell praised the Court's decision as the "greatest advance in civil rights in my lifetime."[9]

As blacks migrated northward in greater numbers and found themselves excluded from expanding job opportunities, they became increasingly discontent and bitter. The migration itself was viewed with increasing alarm and soon attracted mounting opposition in the North. Racial clashes broke out in factories, schools, and neighborhoods in cities both large and small. In the big cities, especially in New York, a wave of violent crimes by young blacks against whites spread fear and panic throughout the white neighborhoods.

One of the problems that continued to plague black families was the difficulty of securing adequate housing. The construction of new homes during the war years was for the most part limited to white neighborhoods. When public housing for blacks was proposed, political battles generally erupted over location and funding. In the winter of 1940/1941, race riots—replete with bombings and burnings—broke out in Dallas in response to the white community's attempts to stop what it believed was a black neighborhood's encroachment on an all-white area. In 1942 riots broke out in Detroit when the Sojourner Truth Housing Project was built in a white area. Hundreds of whites beat and stoned blacks, and police assisted by turning their clubs on the blacks. When the skirmish ended, the twenty people injured and the one hundred arrested were all black.[10]

With the racial conflict escalating, A. Philip Randolph, president of the Brotherhood of Sleeping Car Porters, the first black trade union group in organized labor, decided to provide the leadership for a protest march for equal employment opportunity. Supported by the NAACP and the National Urban League, Randolph put out an appeal throughout the country, urging infuriated black Americans to march on Washington and demand their right to wartime jobs.[11]

The Presidential Remedy: Executive Order 8802

In June 1941, President Franklin Roosevelt, seeing the distinct possibility that one hundred thousand blacks might march on Washington, issued Executive Order 8802 establishing the Committee on Fair Employment Practices (FEPC). This order mandated that federal contracts would be awarded only to those industries that would hire black and white workers on an equal basis. Nothing in the executive order banned segregation; it simply insisted on equality. Even with this narrowly circumscribed power, FEPC did not develop a strong record in settling complaints. Twenty-six of the thirty-five nondiscrimination compliance orders issued to employers in 1945 were simply ignored. In addition, nine of ten unions cited for discrimination by FEPC declined to follow compliance orders.[12]

In spite of this weak enforcement, government pressure and wartime labor shortages led to increased hiring of blacks in defense industries. Indeed, political pressure was basically all that Executive Order 8802 could provide. Compliance could be ordered by FEPC officials, and in theory government contractors who did not heed the order could lose their contracts. However, both the government officials and those they regulated knew that Congress and the public would never allow any major contract to be canceled.

In an effort to bring public attention to the grave difficulties blacks were having in securing employment, members of the FEPC used the meager funds appropriated to them to hold public hearings across the nation, at which employers were brought in and asked to give their reasons for hiring only a few blacks or none at all.[13] This process simply frustrated most members of the black community. They had already heard the reasons firsthand from employers; they wanted jobs, not publicity. In spite of their lack of faith in FEPC's ability to make substantive changes in the hiring practices of white employers, during the five-year period following the implementation of the Executive Order 8802, blacks filed fourteen thousand complaints of continued hiring discrimination.[14]

In 1944 blacks won an important victory in the judicial arena. In *Smith* v. *Allwright*, the Supreme Court ruled that excluding blacks from voting in Democratic Party primaries in the South was an unconstitutional infringment of their civil rights. Paradoxically, this victory led to more incidents of violence against southern black voters, thereby increasing the migration of blacks to the North.[15]

The African-American Male and Military Service

While FEPC was directing attention to discrimination in industry, the question of who would put an end to discrimination in the military remained unanswered. Black organizations such as the NAACP and the National Urban League, founded in 1909 and 1911 respectively, were just beginning to formulate their organizational policies when America entered World War I in 1917. The Selective Service Act of May 1917 did not exclude blacks, and almost three million were registered under the Act. Theywere accepted for service in the four black army regiments, but once those regiments were filled, they were turned away.[16]

By 1939, the United States Army had only 3,640 black regular soldiers and only five black officers, three of whom were chaplains. African-Americans were excluded entirely from the Marine Corps and the Army Air Corps, and the navy and the Coast Guard were permitting blacks to participate only on a limited basis.[17] With the war imminent, black men wanted to demonstrate their patriotism through military service. But they also wanted to bring an end to segregation by participating fully and equally in the armed forces. Neil Wynn, a historian who has studied blacks in World War II, asserts that "military service thus became central to the whole campaign for civil rights."[18]

Significant changes in the black community between World Wars I and II had increased the chance that racial restrictions on military service could be eliminated. Not only was the black community more urbanized, but its greater sophistication and race consciousness were reflected in the growing circulation of black newspapers and increased membership in civil rights organizations. By 1940, the NAACP had a membership approaching ninety thousand and a budget of over $60,000, and the combined circulation of more than 150 black newspapers totaled 1,276,600.[19]

African-American organizational efforts were most clearly evident in the Committee for the Participation of Negroes in National Defense, created specifically to ensure black participation in the war effort. With primary sponsorship from the *Pittsburg Courier*, an influential black newspaper, and under the leadership of Rayford W. Logan, a veteran of World War I, the committee begin a campaign to end discrimination. With the primary goal of changing military poilicies, the committee set out to coordinate the efforts of individuals and organizations during the years 1939 through 1941.

In 1941 local draft boards were inducting black men, but only when necessary to meet their quotas; only two thousand blacks were drafted during the first year of Selective Service. By December 1941, however, one hundred thousand black soldiers had enlisted in the army, in that enlisting was easier than waiting to be drafted. The army still held to its policy of segregated units, however, and hospitals, mess halls, and recreational facilities—including theatres, post exchanges, and canteens on the bases—were roughly equal but always separate. The policy that was most offensive to black men, however, was the one that prevented them from serving in combat units.[20]

Racial violence erupted at army bases, and both black and white soldiers were left dead and wounded as blacks begin to demand greater opportunities within the military establishment. In a typical incident, reported in the *New York Times* on April 3, 1942, three soldiers were killed and five others wounded after an argument between black and white soldiers over who would have first use of a telephone booth. A racial outburst in Fayetteville, North Carolina, in August 1941 left two soldiers dead and five wounded. At another army post an hour-long gun battle, between an entire company of black soldiers and a company of military police, left a dozen dead and wounded. Ironically, the first man in the United States Army to be killed in World War II was a black sergeant, brought down by a U.S. M-1 rifle.[21]

Black Women Seize Economic Opportunities

As local economies expanded and large numbers of men went into the armed services, the ensuing labor shortage opened up many traditionally male fields to women.[22] Aware of women's potential contributions to national goals, four state legislatures enacted equal pay laws during the war, and a number of states passed laws protecting married women from discrimination in employment. For the first time, Congress considered an equal pay bill and an equal rights amendment to the Constitution.[23]

The wartime expansion of the economy brought important changes in the labor force participation of both black and white females. The employment of black women increased from 1.5 million to 2.1 million between 1940 and 1944, but their share of the total female labor force declined from 13.8 to 12.5 percent. These changes reflect three primary factors:

1. Before the war, the labor force participation of black women was relatively higher than that of white women.
2. The war economy improved the the employment prospects of black men, thereby decreasing the need for black women to go into the labor market.[24]
3. Black women entered the labor force much more slowly because of the persistence of racial discrimination.[25]

Although a 1943 poll found that black women were more willing to accept un-appealing jobs than white women, they were still at a distinct disadvantage in the burgeoning labor market for several reasons.[26] Charles S. Johnson noted that black women remained in "the most marginal position of all classes of labor."[27]

First, because of the kinds of jobs created in the defense industries, employers had a clear preference for male workers, and even in the face of critical labor shortages, they were reluctant to hire women to fill jobs that had traditionally been held by men.[28] When women were actually hired to fill such positions, they were expected to retain their "femininity"; and since black women were perceived as less "feminine" than white women, they were generally given the most demanding and lowest-paying jobs. Denying black women jobs in the newly opened war in-dustries was one means of "keeping them in their place."[29]

Second, many employers were unwilling to integrate the working areas inside their plants and often defended their actions by claiming that were not enough black women workers to warrant setting up separate facilities. Work stoppages did occur in many plants where black women were hired; but Karen Anderson has noted that when union–management education efforts among whites were coupled with a firm commitment by employers, the result was a smooth integration of black workers.[30]

Finally, black women went into the newly created war industries in such large numbers that nearly half of all white housewives lost their black domestics. One domestic who left work for a higher-paying factory job put it this way: "Lincoln freed the Negroes from cotton picking and Hitler was the one that got us out of

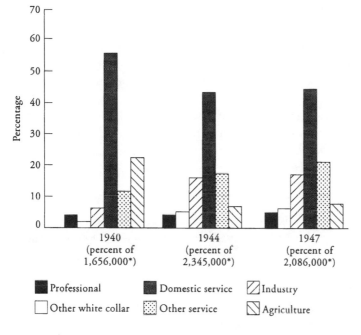

FIGURE 5.1   Black women's employment patterns, by type of employment, 1940–1947. (From D'Ann Campbell, *Women at War with America: Private Lives in a Patriotic Era* [Cambridge, Mass.: Harvard University Press, 1984], 240)

the white folks' kitchen."[31] The black domestics who were still willing to work in white households during the war charged twice as much, were less willing to live in, and refused to do many of the chores (such as window washing) they had done before the war. Susan Hartmann has noted that domestic workers who found better-paying jobs in factories, offices, and service industries "enjoyed the higher wages and better conditions as well as the independence, social contacts, and 'self-respect' that attended their new occupations."[32]

Although the war opened up new areas of employment to black women (Figure 5.1), racial discrimination kept them at a disadvantage in their competition with white women. They had difficulty getting admitted to training programs, and found that even training courses did not remove the difficulty of getting hired. For instance, in Cape Girardeau, Missouri, ten black women applied for jobs at a clothing plant that made WAC uniforms. Because their previous experience had been in domestic service and home sewing, plant officials refused to hire them on the grounds that they had no experience with power sewing machines. Yet when another group of black women in St. Louis completed 200 to 600 hours of training on power sewing machines, they were nevertheless refused jobs by firms producing military uniforms. (Three of them found work in a cartridge plant, where their training was irrelevant.) The managers of the St. Louis firms defended their actions by pointing to work stoppages that had occurred in other midwestern plants when black women were employed.[33]

After an FEPC investigation found that the highest salaried black employee in one federal agency was the director's chauffeur, and that only 2 percent of another agency's employees were black, the federal government undertook an aggressive campaign to recruit for black employees.[34] Between 1940 and 1942, a large number of black women were hired for federal clerical positions, though they were segregated from white clerks.[35] When black women were recruited and hired for certain positions, they had found it harder to get promotions than white women. In a survey that followed blacks and whites with similar efficiency ratings, it was found that whites received promotions six times more often than blacks.[36]

As noted earlier, black women who were lucky enough to be hired were assigned to the hardest, least desirable jobs. For example, the Pennsylvania Railroad in Baltimore hired about fifty black women in 1943 for work that was sweltering, burdensome, and sometimes hazardous: Some served as water and fire tenders, keeping up the fire and steam in the locomotives, and others did various kinds of unskilled physical labor. Similarly, a black woman interviewed by the Women's Bureau in Baltimore reported that her job as a loader at the arsenal entailed lifting fifty-five-pound boxes of TNT all day for the meager wage of $18 a week. Although their participation in factory work quadrupled, black women were heavily concentrated in positions of janitors, sweepers, and material handlers.[37]

Although the federal government had established FEPC to safeguard employment opportunities for racial minorities, government agencies themselves were often guilty of discrimination. For example, the War Department allowed the supervisors of armories, plants, and warehouses under its supervision to refuse jobs to black women. In 1943, an advertisement was reportedly posted in the Pentagon cafeterias and dining rooms for "competent white female help." In Cincinnati, Ohio, black women who applied to the United States Employment Service for work indicated that they were either ignored or referred to domestic or maintenance jobs.[38]

The challenges that black women faced in the workplace during the war years were not ameliorated by the domestic propaganda campaigns engaged in by the Office of War Information (OWI). In films, newsreels, newspapers, and magazines, the OWI sought to boost home-front morale and encourage industry to deal with

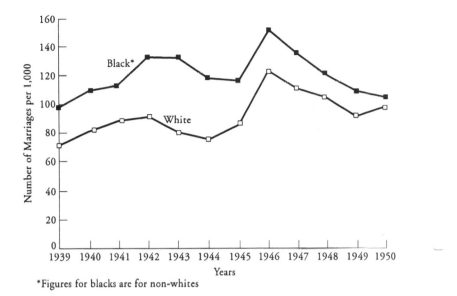

FIGURE 5.2 Marriages per 1,000 eligible males, 1939–1950. Marriage eligibles represent single men fifteen years or older and all divorced or widowed men, as of July 1 of each year. (From Paul Jacobson, *American Marriage and Divorce* [New York: Rinehart, 1959], 102)

labor shortages equitably, in part by hiring more women. According to Maureen Honey, this propaganda improved the images of white women as workers but did nothing for blacks:

> In wartime stories, no blacks appeared as heroes or heroines, and they were cast in the lowest occupational ratings of all groups surveyed. Furthermore, they (along with Jews) were the only group to possess more disapproved than approved character traits. In short, . . . the war had no positive impact on the fictional treatment of black people.[39]

Marriage and Marital Dissolution During the War

During the economic crisis of the 1930s, many marriages had been postponed. In 1946 more than 2.2 million couples said their vows, twice as many as in any year before the war, and set a nuptial record that was not equaled for 33 years.[40] And while the economic boom brought in by the war was the catalyst for a rush to the altar for blacks and whites, Figure 5.2 demonstrates that the marriage rates were even higher for black males than for white males. Although the marriage rate for black males were considerably higher prior to the war, both black and white males had similar increases from 1939 to 1941 (about 16 percent). In 1942, however, with the increased tempo of the draft and the favorable opportunity for black male employment for the first time in war industries, the rise in the marriage rate was much more significant for blacks than for whites.

Clearly, the marriage boom reflected the influence of the war. Many young people married in order to experience marital intimacy before the husband was shipped overseas. While some married to avoid the draft, others wed to acquire the benefits provided to dependents of military personnel.[41] For example, a monthly allotment check of $50 and a life insurance policy of $10,000 was given to the wife of each enlisted man. Women who married for these reasons were sometimes referred to as "Allotment Annies."[42] The marriage rates were highest for blacks and whites, however, during 1946 and 1947, when soldiers were returning home from the war.

Black marriage rates were increasing for another reason. With the enlistment of black men in the armed services and the increase in the total number of employees required for the booming war industries, the black male employment rate rose sharply almost overnight. Equally important, the new jobs were no longer confined to semiskilled work; thousands of blacks were now integrated into the manufacturing and industrial sector of the economy as skilled laborers. Black men had employment opportunities that were unparalleled at any other time in American history.[43]

While the war and the growth it created in the economy was an impetus for marriage, the opening up of higher-paying jobs to women narrowed the gap in income levels between males and females and created more tension in marital relationships. According to one study that examined the effects of working wives on family power relationships, the stresses were greater in working-class households than in middle-class ones.[44]

Even though a disproportionate number of black marriages would be classified as working-class, two different patterns emerged among blacks, both placing strain on their marriages. First, black males made greater economic gains than black females during the war years, thereby enhancing their authority within the family; this shift decreased the marital power of many black women who had previously "controlled the purse strings." Second, many black women were able to move up from domestic work to higher-paying industrial jobs, thereby increasing further their economic independence and paradoxically placing additional strain on the marriages.

In a minority of the black families, stressful marriages were rejuvenated as the result of the war. Before the war, the Brown family lived in Des Moines, Iowa. Howard Brown was an unemployed porter, with a wife and three children, who yearned for a law degree that seemed far beyond his reach. Sarah Brown became the sole provider of the family and amassed a great deal of anger and resentment toward Howard and became emotionally distant from him. She turned to her children both for help in the home and for the companionship her husband failed to give. She also came to enjoy the freedom and independence her job gave her. Sarah did not seek a divorce, however, "for the sake of the children." Howard enlisted in the army and spent his military years in New York, where he was drawn into the excitement of the Harlem scene. He wrote long letters home, full of longing for Sarah and dreams for the future. The new mood continued upon his return to Des Moines, and he enrolled in a local college on the GI bill to pursue his dream of becoming a lawyer. In addition, he spent much more time in the home being helpful to Sarah and playing with the children.[45]

In many cases wartime brides and grooms hardly got to know each other before the husband left for active duty; many such marriages were predictably undone when the veterans returned home. In the late 1930s, 85 marriages in 10,000 had ended in divorce, whereas between 1941 and 1945 the figure rose to 114. And in 1946 and 1947, the years when many veterans returned from the war, the annual rate climbed to 158 per 10,000, the same years in which marriage rates skyrocketed.[46]

When we look at the number of divorces per one thousand married males by race, however, somewhat different patterns emerge. The divorce rate for both black and white males hit its peak in 1946, at 18.7 and 18.1 per thousand, respectively; but the rates for whites dropped every year thereafter until 1950 (Figure 5.3), while for blacks, although the divorce rates declined somewhat, from 1948 to 1950 there was very little change. In 1939 white males had a divorce rate of 8.6 per thousand, compared to 6.6 for black males. By 1950 this rate had climbed to 13.9 for black males and had stabilized at 9.8 for white males.

As these figures suggest, divorce among black males was relatively infrequent during the early part of the century: Until the war years, desertion or informal separation were still the accepted means of dissolving a marriage. This was especially the case in the rural South, and these practices were probably carried to urban centers as blacks migrated north. Paul Jacobson has maintained that the "relatively greater upswing" in the black divorce rate since World War II has also been due in large measure to economic factors. As black males gained more financial security vis-à-vis black women during the 1940s, they emulated the practice of white males by retaining lawyers and filing divorce petitions to safeguard their earnings from their separated wives.[47]

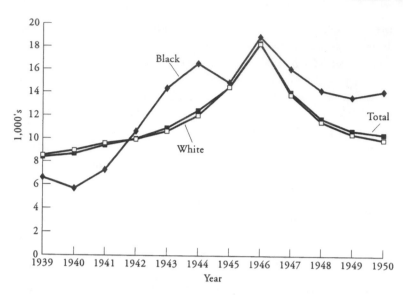

FIGURE 5.3   Divorces per 1,000 married males. (From Paul Jacobson, *American Marriage and Divorce* [New York: Rinehart, 1959], 102)

The Destabilization of the Black Family

During the 1940s, several developments were drawing attention to the metamorphosis of the American family. Births to single women doubled during the decade, and there was a dramatic increase in juvenile delinquency.[48] A sample of eighty-three municipal courts showed an increase in cases from 65,000 to 75,500 between 1940 and 1942. Delinquency increased twice as fast among white girls as black girls and three times as fast among white boys as black boys. Delinquency reached a peak in 1943, the year in which the most mothers were employed.[49]

Obviously, the prolonged separation of husbands from wives was a major disruptive factor. In 1948, John Durand tabulated the percentage of husbands absent from their wives and controlled for race. He found that in 1944, in the age category 20–24, 19.3 percent of white women and 19.4 percent of black women had an absent spouse. In the age categories 25–29 and 30–34, however, these percentages dropped sharply for white women to 13.3 and 13.1; for black women, however, they declined only slightly to 16.1 and 18.4, respectively.[50] (Figure 4.1 describing husband absenteeism can be found on page 80).

These higher rates of absence encouraged infidelity of both spouses.[51] But the double standard prevailed: Infidelity on the part of a soldier/husband was viewed as natural and inevitable, but a wife's infidelity was harshly censured. For example, an army chaplain, Captain H. A. Robinson, wrote a column in the *Baltimore Afro-*

American in which he warned that servicemen's wives who were not faithful to their husbands could have their allotments terminated or be divorced by their husbands.[52]

World War II brought about unprecedented opportunities for extramarital and premarital experiences, by facilitating the shift to urban living and providing youth with more economic autonomy and freedom from adult supervision. As many young men left home to join the armed services, many young women left home in search of jobs. During the 1940s, moral reformers were most concerned with the behavior of "victory girls" or "good-time Charlottes," whereas during World War I their attention had been focused on the dangers presented to young men by prostitution.[53]

The moral reformers were likewise alarmed at the skyrocketing birthrates to unmarried women. In 1940, the rate for unmarried white women in the 15–44 age group was 3.6 per thousand, but it increased to 5.1 in 1945 and stabilized at 5.8 in 1950. For unmarried blacks, the rate was 39.7 in 1940, then 45.3 in 1945, and 69.1 in 1950. Thus, births to unmarried black women, already much higher, increased dramatically from 1945 to 1950, a time when births to unmarried white women were stabilizing.[54]

Among unmarried black women, the age cohort that had the highest increase were the adolescents. When Cutright conducted a more detailed analysis of trends in births to unmarried black teenagers aged 14, 15–17, and 18–19, he found that among those aged 14 and under the rate increased by about six per thousand between 1940 and 1950, whereas for whites the change was insignificant. In addition, for blacks in the age category 15–17, the rate increased from 38 to 53 per thousand, and for whites the rate rose from four to five. During the 1940s there was a precipitous increase in adolescent childbearing among unmarried blacks, although it would not be formally identified as a social problem until the 1970s.[55]

On the positive side, African-Americans benefited in at least two ways during the war years. First, the average income of black families more than doubled between 1939 and 1945, even though it still fell far below that of whites.[56] A study conducted by the Harlem Children's Center in 1942 found that the number of black households on public welfare, as well as the number of undernourished children, had diminished. It also claimed that better employment opportunities had given black men a new measure of self-respect, which it viewed as having a positive influence on family relationships.[57]

Second, maternal and infant mortality rates took an especially sharp plunge in the 1940s, for blacks and whites alike. While the drop was due in part to the increasing incidence of hospital delivery and new medical procedures, another factor was congressional authorization of the Emergency Maternity and Infant Care (EMIC) program in 1943. Through this program, the federal government subsidized the cost of medical care for the wives and infants of enlisted men.[58] The rates of infant and maternal mortality for blacks plummeted in the 1940s, although the maternal mortality rate for black women remained three times higher than the rate for white women.[59] These gains for black women were a direct result of their having husbands in the military; the risks in pregnancy and childbearing for all other black women remained unchanged.[60]

Postwar Adjustment

After the defeat of Germany and the surrender of Japan, employment in defense industries was cut in half. Within a year of Japan's surrender in August 1945, nine million servicemen and women were discharged, and the government canceled war contracts worth more than $35 billion. In 1946 the weakening position of African-American workers became more precarious when Congress refused to appropriate funds for FEPC. President Truman refused to establish another such commission but instead ordered the inclusion of nondiscrimination clauses in defense contracts.

The limited protection FEPC had provided was sorely needed in the aftermath of the war, for various blatant forms of discrimination reappeared. A report published in 1947 by the National Committee on Segregation in the Nation's Capital found that discrimination remained as prevalent as ever.[61] In a particularly flagrant example, federal agencies that had aggressively recruited black clerical workers during the war now posted flyers listing clerical job openings for "whites only."[62]

Blacks remained optimistic, however, that during these postwar years black women would be able to retreat to their homes and take care of their families. In March 1947, an editorial in *Ebony* entitled "Goodbye Mammy, Hello Mom," pointed out that black women had never historically had the opportunity to devote their full attention to their families, but now for the first time "since 1619" they would enjoy the benefits derived from their husbands' high wages. The article ended by noting that "the cooking over which the 'white folks' used to go into ecstasies is now reserved for her own family and they really appreciate it."[63]

What this writer did not anticipate, however, was that the stressors that had burdened the black family "since 1619" would finally take their toll, and many black women would retreat to homes without husbands and the benefits derived from their wages. By 1950, African-American mothers were single parents at twice the rate of white women: In that year 17.6 percent of black families were headed by a woman, compared to 8.5 percent of white families.[64]

Not only were black women more likely to be without husbands, but the war had done little to enhance their position in the labor force. By the end of the decade, black women continued to be the lowest paid workers, with incomes lagging behind both white women and black men. Whereas black women continued to earn less than half the income of white women, the income of black men relative to white men grew from just 41 percent in 1939 to 61 percent by 1950. Even with husbands present, 30.2 percent of black wives worked, compared to only 19.6 percent of their white counterparts.[65]

The wartime labor shortage did make it possible for black women to prove their capabilities in skilled and semiskilled jobs that had once been closed to them, but most of them were not able to hold on to those jobs.[66] In 1950 the percentage of black women in domestic service was greater than it had been in 1940, and their labor force participation remained steady at about 37 percent.[67] In contrast, the rate for white women rose from 24.5 to 28.4 percent. In most major northern cities, the jobless rate for black women was three to four times higher than for foreign-born white women.[68]

During the postwar years, black migrants continued to flow into the northern cities, where white neighborhoods used restrictive real estate covenants and acts of violence to keep them confined to certain sections of town. The declining conditions in the ghettos, coupled with tenuous access to adequate health care, increased the prevalence of disease among blacks and pushed mortality rates for blacks higher in the cities than in rural areas.

Stanley Lieberson has found that between 1930 and 1950 there was "substantial deterioration in the unemployment situation of blacks" compared to whites, both immigrant and native. And while he found "no deterioration in the black educational position in the North through 1930," he has shown that by the 1950s the relatively favorable educational position of blacks compared to new immigrants had largely eroded.[69]

Perhaps the assault on black families during the postwar years is most clearly reflected in the divorce and separation rates for black couples, which were four times as high as whites'. This greater incidence of marital disruption was directly related to the high rate of black male unemployment.[70] And, of course, the problems of black families were exacerbated by a fertility rate much higher than that reported for whites.[71]

Many black women expressed an unwillingness to return to domestic service after having worked in industry. Here are the reasons given by one of them:

> [Some people say] they can't be as bad as they seem to me—these women I have worked for as a domestic . . . so overbearing, so much a slavedriver, so unwilling to grant us even a small measure of human dignity. But I have had three years of experience in at least a dozen households to bear eloquent witness to the contrary.
>
> Take this matter of inconsiderateness, of downright selfishness. No other women workers have the slave hours we domestics have. We usually work

twelve and fourteen hours a day, seven days a week, except for our pitiful little "Thursday afternoon off . . ." See how your legs ache after being on them from 7:00 a.m. to 9:00 p.m., when you are finishing the last mountain of dishes in the pantry!

. . . It is not only the long hours, the small pay, and the lack of privacy—we often have to share a room with the children—that we maids find hardest to bear. It is being treated most of the time as though we are completely lacking in human dignity and self respect. During my first years at this work I was continually hopeful. But now I know that when I enter the service elevator I should park my self-respect there along with the garbage that clutters it.[72]

With few alternatives available to them, many destitute black mothers applied to ADC for financial assistance. (After 1950, ADC became AFDC, or Aid to Families with Dependent Children.) There was likewise a precipitious increase in the number of black adolescent mothers applying for AFDC, in that adolescent childbearing among blacks proliferated for the first time during the 1950s. As the welfare rolls expanded, the late 1940s had brought violent pervasive attacks on ADC. As Harold Silver of Detroit noted in his address to the Family Service Association of America in 1950, "the headlines and impressions created by the press were that from 30 to 50 percent of the AFDC program's clientele were 'fraud' and 'chiselers,' that millions of dollars of tax funds were being wasted through carelessness and negligence of administration." Silver then points out that in 1948, an exhaustive investigation of the Department of Public Welfare in Detroit had found that only two warrants for fraud had been issued, and that neither one had resulted in conviction.[73]

Conclusion

World War II placed severe strains on all American families, but its heaviest impact was felt by the African-American family, weakened by slavery, sharecropping, and the northern migration. During the 1940s, twice the number of blacks migrated to the North than had relocated there between 1910 and 1930. By the end of the postwar decade, the proportion of blacks in urban areas would finally exceed those in rural areas—a shift that had been made by whites some 30 years before.

The war catalyzed an unprecedented tide of migration for whites as well. The federal government's efforts to remedy shortages in housing and schools were not only inadequate but were aimed primarily at white communities. And occasional attempts to assist the black community were met with strong resistance from whites. Race riots broke out in many cities when black neighborhoods were perceived as encroaching on all-white areas. In these skirmishes, blacks were invariably the ones injured or arrested.

With FEPC abandoned and defense industries shutting down, discrimination in the labor market proliferated, and black employment rates plummeted. By the end of the war, the proportion of black women in domestic service was greater than it had been in 1941. The jobless rate for black women was three to four times greater than for foreign-born white women. By 1948 most of the gains that blacks had made during the wartime boom had been wiped out, and labor analysts predicted that the security of the black worker would depend almost entirely on a strong economy.

Facing a weakened economy without the social controls once provided by the communal aspects of southern life, black marriages disintegrated, and out-of-wedlock births proliferated, especially among adolescents. Although clearly disadvantaged in their competition with white women for jobs in the labor market, many black women opted not to return to the paltry wages and irregular hours of the domestic service jobs they had held before the war. In an effort to cope with their much higher rates of desertion, separation, and divorce from black men, and with the difficulty of securing support from the financially beleaguered fathers, black mothers became more reliant on welfare.

In the postwar political climate of patriotic fervor and obsession with the threat of communism, government programs to help the poor were often criticized as "creeping socialism," and were attacked with little abatement until the presidential election of 1952. Although many of these attacks were groundless and inaccurately documented, welfare leaders found it difficult to rebut them, because the real problem was not the socialistic nature of government programs but the failure of black family patterns, with all their handicaps, to conform to mainstream norms. Unfortunately, public ignorance about the complexity of these handicaps would persist for decades, and the plight of poor black families would become increasingly distinct and desperate.

Notes

1. Arthur Marwick, *War and Social Change in the Twentieth Century* (New York: St. Martin's Press, 1974), 6–14.

2. Reynolds Farley, *The Growth of the Black Population* (Chicago: Markham, 1970), 42. Jack T. Kirby, "The Southern Exodus, 1910–60: A Primer for Historians," *Journal of Southern History* 49 (November 1983): 585–600. Kirby argues that the earlier migration was partly responsible for the direction and volume of the larger migration that followed, because it established "interregional networks of family and friends" (592).

3. Robert C. Weaver, *Negro Labor: A National Problem* (New York: Harcourt, Brace

& Co, 1946), 91. Although some social analysts had argued that this boom in the nation's economy spurred the migration patterns for blacks as well as whites, a closer analysis revealed that it applied only to whites. See Harold B. Myers for the argument that the 1930s was a "depression" migration and the 1940s was an "economic boom" migration, making no distinctions between blacks and whites "Defense Migration and Labor Supply," *Journal of the American Statistical Association* 37 (March 1942). This analysis was challenged by Daniel M. Johnson and Rex R. Campbell, *Black Migration in America: A Social Demographic History* (Durham, N.C.: Duke University Press, 1981), ch. 8. For figures on the growth of black migration to the North, see Robert C. Weaver, *Negro Labor: A National Problem* (New York: Harcourt, Brace, 1946), 91. On the competition between whites and blacks for jobs in southern cities, see T. J. Woofter, Jr., "Southern Population and Social Planning," *Social Forces* 14(October 1935): 609–18.

4. Gunnar Myrdal, *An America Dilemma* (New York: Harper, 1944), 997.

5. For further details on migration to areas with a sizable number of defense industries, see Department of Commerce, Census Bureau, *Current Population Reports*, series P-23, no. 42, *The Social and Economic Status of the Black Population in the United States, 1971* (Washington, D.C.: Government Printing Office, 1972), 18. See also Weaver, *Negro Labor*.

6. Quoted in T. B. Bottomore, *Karl Marx* (Glencoe, Ill.: Free Press, 1950), 64.

7. As late as 1949, only eighteen states had passed laws that would make it illegal to discriminate on the basis of race in public facilities, and even those laws were limited in application. For a closer examination of the various forms of segregation in most states and the laws that enforced them, see Richard Bardolph, ed., *The Civil Rights Record: Black Americans and the Law, 1849–1970* (New York: Crowell, 1970).

8. Blacks did not accept the social humiliation of segregation passively. When more forceful forms of opposition were blocked, they used other means, like placing "out of order" signs on white restrooms (to force whites to use the same facilities) or painting over the signs designating "colored" or "white." See Benjamin Muse, *American Negro Revolution* (Bloomington: University of Indiana Press, 1968); Frank A. Aukofer, *City With a Chance: A Case History of Civil Rights Revolution* (Milwaukee: Bruce, 1968).

9. Quoted in Geoffrey Perrett, *Days of Sadness, Years of Triumph: The American People 1939–1945* (New York: Coward, McCann & Geoghegan 1973 148.

10. Karen Tucker Anderson, *Wartime Women: Sex Roles, Family Relations and the Status of Women During WW II* (Westport, Conn., Greenwood Press, 1981), 80. Perrett, *Days of Sadness,* 312.

11. For a discussion on social action taken by blacks during the wartime period for jobs, see Herbert Garfinkel, *When Negroes March: The March on Washington Movement in the Organizational Politics for FEPC* (Glencoe, Ill.: Free Press, 1959). For a discussion of the role of FEPC and the leadership of A. Philip Randolph, see Louis C. Kesselman, *The Social Politics of FEPC: A Study in Reform Movements* (Chapel Hill: University of North Carolina Press, 1948).

12. Kesselman, *Social Politics of FEPC,* 23n; Harvard Sitkoff, *A New Deal for Blacks: The Emergence of Civil Rights as a National Issue* (New York: Oxford University Press, 1978).

13. On the efforts of local black workers to put pressure on FEPC, see Lester B. Granger,

"A Hopeful Sign in Race Relations," *Survey Graphic* 23(November 1944), 355–56.; William H. Harris, "Federal Intervention in Union Discrimination: FEPC and West Coast Shipyards during World War II," *Labor History* 22 (Summer 1981):325–47; John C. Walter, "Frank R. Crosswaith and Labor Unionization in Harlem, 1939–45," *Afro-Americans in New York Life and History* 7 (July 1983):47–58.

14. It should be noted that black women filed more than one of every four discrimination complaints heard by FEPC between July 1943 and December 1944. But even when black women were hired, they were the first to be laid off. These FEPC figures are taken from George E. Demar, "Negro Women Are American Workers, Too," *Opportunity: Journal of Negro Life* 21 (April 1943): 41–42.On the complaints filed for continued discrimination and the challenges that the FEPC faced as it endeavored to settle complaints, see Malcolm Ross, *All Manner of Men* (New York: Reynal and Hitchcock, 1948) and Philip S. Foner, *Organized Labor and the Black Worker, 1916–1973* (New York: Praeger, 1973).

15. For a closer examination of the struggle for black voting rights in the South during the 1940s, see John Hope Franklin, *From Slavery to Freedom,* 7th ed. (New York: Knopf, 1994); Thomas R. Brooks, *Walls Come Tumbling Down: A History of the Civil Rights Movement 1940–1970* (Englewood Cliffs, N.J.: Prentice-Hall, 1994).

16. For an analysis of the black experience in World War I, from the perspective of the black soldier, see Kingsley Moses, "The Negro Comes North," and John Richards, "Some Experiences with Colored Soldiers," in *World War I at Home: Readings on American Life, 1914–1920,* ed. David F. Trask (New York: Wiley, 1970). The problems the black men faced in the army during World War I were aggravated by an Army Signal Corps film entitled *Training of Colored Troops,* which presented stereotypic images of blacks. This film, a dramatized portrayal of a black soldier from induction to training, contributed further to the negative image of the black soldiers by highlighting a watermelon-eating and dancing competition; National Archives Film Library, NA 111H-1211–PPSA-1.

17. Ulysses G. Lee, *The Employment of Negro Troops: The U.S. Army in World War II,* (Washington, D.C., Center for Military History, U.S. Army 1966), 29–38; Richard M. Dalfiume, "The Forgotten Years of the Negro Revolutions," in *The Negro in Depression and War,* ed. Bernard Sternsher (Chicago: Quadrangle Books, 1969); John W. Davis, "The Negro in the United States Navy, Marine Corps, and Coast Guard," *Journal of Negro Education* 12 (Summer 1943): 345–349.

18. Neil A. Wynn, *The Afro-American Experience and the Second World War,* rev. ed. (New York: Holmes & Meier, 1993), 21. On the status of black servicemen during the war, see also W. Y. Bell, Jr., "The Negro Warrior's Home Front," *Phylon* 5 (Third Quarter 1944): 271–78; Mary Frances Berry and John W. Blassingame, *Long Memory: The Black Experience in America* (New York: Oxford University Press, 1992): 320–30.

19. Langston Hughes, *Fight for Freedom: The Story of the NAACP* (New York, 1962), 197–98; Wynn, *Afro-American Experience,* 19. In 1943 the NAACP received over $5,000 from servicemen, and by the end of the war donations from soldiers amounted to $25,000, and some fifteen thousand had joined the organization.

20. One survey found that all blacks were not opposed to segregation. As many as 40 percent thought separate post exchanges were a good idea, 48 per cent thought them a poor

idea, and 12 percent were undecided. Thirty-eight percent of those questioned favored racially separate units, 36 percent wanted integrated ones, and 26 percent were undecided; Wynn, *Afro-American Experiences*, 28–29.

21. Perrett, *Days of Sadness*, 153.

22. For a review of the changing opportunity structure for women during the Second World War, see Joan Ellen Trey, "Women in the War Economy," *Review of Radical Political Economics* 4 (July 1972); Eleanor Straub, "Government Policy toward Civilian Women during World War II" (Ph.D. diss., Emory University, 1973); Leila Rupp, *Mobilizing Women for War: German and American Propaganda, 1939–1945* (Princeton: Princeton University Press, 1978); William Chafe, *The American Woman: Her Changing Social, Economic, and Political Roles, 1920–1970* (New York: Oxford University Press, 1972); D'Ann Campbell, *Women at War with America: Private Lives in a Patriotic Era* (Cambridge, Mass.: Harvard University Press, 1984); Susan M. Hartmann, *The Home Front and Beyond: American Women in the 1940s* (Boston: Twayne Publishers, 1982).

23. Hartmann, *Home Front and Beyond*, 22.

24. A Florida survey found that "since the war started the Negro men had higher incomes and they could afford to have a higher standard of living. Therefore, their wives and children no longer had to cook for the whites." For the Florida survey results in their entirety see Howard W. Odum, *Folk, Region, and Society* (Chapel Hill: University of North Carolina Press, 1964), 63.

25. Nora R. Tucker and Thomasina W. Norford, "Ten Years of Progress: The Negro Woman in the Labor Force," in *Women United*, Souvenir Year Book (National Council of Negro Women, 1951); Mary S. Bedell, "Employment and Income of Negro Workers— 1940–52," *Monthly Labor Review* 76 (June 1953): 596–601; Department of Labor, Women's Bureau *Negro Women War Workers*, Bulletin no. 202 (Washington, D.C., 1945). For a comprehensive analysis of black women's employment experiences during World War II, see Jacqueline Jones, *Labor of Love, Labor of Sorrow, Black Women's Work and the Family from Slavery to the Present* (New York: Basic Books, 1985), ch. 7; Karen Tucker Anderson, "Last Hired, First Fired: Black Women Workers During World War II," *Journal of American History* 69 (June 1982): 82–97.

26. A Roper poll found that three out of four black women were willing to take factory jobs, whereas only one in eight white women found factory work acceptable. Factory work was also acceptable to those with only an elementary education (37 percent), in contrast to its rejection by better-educated women (2 percent). Education and socioeconomic/racial status clearly overlapped, in that most black women had attained less education than white women. The analysis of variance demonstrated that both race and class had a strong independent effect; Roper-*Fortune* poll 35, May 1943, Roper Center, Williams College.

27. Quoted in Philip S. Foner, *Women and the American Labor Movement: From World War I to the Present* (New York: Free Press, 1980), 344.

28. Campbell, *Women at War*, chapter 4 provides an excellent overview of attitudes and practices of male employers and workers.

29. For popular attitudes regarding women and employment during the 1930s and 1940s, see Rupp, *Mobilizing Women for War*; Lois Scharf, *To Work and to Wed: Female*

Employment, Feminism, and the Great Depression (Westport, Conn.: Greenwood Press, 1980); Mary Kelly, ed., *Woman's Being, Woman's Place: Female Identity and Vocation in American History* (Boston: Hall, 1979).

30. Straub, "Government Policy toward Civilian Women," pp. 297–300; Anderson, "Last Hired, First Fired," 7.

31. Quoted in Odum, *Folk, Region, and Society,* 63.

32. Hartmann, *Home Front and Beyond,* 90

33. Straub, "Government Policy toward Civilian Women," 302.

34. For examples of discrimination in federal agencies during the pre- and postwar years, see Samuel Krislov, *The Negro in Federal Employment: The Quest for Equal Opportunity* (Minneapolis: University of Minnesota Press, 1967); L.J.W. Hayes, *The Negro Government Worker* (Washington, D.C.: Howard University Graduate School, 1941); Dorothy K. Newman, Nancy J. Amidei, Barbara Carter, *Protest, Politics, and Prosperity: Black Americans and White Institutions 1940–75* (New York: Pantheon, 1978).

35. A group of black secretaries entering a government lunchroom in 1945 found all the tables full except one partly occupied by white men. When they took the empty seats, their lunch trays were swept to the floor by one of the men, who insisted that no blacks were going to eat at his table; Newman, *Protest, Politics, and Prosperity,* 306.

36. Kenesaw M. Landis, *Segregation in Washington: A Report of the National Committee on Segregation in the Nation's Capital* (Chicago: , 1948), 60–74.

37. Karen Anderson, *Wartime Women: Sex Roles, Family Relations. amd the Status of Women during World War II* (Westport, Conn.: Greenwood Press, 1981), 35–39; Alice Kessler-Harris, *Out to Work: a History of Wage-Earning Women in the United States* (New York: Oxford University Press, 1982), 273–99.

38. Anderson, "Last Hired, First Fired," 82–97; Hartmann, *Home Front and Beyond.*

39. Maureen Honey, *Creating Rosie the Riveter: Class, Gender, and Propaganda during World War II* (Amherst: University of Massachusetts Press, 1984), 28–29, 83. For a more in-depth discussion of the propaganda on African-Americans generated during the war, see Bernard Berelson and Patricia J. Salter, "Majority and Minority Americans: An Analysis of Magazine Fiction," *Public Opinion Quarterly* 10 (Summer 1946): 168–97.

40. Landon Y. Jones, *Great Expectations: America and the Baby Boom Generation* (New York: Coward, McCann & Geoghegan, 1980), 11. According to an analysis conducted by Thomas Espenshade, as of 1940–45, white women were spending 49.4 percent of their total lifetime married, compared to 41.9 percent for black women. For 1945–50 this figure increased to 53.7 percent for white women and decreased to 40.2 percent for black women. The percent of time in a first marriage increased for both groups in 1945–1950. However, for whites the percent of time in remarriages increased in 1945–50, but it dropped precipitiously for blacks during the same time frame. The proportion of their lifetime that black women can expect to spend in an intact marriage or a remarriage was analyzed in 1975–1980 and the percentage had declined from 40 percent at the rates prevalent in 1945–1950 to 22 percent; "The Recent Decline of American Marriage: Blacks and White in Comparative Perspective," in *Contemporary Marriage,* eds. Kingsley Davis and Amyra Grossbard-Schechtman (New York: Russell Sage Foundation, 1986), 56–64.

41. Men with dependents were deferred until 1942. It should be noted that this was not as much the case for black couples; for the most part, black men voluntarily enlisted in that many were being overlooked by their local draft boards.

42. For more information on Allotment Annies, see Ronald H. Bailey, *The Home Front: U.S.A.* (Alexandria, Va.: 1978), 51.

43. On the growth of blacks in industry and the conflicts they experienced as they made attempts to join forces with organized labor in the 1940s, see Neil Lichtenstein, *Labor's War at Home: The CIO in World War II* (New York: Cambridge University Press, 1982); Sumner M. Rosen, "The CIO Era, 1935–55," in *The Negro and the American Labor Movement* ed. Julius Jacobson (Garden City, N.Y.: Anchor/Doubleday, 1968); August Meier and Elliott Rudwick, *Black Detroit and the Rise of the UAW* (New York: Oxford University Press, 1979); Alma Herbst, *The Negro in the Slaughtering and Meat-Packing Industry in Chicago* (New York: Arno Press, 1971); Herbert R. Northrup, *Organized Labor and the Negro* (New York: Harper, 1944). The labor force participation of black men simultaneously declined during this period. William J. Wilson analyzed a similar pattern during the postwar years through the early 1980s and has asserted that "the increasing delay of first marriage and the low rate of remarriage among black women seem to be directly tied to the increasing labor force problems of men"; *The Truly Disadvantaged: The Inner City, the Underclass, and Public Policy* (Chicago: University of Chicago Press), 84.

44. Mirra Komarovsky, *Blue-Collar Marriage* (New York: Random House, 1967), 70–74.

45. Reuben Hill and Elise Boulding, *Families Under Stress: Adjustment to the Crises of War Separation and Reunion* (New York: Harper Brothers, 1949), 275–77.

46. Frances E. Merrill, *Social Problems on the Home Front* (New York: Harper & Row, 1948), chap. 2; Paul H. Jacobson, "Differentials in Divorce by Duration of Marriages and Size of Family," *American Sociological Review* 15 (April 1950): 235–44.

47. Paul H. Jacobson, *American Marriage and Divorce* (New York: Rinehart, 1959), 102.

48. Abbott L. Ferris, *Indicators of Trends in the Status of Women* (New York: Russell Sage Foundation, 1971), 351. In 1940 single women bore children at the rate of 7.1 per thousand women aged 15–44; by 1950 the rate had reached 14.1.

49. Campbell, *Women at War*, 203; Hartmann, *The Home Front and Beyond*, 179. Social scientists and experts on the family, not surprisingly, identified the working mothers as one of the primary causes. For comprehensive analyses of social problems and the role of women, see Merrill, *Social Problems*; Chafe, *American Woman*; Glick, *American Families* (New York: Wiley, 1957).

50. John Durand, *The Labor Force in the United States, 1890–1960* (New York: Gordon and Breach, 1948): 224–26. See also Table 4.2, which compares black and white husband absenteeism for the years 1930, 1940, and 1944.

51. When Drake and Cayton studied the changes in the marital status among African-Americans living in poverty during the war, they found that about forty out of every hundred black women were "available" in the sense that they did not have husbands. They also found that nearly all of the men reported themselves as "single" even though in many cases they

may have been previously married. They noted that individuals from the ranks of the "sixty per cent married" were continuously dropping into the ranks of the "forty per cent available," and vice versa; *The Black Metropolis* (New York: Harcourt, Brace, 1945) 585; St. Clair Drake, "The Negro in the North During Wartime Chicago," *Journal of Educational Sociology* 17 (January, 1944): 266.

52. Quoted in Anderson, *Wartime Women*, 81.

53. For an analysis of the sexual norms during the 1940s, see John D'Emilio and Estelle B. Freedman, *Intimate Matters: A History of Sexuality in America* (New York: Harper & Row), 260–62; Allan M. Brandt, *No Magic Bullet: A Social History of Venereal Disease in the United States since 1880* (New York: Oxford University Press 1985), 164, 167–68.

54. Phillips Cutright, "Illegitimacy in the United States: 1920–1968," in *Demographic and Social Aspects of Population Growth*, ed. Charles F. Westoff and Robert Parke, Jr., U. S. Commission on Population Growth and the American Future, Research Reports, vol. 1 (Washington, D.C.: Government Printing Office, 1972), 381–438. It should also be noted that when out-of-wedlock ratios are calculated by the number of births rather than the number of women, in 1940 the figure was 40.3 per thousand for all births and by 1950 that figure was 40.9 births, reflecting no growth. However, when these figures are broken down by race some differences emerge. For whites the ratios were 19.8 in 1940 and 23.6 in 1945 but dropped to 17.5 by 1950, whereas for blacks the ratios were 166.4 in 1940 and 179.3 in 1945, and they held constant in 1950 at 179.5.

55. Ibid.

56. Figures on the employment gains of black men: Susan Hartmann, *Home Front and Beyond*, 5. Figures on the income increase for black families: Campbell, *Women at War*, 218. For a distribution of employees in the auto industry during the war years by gender and race see Ruth Milkman, 'Redefining 'Women's Work': "Organizing the Sexual Division of Labor: Historical Perspectives on 'Women Work' and the Am. Labor Movement, *Socialist Review* 49 (Jan-Feb, 1980):128–33.; Alan Clive, "Women Workers in World War II: Michigan as a Test Case," *Labor History* 20 (Winter, 1979):44–69; Meier and Rudwick, *Black Detroit*.

57. Reported in George Gregory, Jr., "Wartime Guidance for Tomorrow's Citizens," *Opportunity* 21 (Aril 1943): 70–71, 90–91.

58. Martha M. Eliot and Lillian R. Freedman, "Four Years of the EMIC Program," *Yale Journal of Biology and Medicine* 19 (March 1947):621–35.

59. Sam Shapiro, Edward R. Schlesinger, and Robert E. L. Nesbit, Jr., *Infant, Perinatal, Maternal and Childhood Mortality in the United States* (Cambridge, Mass.:Harvard University Press, 1968), 248, 329; Richard C. Wertz and Dorothy C. Wertz, *Lying-In: A History of Childbirth in America* (New York: Free Press, 1977), 164–73.

60. The difference in mortality rates between blacks and whites can be explained in part by the persistence of midwifery and home deliveries in southern black communities. For example, in 1942 in a small town in Mississippi 119 black babies were delivered by midwives and 37 by physicians, and of those 37 deliveries by physicians, 26 were delivered at home. In 1941 and 1942 in Alabama and South Carolina, 62 percent and 80 percent of the black babies were delivered by midwives, respectively; Campbell, *Women at War*, 179.

61. President's Committee on Civil Rights, *To Secure These Rights* (Washington, D.C.: Government Printing Office, 1947), 58.

62. Newman, *Protest, Politics, and Prosperity*, 103. See also Thomas Richardson, "Negro Discrimination by Uncle Sam," *March of Labor* 1 (July 1949): 22.

63. *Ebony* March, 1947, 36.

64. Department of Commerce, Census Bureau, "Characteristics of Single, Married, and Widowed Divorced Persons in 1947" *Current Population Reports*, series P-20, no. 10 (Washington, D.C.: Government Printing, 1948).

65. Hartmann, *Home Front and Beyond*, 5–6.

66. The proportion of women of all races employed in domestic service was reduced again, by more than half a million—from nearly 20 percent to 10 percent. White women gained more from this shift than black women. For information on changes in black and white women's occupational status during the 1940s, see Department of Labor, Women's Bureau, "Changes in Women's Occupations, 1940–1950," *Bulletin* no. 153 (Washington, D.C.: Government Printing office, 1954); C. Arnold Anderson and Mary Jean Bowman, "The Vanishing Servant and the Contemporary Status System of the American South," *American Journal of Sociology* 59 (November 1953). Figures on the median income of black women compared to white women are from George E. Demar, "Negro Women are American Workers, Too," *Opportunity: Journal of Negro Life* 21 (April 1943): 41–42.

67. A black woman who preferred her job as a machine operator in a can company was "beginning to accept the fact that Negro women will be forced to return to domestic work." For in-depth interviews with black women who were employed as domestics during the 1940s and sought to reconcile their jobs with their feelings of dignity and self-worth, see Bonnie Thornton Dill, "Across the Barriers of Race and Class: An Exploration of the Relationship between Work and Family among Black Female Domestics" (Ph.D. diss., New York University, 1979); Robert Hamburger, *A Stranger in the House* (New York: Collier, 1978).

68. Phyllis A. Wallace, *Black Women in the Labor Force* (Cambridge, Mass.: MIT Press, 1980), 44; Valerie Kincaide Oppenheimer, *The Female Labor Force in the United States: Demographic and Economic Factors Governing Its Growth and Changing Composition* (Westport, Conn.: Greenwood Press, 1970), 78–79.

69. Stanley Lieberson, *A Piece of the Pie: Blacks and White Immigrants Since 1880* (Berkeley: University of California Press, 1980), 200–250.

70. For a comprehensive discussion and analysis, see Phillips Cutright, "Components of Change in the Number of Female Family Heads Aged 15–44: United States, 1940–1970," *Journal of Marriage and the Family* 36 (November 1974):714–22; La Frances Rodgers-Rose, "Some Demographic Characteristics of Black Women: 1940 to 1975," in *The Black Woman*, ed. La Frances Rodgers-Rose (Beverly Hills: Sage Publications, 1980).

71. In the early 1940s black organizations had cooperated with the Planned Parenthood Federation in campaigns to make contraceptives available to black families, but to little avail. When researchers surveyed 357 black women in rural Maryland in 1950 and 1951 they found that just one in five practiced birth control. See Christopher Tietze and Sarah Lewit,

"Patterns of Family Limitation in a Rural Negro Community," *American Sociological Review* 18 (October 1953):563–64; Myrdal, *America Dilemma*, 178–81.

72. Quoted in Herbert Aptheker, ed., *A Documentary History of the Negro People in the United States*, vol. 3, *From the Beginning of the New Deal to the End of the Second World War, 1933–1945* (Secaucus, N.J.: Citadel Press, 1974), 382–84.

73. Quoted in Winifred Bell, *Aid to Dependent Children* (New York: Columbia University Press, 1965), 62.

CHAPTER SIX

THE CALM
BEFORE THE STORM

Scientific interest in a social problem emerges only when the moral norms by which the thing is judged evil are themselves subjected to analysis rather than taken for granted.

Kingsley Davis, "Illegitimacy and the Social Structure"

Customs persist and preserve their external forms after they have lost their original meaning and functions. Institutions are imposed upon people to whose traditions, instincts, and actual needs they are quite foreign, or have not yet been fully assimilated. Fashions change, and with the change institutions, though they persist, are looked upon with profoundly changed attitudes.

Robert E. Park, in Johnson, Shadow of the Plantation

The 1950s, often thought of as the "golden age of the American family," brought a period of stability to family life after two decades of disruption caused by the depression and the war effort. For blacks, these disruptions had been exacerbated by a shift in migratory patterns and the intensification of racial bigotry as they moved into the North. Anticipating a decline in these problems, both black and white Americans placed a renewed emphasis on family life as a national ideal. By 1960 the average marriage age of women had dropped to twenty, and 14 million were engaged by the age of seventeen.[1]

But there were differences in the emphasis that black and white communities put on the family. *Life*, one of the nation's most popular magazines, ran a thirteen-page article in 1947 entitled "The American Woman's Dilemma." In the past, it said, women had only one big decision to make—the choice of a husband. Now, it warned, women who devoted themselves exclusively to the home risked isolating themselves from the world of ideas and experiences encountered by their husbands.[2]

In contrast, *Life*'s analogue in the black community, *Ebony*, featured an article entitled "800,000 Negro Girls Will Never Go to the Altar," in which it analyzed geographic variations in gender-ratio imbalances throughout the country. Whereas

Life assumed that all white women would marry, and defined their major challenge as finding ways to become increasingly involved in the world around them, *Ebony* made no such assumption and highlighted the difficulty that many black women would have in finding a husband.[3]

During the 1950s there was a cultural uneasiness about the role of single women, so many of whom had become more emancipated by their experiences of living and working without husbands during the war. While marriage and child-rearing were the ethical goals regulating the behavior of most Americans, a minority of women and men began to bear children out of wedlock and mother-only families emerged as social problem. And, as in earlier periods, circumstances shaped different marriage and family experiences for whites and blacks during this period in American history.

The Baby Boom and Economic Expansion

The rate of the American population's growth during the 1950s was twice what it had been before the war; various theories have been advanced to explain this baby boom. Although most of them have focused on the economic aspects of the boom, a psychological perspective set forth by Glen Elder is worth noting at the outset. Elder studied people who grew up during the depression, in an effort to determine how their experiences shaped their values. In that period many husbands were unable to support their families; some left permanently to avoid embarrassment, and others left temporarily until they could secure employment. Many wives and children were forced to devise ways to support themselves and sought employment outside the home.

In Elder's view, during the depression decade teenagers often assumed adult responsibilities, and these experiences had lasting consequences, such as a reluctance to have large families. Those who started their own families after World War II generally had favorable attitudes toward marriage and family life; they married at an early age, bore numerous children, and had lower divorce rates.[4]

Although many demographers contend that it is not possible to attribute changes in the fertility patterns of women to a single economic or psychological factor, the fertility boom coincided with a period of great economic expansion in this country. Fred Vinson, the director of War Mobilization and Reconversion, exulted that the "American people are in the pleasant predicament of having to learn to live fifty percent better than they ever have before." Such optimism was understandable: Between 1940 and 1955 the personal income of Americans had increased by 293 percent, and the gross national product had doubled.[5]

The prosperity of the forties and fifties was widespread. Mass unemployment ended, and wages—especially for workers in strongly unionized industries such as steel and automobiles—rose dramatically. There was also a precipitous increase in the consumption of the most visible commodities such as clothes, cars, and electrical appliances. The use of electricity tripled in the 1950s, in large part because of the appliances purchased. These purchases were likewise influenced by the advertising industry, which increased its expenditures by 400 percent between 1945 and 1960.[6]

Consumerism was fostered not only by the booming construction in the suburbs but by the building of a massive network of highways created to get people to work in the cities. Under the Highways Act of 1956, Congress appropriated $32 billion to build forty-one thousand miles of roads. This transformation of the American landscape increased its reliance on automobiles and the ancillary industries of oil, rubber, and gasoline. John Kenneth Galbraith explained these consumption patterns further when he noted that the modern economy was one in which consumer industries met a demand for products which they themselves had generated. As shopping centers proliferated and a new culture of buying took control, suburban residents were bombarded with the message that they could not enjoy the good life without a motorized lawnmower, a new convertible, or the latest imported wine.[7]

During this period of rapid economic expansion there were relatively low levels of immigration—and as educational opportunities expanded and opportunities for service employment grew, the children of foreign-born whites increasingly left the ranks of manual laborers. Under these conditions, industry once again turned to black migrants from the South to fill low-wage jobs, and during the 1950s, approximately 1.5 million more blacks relocated to the North.[8]

The New American Frontier for Whites: Suburbs

While the internal migration pattern for blacks remained the same—from the South to the North—during the 1950s the migration pattern for whites was from the cities to the suburbs. In the twenty years between 1950 and 1970, the population of the suburbs doubled from 36 million to 72 million. During the 1950s alone, the suburbs grew fifteen times faster than any other segment of the country.[9]

Although middle-class whites may have fled to the suburbs to escape the rising tide of poor blacks entering cities from the South, as William Frey has argued, there were additional factors activating this flight pattern.[10] The combination of Federal Housing Administration (FHA) financing and new construction methods made it less expensive to purchase new suburban homes than to rent comparable older dwellings in the central city. Loan programs created by the FHA, along with the Veterans Administration (VA) program authorized by the Servicemen's Readjustment Act of 1944, pumped millions of dollars into the housing industry and provided the major impetus for a reshaping of the residential market in the United States.[11]

Before the FHA program, mortgages were not usually granted for more than two-thirds of the appraised value of a property, which meant that a buyer might be required to raise cash to cover the other third. With the FHA guaranteeing upwards of 90 percent of the assessed value of a property, prospective buyers needed much less cash for a down payment. The FHA also extended the loan repayment period to twenty-five or thirty years, thus lowering monthly payments for buyers. In addition, the guarantees provided by the FHA minimized the risks to lender banks, making it possible for them to pass their savings on to customers in the form of lower interest rates. The VA policies duplicated those already established by the FHA.

Douglas Massey and Nancy Denton have argued that the FHA and the VA "contributed significantly to the decline of the inner city by encouraging the se-lective out-migration of middle-class whites to the suburbs."[12] In their view, the bias in favor of the suburbs was evident in numerous FHA policies, notably those that favored construction of single-family homes but discouraged multifamily units, and those that required a professional appraisal of insured properties, which nat-urally included an evaluation of the neighborhood. In evaluating neighborhoods, the FHA used the Home Owners' Loan Corporation (HOLC) rating system, which stated that "if a neighborhood is to retain stability, it is necessary that the properties shall continue to be occupied by the same social and racial classes."[13]

With numerous inducements provided by the federal government, white fam-ilies moved in massive numbers to the suburbs and achieved a new level of racial and gender polarization. Gender roles were altered further: A commuter father often left the home before daylight and saw very little of his children or his home-maker wife, who took entire responsibility for the daily activities in the home. A woman's life, according to one humorist, "was motherhood on wheels, [delivering children] obstetrically once and by car forever after."[14]

Although Betty Friedan would not write *The Feminine Mystique* until 1963, what she described was male contempt for women's domestic endeavors that she had witnessed during the 1950s. Most housework, she suggested, could be ade-quately performed by "feeble-minded girls" or eight-year-old children. What made Friedan's book a bestseller was her compassionate documentation of the malaise of the middle-class housewife. She also described the pernicious effects of dependent housewives on those around them, arguing that the rising divorce rate confirmed "the growing aversion and hostility that men have for the feminine millstones hanging around their necks."[15]

A dramatic social transformation occurred during this period among white mid-dle-class women. In households where the husband earned from $7,000 to $10,000 a year, the rate of women's labor force participation increased from 7 percent in 1950 to 25 percent in 1960. The proportion of women receiving college degrees rose from just 24 percent in 1950 to over 30 percent fifteen years later.[16] Social scientists during this period were puzzled by the fact that women's education and employment were increasing at the very time women were finding new contentment in the domestic arena. Clearly, the nature of suburban life was more complex than the popular images of the 1950s suggested. This generation of white women in the suburbs would be the first to experience the contemporary economic and social pressure to find meaning in their lives beyond the traditional obligations of childbearing and homemaking.

The Making of the "Second Ghetto"

While white families were moving to the sprawling suburbs and savoring their economic prosperity, black families were experiencing economic adversity and increasing confinement to urban ghettos.[17] The growing disparity between blacks and whites during this period was clearly reflected in aggregate family incomes. In 1959 the median family income for whites was $5,600, but for blacks it was only $2,900. Furthermore, black income remained stagnant in the postwar years—54 percent of that of white workers in 1947, 55 percent in 1962.[18]

The irony of the home-ownership quest for all Americans was that the same government policies that made it possible for whites to purchase homes in the suburbs served to confine blacks to inner-city neighborhoods by sanctioning the use of redlining. The practice of redlining was introduced when the HOLC program was initiated by the federal government during the 1930s. The HOLC developed a rating system to measure the risks associated with loans made to particular communities, and categories of neighborhood quality were established. The majority of home mortages went to the top categories, which included areas that were "homogeneous" or had reached their peak, in terms of risk, and could be expected to remain stable. The HOLC rating method systematically underrated central city neighborhoods that housed stigmatized (nonwhite) racial groups and coded them with the color red. Black neighborhoods were invariably redlined. While the HOLC had not invented this method, its use of it bureaucratized racial discrimination in the federal home mortgage industry.[19]

Restrictive covenants were another discriminatory practice used by whites to preserve the homogeneity of their neighborhoods. These charters were contractual agreements among property owners stating that they would not permit a black to own, occupy, or lease their property. Those signing the document bound themselves and their heirs to exclude blacks from the designated locality for a specified period of time. On average, a covenant agreement lasted twenty years, and if it was breached the transgressor could be sued for damages.

With the massive population shifts of blacks during the postwar era, practices such as redlining and restrictive covenants brought about a geographic concentration of blacks in urban areas. With white flight to the suburbs, racial clusters became more imbalanced in the inner cities. In addition to the concern that large concentrations of blacks in urban areas would jeopardize white commercial interests, there was a growing demand for social services to help poor blacks. Such services raised the cost of local government, and politicians looking for new sources of revenue were compelled to turn to the federal government.

Local politicians found this much-needed revenue when Congress passed the Housing Act of 1949, which provided funds to communities to acquire slum properties and "redevelop" them. Included in this legislative package was approval for the construction of 810,000 new units of low-cost housing over a four-year period. In order to qualify for these funds, however, local authorities had to guarantee that adequate and affordable housing would be made available to families displaced by the redevelopment.[20]

Local planning agencies manipulated the new legislation to their own advantage: They used it to demolish black neighborhoods that threatened white business districts or other valuable property, and then, to satisfy the federal mandate, they offered living quarters to displaced black families in new high-density housing projects. In the end, urban "redevelopment" was used to carry out widespread slum clearance and destroyed more housing than it replaced.[21]

Because the newly constructed public housing projects could not absorb everyone displaced by urban "redevelopment," many displaced families moved into established black neighborhoods. This movement offered opportunities for exploitation to slumlords and property owners who were more concerned with profit than community stability. A typical result was described by a black woman who told interviewers what was happening in her neighborhood:

> I hear that the people who are buying the place are going to cut it up into kitchenettes. This will be terrible, but what can we do? I wish that we could petition and protest against their making kitchenettes here. Kitchenettes usually bring a lower class of people into the neighborhood. So many fine homes have been ruined by cutting them up into kitchenettes.[22]

Replacing low-density black neighborhoods that had some class diversity with high-density slums for poor families speeded up the concentration of poverty and the concomitant growth of social problems. Arnold Hirsch, a historian, has described public housing as "solidly institutionalized and frozen in concrete" and the federal government as taking "an active hand not merely in reinforcing prevailing patterns of segregation, but in lending them a permanence never seen before."[23]

Kenneth B. Clark, a psychologist, went further than Hirsch. In *Dark Ghetto*, he described these new slums as "pathologies" that "perpetuate themselves through cumulative ugliness, deterioration, and isolation and strengthen the Negro's sense of worthlessness, giving testimony to his impotence."[24] During the years that Clark was studying these communities, a report developed by the Labor Department found that joblessness was three times higher for black than white male heads of household; that only 17 percent of blacks had white-collar jobs in contrast to 47 percent of whites; and black adolescents endured unemployment at twice the rate of white adolescents.[25]

Youth Culture and Its Consequences

In her autobiography *I Know Why the Caged Bird Sings*, Maya Angelou describes an incident that occurred shortly after World War II when she was fourteen. After a distressing visit with her divorced father, she ran away from his house. Without money or any particular destination in mind, she stumbled upon a vacant lot filled with abandoned cars and climbed into one and fell asleep for the night. The next morning, she opened her eyes to find a "collage of Negro, Mexican, and white faces" peering in through the car window. These faces belonged to the other un-deraged youth who were living in the junkyard.[26]

These wayward children were products of changing social currents inflamed by World World II and of the changing migration patterns of many Americans, es-pecially the poor. Beyond the fact that they were living away from adult supervision, they symbolized a youth culture that was emerging to challenge family ideology. Experts in adolescent behavior concluded that the socialization process had changed dramatically after World War II. The new youth culture had encroached on the parent-child relationship, and teenagers appeared to listen to no one but their peers.[27]

To many Americans, teenage culture seemed to threaten normal forms of in-stitutional socialization, while more optimistic discussions noted that there was a lack of understanding between adults and adolescents. In 1957 an article in *Collier's* pondered this leading topic of discussion: "Never in our 180-year history has the United States been so aware of—or confused about—its teenagers."[28] As the fren-zied dances, blaring music, outlandish clothes, and language fads of teenagers swept across the nation, many adults feared that an entire generation had turned rebel-lious.[29]

One of the greatest concerns during this period was expressed in the increasing reports of teenage crime and delinquency. Court records and FBI reports described the following trend: a rise in delinquency during World War II, a sharp but brief decline, and then a rise during the 1950s. As one member of a Senate subcommittee on delinquency put it: "Elvis Presley is a symbol, of course, but a dangerous one. His strip-tease antics threaten to 'rock-n-roll' the juvenile world into open revolt against society. The gangster of tommorrow is the Elvis Presley type of today."[30]

What was most perplexing to social commentators during this period was that delinquent behavior among young people transcended class lines. Bertram Beck voiced these concerns in his 1954 speech to the National Congress of Parents and Teachers, noting that delinquency had spread during the previous ten years from the "wrong side of the tracks" to middle-class areas. This phenomenon, he concluded, was a sign of "social decay."[31] Kenneth Keniston, in discussing the problems of alienated youth, argued that changes in the American middle-class family, especially the mother's "overinvestment" in the children and the father's physical absence, were increasing the probability of estranged family patterns.[32] These statements reflect the fears of many Americans that a youth culture that originated in the lower classes was now spreading into middle class terrain.

Despite all the postwar enthusiasm for family life, there was increasing recognition that the family now exercised less influence on young people than other societal institutions, such as schools. As the baby boom pulled the population's center of gravity downward and mothers were increasingly working outside the home, the school seemed to be replacing the family as the institution that would mold the values of young people. In his 1954 opinion in *Brown* v. *Board of Education*, which desegregated American public schools, Chief Justice Earl Warren wrote that "education represented a central experience in life" because it alerted children to cultural values. In Warren's view, the ideas that children learned in school remained with them for the rest of their lives.[33]

The modern high school, in particular, was becoming the central laboratory in which diverse groups came together and interacted. For example, in the 1930s about 50 percent of working-class students attended high school, whereas by the 1960s this figure exceeded 90 percent. And between the early 1940s and the late 1950s the percentage of black students who finished high school doubled.[34] But if the high school was becoming more heterogeneous, It was more along class than race lines, even though the Supreme Court had unanimously ruled in *Brown* v. *Board of Education* that the Fourteenth Amendment required equal admission of all students to public schools.[35]

The most perplexing transformations in adolescent behavior during the 1950s occurred in the areas of sexual mores and marriage. In 1956 the median year for first marriages fell to its lowest point—22.5 for men and 20.1 for women. In fact, during the 1950s Americans had an earlier average age of first marriage than people in any other Western nation.[36] Working-class couples would generally marry soon after high school, often hastened by peer pressures for early sexual involvement.

Experts on adolescent behavior seemed to agree that these early marriages were being kindled by premarital sex, and popular magazine articles focused on the practices of "going steady" and "petting." Writing during these years, Albert Kinsey noted that "on doorsteps and on street corners, and on high school and college campuses . . . [petting] may be observed in the daytime as well as the evening hours."[37] Adolescents were expanding their premature adult culture into another area that was overlooked by Kinsey—automobiles. In 1961, a Gallup poll found that 44 percent of adolescent boys and 19 percent of girls either owned or had the use of a car.[38]

For adolescents during the 1950s the experience of going steady, seen as a higher level of commitment than simply dating, granted them permission to explore the carnal aspects of the relationship. One teenager conceded that she and her peers "do a lot of petting" but felt that the steady relationship justified a deeper sexual involvement: "[S]omething you go all the way in should only be with someone you really love."[39] And though experts on human sexuality could not prove that adolecents had suddenly increased their level of premarital sexual activity, they did conclude that early sexual relationships often led to early marriages.[40] One study specifically found that more than one-third of the girls involved in teenage marriages were pregnant at the time of their marriage.[41]

In *The American Sex Revolution*, the sociologist Pitrim Sorokin argued that American culture had become "sexualized," which threatened to have dire physical and mental effects on youth. He admonished parents to protect children by prohibiting rock-and-roll, dancing, and certain radio and television shows.[42] His view was myopic. Seen from a wider perspective, the unprecedented opportunities for premarital sex among young people were clearly influenced by many other factors, such as the accelerated shift to city and suburban living, increased economic autonomy, and more freedom from adult supervision. Increased economic automony, for instance, could be seen in the labor force participation of the high-school-age population, which by the mid-1950s had reached 50 percent on at least a part-time basis.[43]

The Proliferation of Black Adolescent Childbearing

The effects of premarital sexual activity were reflected not only in the number of early marriages but also in the increasing number of unmarried teenaged mothers.[44] When Leontine Young wrote *Out of Wedlock* in 1954, she noted a "considerable number—the best estimate is two out of five—of our unmarried mothers do come from the young adolescent group."[45] And whereas social analysts during this period were blaming premature sexual activity and the accidental pregnancies at least partly on youth culture, Young disagreed:

> There is a popular conception that the very young girl may easily have sexual relations with a resultant pregnancy out of either ignorance or lack of adult self-control. . . . But experience with young unmarried mothers does not bear this out. In every case observed, the girl has had unhappiness and problems in her life which have led directly to this action.[46]

Challenging the generalizations being made about the higher number of unmarried black mothers among adolescents, Young argued that patterns of black culture are not the same "in all places and under all circumstances":

> The Negro girl in a backward area of the rural South has a very different environment from the Negro girl growing up in an industrial city in the North. The matriarchal system and the difficulty of maintaining a strong, enduring family structure, both conditions bred and fostered by slavery, in general promoted an attitude of acceptance of the unmarried mother and her child without exacting either personal or social penalties. . . . The child is accepted for himself and is happily spared any such stigma as that emblazoned by our labels "bastard" or "child of sin."[47]

What Young overlooked was the effect of the huge migration of young blacks from the rural South to the industrial North in search of work, and the effect this was having on the increase in black unmarried mothers. During the 1940s Alabama and Georgia lost nearly a third of their young black men between the ages of fifteen and thirty-four, and Mississippi lost nearly half. On the other hand, Illinois increased its young black male population by nearly 60 percent, Michigan by over 80 percent, and New York by nearly 55 percent.[48] Drake and Cayton confirmed these migratory shifts when they observed that "roving masses of Negro men" were "an important factor . . . in preventing the formation of stable, conventional family units."[49]

These young men were making a transition away from the southern communities' with their time honored norms related to marriage and the family, and this factor was also a major one in family instability. In the South, rigidly enforced community sanctions had helped ensure that young black men acted responsibly when children resulted from brief sexual encounters. Thus Charles Johnson wrote that in the southern community he investigated, when "children resulted from the deliberate philandering" the men responsible "*are universally condemned.*"[50] Needless to say, such social controls were not in place in the northern communities to which young black men migrated.

Drake and Cayton had also observed that the young women most vulnerable to unmarried motherhood were poor and were new arrivals from the South.[51] In understanding the greater vulnerability of these young women to early pregnancy, it is important to understand that boundaries of acceptable female sexual behavior based on social class did in fact exist in southern black communities. When Johnson studied black youth in the rural south he uncovered the age-old double standard of "good" and "bad" girls. One southern young black man describes his decision-making process for whether or not to engage in sexual activity:

> There are some that I run around with and can do anything to and there are some who won't let you mess with them. I don't mess with girls I go with because they are nice girls, and I don't believe it's nice to bother nice girls.[52]

Thus while the condemnation of a young man's sexual improprieties may have been "universal," the force of its application depended heavily on the social class background of the girl he impregnated.

This theme was reiterated by Hylan Lewis, when he conducted a participant observation study of black families in a rural southern community in the mid-1950s.[53] Discussing community sanctions on out-of-wedlock childbearing, he observed:

> Given the fact that practically every knows everyone else, instances of illegitimacy and alleged illegitimacy are generally known and talked about freely. In most cases, the father or alleged father is identified . . . However, there are many girls and many parents whose views are more conventional; once pregnancy ensues—barring abortion or miscarriage—individual, family, and community pressures begin to operate. It is considered the right thing for the man to marry the girl, and if he does, he is commended. The chances of the man marrying her are high if she has not been promiscuous.[54]

A variety of studies conducted during this period demonstrate the variability in individual, family, and community reactions to unmarried mothers. For every study that reported a relaxed acceptance of unmarried motherhood, there was another that reported that out-of-wedlock childbearing was censured, and most of the studies found a range of responses. For example, one study of forty-four unmarried black mothers in St. Louis reported that "in twenty-nine cases the girl's family rejected her and the child after the birth of the child," whereas another study conducted on forty-nine unmarried black mothers in Washington, D.C., around the same time found three distinct groupings. One group had "great concern and anxiety," another showed "no apparent discomfort, neither guilt nor anxiety," and the final group felt that the mother "had made a mistake and ought to be punished, but this was not an intense feeling."[55]

Hylan Lewis provided a specific explanation for this variability when he discussed values and class stratification:

> Since pride, respectability and the approach to conventional morals tend to be earmarks of the respectable family, this group tends to frown upon, is ashamed of, and seeks to disassociate itself from "lower class" behavior. . . . These respectable parents seek to offset the threat [of contamination by a 'lower class'] by rigid discipline and supervision as well as by "getting the children out of the situation," if possible by sending them away. Some of the respectable families have not escaped what for them is the acute shame of illegitimacy.[56]

And while there were sanctions that governed the behavior of the black residents in rural communities in the South, even these standards were changing, and one older black woman shared her observations with Lewis:

> These younger girls get out sooner and does more than we use to do. We never drank whisky and went out with mens that young. . . . Some of these girls ain't nothing but babies; they starts when they's twelve and thirteen years old and before you can turn around they's having babies by some of these old men and having to stop school.[57]

In northern cities, however, and especially for young black men and women living in disorganized ghetto neighborhoods, the sexual debauchery found among a minority of adolescents in the South was normative in the North. Kenneth Clark, in his classic study *Dark Ghetto*, described the disturbing dynamics in young black male female relationships:

> Young men establish temporary liaisons with a number of different women with no responsibility for any. Among Negro teenagers the cult of going steady has never had the vogue it seems to have among white teenagers. . . . The marginal Negro male tends to identify his masculinity with the number of girls he can attract. . . . In this compensatory distortion of the male image, masculinity is, therefore, equated with alleged sexual prowess.[58]

The ghetto-specific behaviors Clark describes were clearly evident in the rising birthrate of young black women during the years between 1940 and 1960. The birthrate for black teenagers between the ages of fifteen and nineteen increased

Table 6.1 Birthrates for Married and Unmarried Black and White Women,
1940–1984

AGES	Births per 1,000 Married Women					Births per 1,000 Unmarried Women				
	1940	*1950*	*1960*	*1970*	*1984*	*1940*	*1950*	*1960*	*1970*	*1984*
Black Women										
15–19	340	475	713	533	322	43	69	77	97	87
20–24	264	292	364	263	236	46	105	167	131	111
25–29	150	180	224	148	132	33	94	172	101	80
30–34	105	114	142	81	72	23	64	104	72	45
35–44	56	47	54	29	18	9	20	36	22	13
White Women										
15–19	401	399	532	432	409	3	5	7	11	19
20–24	263	281	355	244	201	6	10	18	23	28
25–29	168	193	219	165	145	4	9	18	21	25
30–34	103	116	121	78	81	3	6	11	14	16
35–44	34	39	39	20	16	1	2	4	4	5

SOURCE: Robert D. Grove and Alice M. Hetzel, *Vital Statistics Rates in the United States: 1940–1960*, National Center for Health Statistics, table 28; National Center for Health Statistics, *Vital Statistics of the United States: 1981*, vol. 1, Natality, table 1–32; *Monthly Vital Statistics Reports*, vol. 33, no. 6, supplement (Sept. 28, 1984), table 17; no. 34, no. 6, supplement (Sept. 20, 1985), table 17, vol. 35, no. 4 supplement (July 18, 1986, table 18).

from 43 to 77 per thousand unmarried women, whereas the increases for whites were minuscule—only 3 to 7 per thousand unmarried women (Table 6.1). The escalating birthrates per thousand unmarried black women between the ages of twenty and twenty-four, and twenty-five and twenty-nine, were even more alarming: they increased from 46 to 167 and 33 to 172 respectively. The birthrates of married teenagers shot up during this period as well. Whereas married white teenagers had higher birthrates than blacks in 1940, by 1950 and 1960 the birthrates of married black adolescents had climbed abruptly.

Another confirmation of the precipitous increase in adolescent childbearing among African-Americans can be found in Chapter 2, Table 2.1. These tabulations chart the mean fertility of white and black women born during the years from 1903 to 1956. Black women born between 1940 and 1950 had the lowest mean fertility age. This means that sharecropping and slavery combined with a major war and the transition to the urban north had the effect of bringing the fertility age of black women to its lowest point during this period.

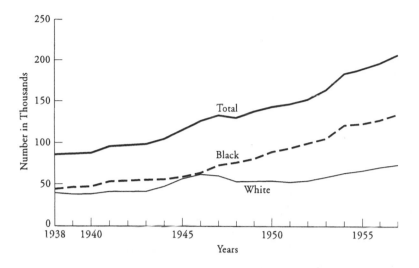

FIGURE 6.1   Estimated number of live births to single mothers, by color, in the United
States, 1938–1957. (From USDHEW Public Health Service, National Office of Vital
Statistics, *Vital Statistics, Special Reports,* vol. 47, no. 8 [September 30, 1960])

The Emergence of the Unmarried Mother as a Social Problem

Although scholars have debated whether or not American society began to experience the opening of an era of sexual liberalism in the 1950s, the fact remains that
there was an exponential growth of unmarried mothers during this time. The
number of children born to unmarried mothers tripled between 1940 and 1957
(Figure 6.1).[59] And while experts further acknowledged that there was a higher
proportion of unmarried mothers among blacks, the out-of-wedlock birthrate for
white women was growing faster than for black women.[60]

Child welfare agencies were initially charged with handling the cases of unmarried mothers, and their policies were focused on ensuring that all children would
remain with their mothers subsequent to their birth. For example, Maryland and
Minnesota were among the first of several states to pass welfare legislation man-
dating that mothers breast-feed their babies for six months, in order to keep mothers and children together. Such policies were at first applied to all unmarried
mothers regardless of race.[61] But as the number of births to unmarried black mothers escalated, agency policies began to change.

In the mid-1940s, child welfare agencies begin to develop special units to deal
with unmarried mothers. In 1944, for example, the United Charities of Chicago
began operating a specialized unit known as the Women's Service Division, with
the objective of offering "a comprehensive program for the unmarried mother."

The division's staff made monthly reports on the deficiencies in community resources that were revealed by their own caseloads. When the summary report for
the first six months was released, it indicated a "lack of maternity homes, boarding
homes, and adequate housing for the Negro unmarried mother."[62]

When Clark Vincent evaluated a maternity homes directory compiled and published by the National Association on Service to Unmarried Parents in 1960, he
found that 25 percent of the homes listed in the directory excluded black mothers.[63]
There was considerable debate as to why this disparity in social services existed,
and Annie Lee Davis discussed these issues in her presentation to the National
Conference on Social Welfare in 1948.[64]

During the 1950s, as many as 70 percent of the children of white unmarried
mothers were given up for adoption, compared to only 3 to 5 percent of black
children.[65] In one of the few studies on black adoptions during this period, David
Fanshel attributed the difference between black and white adoption rates to what
economists would call a "seller's market," where demand exceeds supply, and a
"buyer's market" where supply exceeds demand. He mentioned parenthetically that
"socially and economically-depressed groups [who prefer adoption] tend to easily
give up their goals and to interpret agency neutrality as indifference or rejection."
But he also recommended that adoption agencies put "something special" into
their work in view of the fact that "in the North as well as in the South unwilling
service and outright rejection of Negroes by public and quasi-public institutions
are still not uncommon."[66]

A report released by the Department of Health, Education, and Welfare (HEW)
in 1963, by Helen Martz, an HEW social welfare adviser, attributed the much
lower rates of black adoptions to the fact that "fewer nonwhite families have income
and housing adequate to care for an adopted child and the supply of foster family
homes for them also is limited."[67] However, Rickie Solinger uncovered another
explanation: In the family courts in Chicago, black mothers were routinely threatened with charges of child abandonment and desertion if they tried to put their
child up for adoption. In confirmation, she quoted Ursula Gallagher, director of
the United States Children's Bureau's programs and services for unmarried mothers: "In some courts it is almost impossible for a Negro unmarried mother to give
up her baby for adoption. The general interpretation of this is that the courts
believe the girl should be made to support her children and should be punished
by keeping them."[68]

Black Mothers and Welfare Dependency

As stated earlier, economic condtions worsened for the black poor during the
1950s, especially among those residing in urban ghettos. In 1960, for example, 41

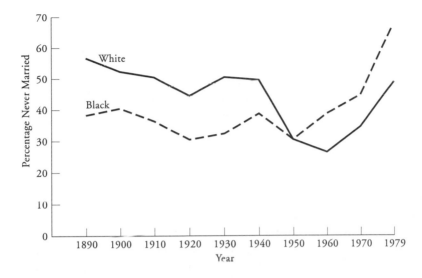

FIGURE 6.2   Percentage of never-married women aged 20–24, by color, in the United
States, 1890–1979. (From A. J. Cherlin, *Marriage, Divorce, Remarriage* [Cambridge,
Mass.: Harvard University Press, 1981], Figure 4-1)

percent of the black men in Detroit in an entirely black-populated census tract
were jobless. In census tracts in Chicago, Los Angeles, and Baltimore where 90
percent or more of the inhabitants were blacks, the rates ranged from 24 to 36
percent.[69] The jobless rates of black men soared, and the number of never-married
black women between the ages of 20 and 24 surpassed that number for white
women for the first time since 1890 (Figure 6.2). As the number of unmarried
black mothers increased, so did the number of black families receiving AFDC.

Michigan's welfare policies became the "litmus test" for northern states when
its longstanding policy against providing assistance to unmarried mothers and their
children became even more restricted.[70] Michigan public welfare bureaucrats were
clear about their desire to maintain AFDC as an "elite" program, and especially
about their wish to protect themselves from criticism that they were supporting
unmarried women who bore children.

In 1955 the Michigan plan called attention to certain "social patterns of adult
behavior which are believed to be particularly harmful to children:"

> When an A[F]DC mother supplements the grant by taking in a male roomer
> or boarder, it should be explained that this practice frequently leads to ques-
> tions concerning suitability. . . . When the Bureau makes a positive deter-
> mination that an A[F]DC recipient is cohabitating with a person to whom
> he or she is not legally married, the home must be considered unsuitable.[71]

In 1959 in Atlantic City, New Jersey, a grand jury reported:

There is no logic, justice, or morality in granting state welfare funds to a mother who has had two, three, four or even five illegitimate children fathered by two or three different men. . . . Immorality, promiscuity, and unwed motherhood seem to be rewarded and encouraged by the easy allowance made upon a simple application of need.[72]

By the late 1950s, in response to escalating public sentiment against welfare payments to unmarried mothers, most states had enacted some type of "suitable homes" policy. In Florida, for example, seven conditions of unsuitability were listed. Six of these could be classified under the traditional concept of neglect; the seventh was "failure of the parent or relative to provide a stable moral environment for the child." During the first year after the law went into effect, approximately half of the homes receiving AFDC in Florida were identified as probably falling below the new standards. Of the 5,927 cases reviewed by Florida's public welfare department, 5,854 had been forwarded from local communities solely because the parents failed to provide a "stable moral environment."[73]

In 1957 a study conducted by several colleges in Mississippi sought to determine why welfare grants had been denied or discontinued between 1954 and 1956. The 323 families in the study were first interviewed at the time of the case closures; when the follow-up interviews were conducted in 1957, the 187 new births included 176 that were out of wedlock. This was a surprising finding: The incidence of births to unmarried mothers actually *increased* after the discontinuance of the welfare grants.[74]

According to reports in the press during this period, much of the evidence of "unsuitability" was flimsy. For example, one grant was discontinued because investigators believed "a shirt they found did not belong to the mother's teenage son, as both she and the boy contended, but rather to a man." And in another case a family was cut off welfare because investigators believed they could not be sure a man was only visiting: He was seen entering but not leaving the three-flat building where a dependent mother and her children lived.[75]

By 1962, eight states and eighteen large cities had established special investigating units to gather information on families receiving welfare.[76] Across the country three levels of surveillance emerged:

1. A home was watched during the day or night or both.
2. Two investigators made a surprise visit, with one at the front door, and one at the back door, in the hope of apprehending a man.
3. The investigators demanded entry and searched the premises for a man or evidence that a man might be included in the family unit.

The "surprise element" was considered one of the outstanding merits of the program.[77] These subversive tactics by the welfare investigators were effective, and this was most apparent in the inconsequential rise in the welfare rolls—from 635,000 families in 1950 to 745,000 in 1960, an increase of only 110,000 families, or 17 percent.[78]

To confront the fact that there was little evidence, empirical or otherwise, for the presumed relationship between welfare receipt and maternal misbehavior, a rigorous study was conducted in 1960 in Cook County, Illinois. Its findings were summarized as follows:

> A typical A[F]DC family . . . consists of a mother and three or four children. The children were born in Illinois, the mother has lived here fifteen years or more. She is between 30 and 35 . . . was born in Mississippi and is Negro. The mother was married and had children by her husband, who deserted. The youngest child is illegitimate. The mother knew the father for more than a year before she became pregnant. The couple thought about marriage, but because the other was already married, this was impossible. The mother did not want to have another child, but did not know what to do to prevent becoming pregnant. When she learned she was pregnant, she did nothing to prevent having the child. Once the baby was born, she accepted it and loves it.[79]

This profile was consistent with the findings of the first national survey conducted during this same period. It compared black and white women in three demographic groups: those raised on southern farms and still living there; those raised on southern farms but living in cities by 1960; and those raised and still living in cities. In the first group, blacks had a fertility rate much higher than whites; in the second group, the fertility differences were much less; and in the third group blacks differed only slightly from whites in their fertility. The researchers concluded that the high birthrate among blacks was largely attributable to their rural background.[80]

Helen Martz's report for HEW summarized the available information on "illegitimacy and dependency" and found that in 1961:

1. Only one in five of all children born to unmarried mothers were receiving welfare and three-fourths of the children on welfare were born to married mothers.
2. The teenage group is the largest group, 55 percent of the total unmarried female population of childbearing age.
3. Thirty-two percent of the children born out-of-wedlock were adopted and about 45 percent were cared for by the mother or relatives. [Martz

did not describe racial differences in these categories, but based on other data collected during this period it seems safe to say that the majority of the adopted children were white and the majority of those cared for by the mother and/or relatives were black.]

4. About 2 percent of the children born out-of-wedlock were cared for by institutions or foster homes, and 21 percent were dependent on AFDC. Of all the children receiving AFDC, 18 percent were deprived of parental support because the father was not married to the mother.[81]

Bifurcated Fertility Trends among Black Women

During the decade of 1945 to 1955, black women gave birth to proportionately more children than white women. After dropping to its lowest point in 1935, the fertility rate of both black and white women began a sharp rise, peaking in 1957. In 1950 fertility rates were 33 percent higher for blacks than for whites. By the end of the decade the total fertility was 4.5 and 3.5, children for blacks and whites respectively.[82] According to Landon Jones, this was the "highest completed fertility of any group since the decade following the Civil War."[83]

While demographers were paying close attention to the widening fertility gap between black and white women, few noticed another significant change: The gap was also widening between highly educated professional black women and younger black women with less education and limited resources. During the 1950s, the number of black women attending college had increased exponentially, and they were receiving 62.4 percent of all degrees from black colleges—a figure substantially higher than that of black men. In addition, more black women than black men were the recipients of graduate degrees, although black men still held the edge in doctoral degrees. Because there was a high probability that even a married black woman would need to find employment outside the home, the impetus for these educational achievements was the desire for occupational mobility, and especially the desire to escape the degradation of domestic service.[84]

Many scholars of the black family during this period noted that a greater premium was placed on the advanced education of young black women than on that of young black men. The general explanation for the more extensive education of black women was that of "getting out of the white folks' kitchen." For black women, working for white families as a domestic represented a continuity of the oppression they had experienced during slavery. On the other hand, the occupational options for the college-trained black male were more limited than for the black female. Referring to the occupational mobility of black males in a southern rural community—and many of these same conditions held in the urban North—Hylan Lewis specifically states: "To reach the maximum security or status in this community, a pattern is prescribed for the Negro in which higher education for the male would be, on the surface, superfluous, wasteful, and undoubtedly frustrating."[85] Lewis goes on to say that a college education for a black man was not a priority because there was little for a college-trained black to do except teach.

During this decade, there was a lag in the educational and professional achievements of white women. Two out of three white women who entered college dropped out before graduating, and 60 percent of those left either to marry or because they feared having a B.A. would diminish their chances of marriage. Two out of five female students at Barnard admitted that they "played dumb" on dates in order to get along with men.[86] In 1955 Adlai E. Stevenson told the graduating women at Smith College that their role in life was to "restore valid, meaningful purpose to life in your home."[87]

The educational accomplishments of black women were reflected in the their occupational achievements from 1940 to 1960: Their numbers in domestic service decreased from 60 to 35 percent but increased from 4 to 6 percent in professional positions. On the other hand, the percentage of white women holding professional positions dropped from 14.9 percent to 13.1 percent in 1960. Black women's educational achievements are most clearly reflected in the shift in their socioeconomic index from 13 to 21 during the years from 1940 to 1960.[88] White women, however, had a socioeconomic index almost three times that of black women in 1940, and their index remained unchanged from 1950 to 1960.[89]

Historically, black women had higher labor force participation rates than white women, but their upward mobility was having an impact on black fertility patterns. Mary Jo Bane analyzed decennial census data and found that 25 percent of never-married black women were childless in 1970, compared to 16.7 percent of never-married white women. When she identified the characteristics of childless women, she found that they were more likely to be black, born in the Northeast, married at older ages, college-educated, living in urban areas, and married to professional or white-collar workers rather than to farmers or laborers.[90] In short, childlessness was highest among the most economically stable and well-educated blacks.

Black women with the highest levels of academic and professional achievement did not participate in the baby boom.[91] Those who completed college and delayed marriage were having about the same number of children as white women. For blacks, as well as for whites and the total population, fertility increased during the 1950s and decreased during the 1960s for every education group. The largest relative fertility increases occurred between 1945 and 1957: 90 percent was recorded for black high-school graduates, followed by 79 percent for black women with nine to eleven years of education, and 57 percent for black women with five to eight years of schooling.[92] When these figures are broken down by college education, the patterns diverge even further (Figure 6.3). Black women with thirteen

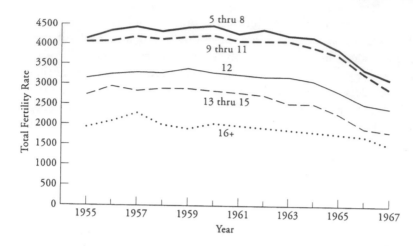

FIGURE 6.3   Total fertility rates for five education groups among blacks, 1955–1967. (From R. R. Rindfus and J. A. Sweet, *Postwar Fertility Trends and Differentials in the United States* [New York: Academic Press, 1977], Figure 3-6)

to fifteen and sixteen or more years of education had the lowest fertility rates of all black women. The conclusion seems obvious: The formidable responsibilities that came with parenting were being foregone by black women with higher educational and occupational attainment.

Although Linda Gordon, a feminist historian, recently documented these patterns of lowered fertility or childlessness among some of the most notable black women, E. Franklin Frazier had made this observation of the black middle class much earlier.[93] Frazier reported numerous studies conducted during the 1920s, 1930s, and 1940s on black professionals and found that although they came from large families, they "voluntarily restricted the size of their families." For example, studies that surveyed black faculty members at Howard and Fisk Universities in the 1930s found that whereas the professors came from families averaging 6.3 children, they themselves averaged only 1.5 children per family.[94]

During the 1950s, there was a continuous rise in the proportion of births to black teenagers. In 1960, for example, black adolescents accounted for 20 percent of the total black births, and this percentage would continue to increase over time.[95] Whereas only 36 percent of black women aged fifteen to forty-four were between fifteen and twenty-four years of age in 1960, that number would climb to 46 percent by 1975.[96]

The higher fertility rates among younger black women would contribute significantly to accelerated changes in the age structure of the African-American population. Changes in age structure increased the number of births to younger, unmarried black women, thereby boosting the proportion of all births occurring outside marriage.[97] These out-of-wedlock births then contributed to the exponential growth of black mother-only families in succeeding decades. From 1940 to the mid-1980s the proportion of black families headed by females tripled. It is now clear that increased childbearing among younger black women has widened the social and economic divisions within the black community by generating an ever-larger proportion of black children born into poverty.

Conclusion

Although the 1950s have been sentimentalized as the "golden age" of the American family, the growing prosperity experienced by whites during this period did not "trickle down" to blacks. Public policies in housing and welfare began to have a devastating impact on blacks and would contribute to the dramatic transformation of the the black family structure in the decades to come.

Residential housing segregation as we know it today was manufactured during the 1950s by the implementation of policies such as redlining and restrictive covenants. This decade also saw the construction of the first high-density public housing projects, which replaced many low-density black neighborhoods that had some class diversity. Besides producing social isolation and psychological alienation among their residents, these projects have become notorious as havens for crime, drugs, destructive gang activities, high rates of welfare dependence, and concentrated poverty.

Public welfare polices were likewise altered during this decade in response to a tide of criticism that AFDC was encouraging immorality and indolence among the poor. "Suitable home" policies were initiated to ensure that there was a "stable moral environment" in the welfare recipient's household. Special investigative units were set up to keep black mothers on welfare under surveillance, which included surprise visits by agency personnel. If welfare investigators observed a man entering or leaving the home of an abandoned mother, her application for welfare could be denied, or if she was already a recipient, her benefits terminated.

The majority of black women receiving welfare during this period were married women who were separated or divorced from their husbands. As black families migrated north and husbands and wives experienced chronic unemployment, many families broke up. Desperate black fathers often left their families, either temporarily or permanently, to search for employment in other regions of the country.

While poor black mothers were getting on welfare in increasing numbers, more and more black women were completing college—and receiving 62 percent of all degrees from black colleges. While the educational and professional achievements of white women were declining slightly, there was a solid increase in the number of black women in professional occupations and a dramatic decrease in their employment as domestic servants. The greater occupational mobility of black women was gained at a price: A large number of the better-educated black women were childless, and those who did bear children had fertility rates considerably lower than that of less-educated, younger black women. This emerging pattern was to have serious consequences for the structure of the black family in subsequent decades.

With a disproportionate number of black women in younger age cohorts compared to white women, the proliferation of black adolescent childbearing accelerated changes in the age structure of the African-American population. These changes were exacerbated by three other trends: There were changes in societal norms regarding sex and marriage; ghettos became increasing isolated from mainstream society; and accomplished blacks had dramatically lower fertility rates. The consequences were exponential increases in the numbers of births to unmarried black women, and the proportion of all births occurring outside of marriage became even greater. From 1940 to the mid-1980s the number of black families headed by females has tripled, and the social and economic gaps within the black community have simultaneously widened.

Notes

1. Douglas T. Miller and Marion Nowak, *The Fifties: The Way We Really Were* (Garden City, N.Y.: Doubleday, 1977), 147.

2. Quoted in William H. Chafe, *The Unfinished Journey: America Since World World II* (New York: Oxford University Press, 1986), 125–26.

3. *Ebony*, June 1947, 4.

4. Glen H. Elder, Jr., *Children of the Great Depression: Social Change in Life Experience* (Chicago: University of Chicago Press, 1974).

5. Quoted in Landon Y. Jones, *Great Expectations: America and the Baby Boom Generation* (New York: Coward, McCann & Geoghegan, 1980), 19, 20. For other analyses of the 1950s, see Peter Lewis, *The Fifties* (Philadelphia: Lippincott, 1978); Eric F. Goldman, *The Crucial Decade—and After: America, 1945–1960* (New York: Vintage, 1960); Lincoln H. Day and Alice Taylor Day, *Too Many Americans* (Boston: Houghton Mifflin, 1964); John Kenneth Galbraith, *The Affluent Society* (New York: New American Library, 1969); Chafe, *Unfinished Journey.*

6. Chafe, *Unfinished Journey,* 119.

7. Galbraith, *Affluent Society,* 142.

8. Neil Fligstein, *Going North: Migration of Blacks and Whites from the South, 1900–1950* (New York: Academic Press, 1981).

9. Jones, *Great Expectations,* 38–39. For the purposes of this section, suburbia refers to areas outside the large central cities. For more on the growth of the suburbs during the

1950s, see Leo F. Schnore, *Class and Race in Cities and Suburbs* (Chicago: Markham, 1972); Karl E. Taeuber and Alma F. Taeuber, "White Migration and Socioeconomic Differences between Cities and Suburbs," *American Sociological Review* 29 (October 1964):718–29; Eugene S. Uyeki, "Residential Distribution and Stratification, 1950–1960," *American Journal of Sociology* 69 (March 1964): 491–98; Gladys K. Bowles and James D. Tarber, *Net Migration of the Population, 1950–1960, by Age, Sex, and Color*, vol. 1 (Washington, D.C.: Government Printing Office; William M. Dobriner, *Class in Suburbia* (Englewood Cliffs, N.J.: Prentice-Hall, 1963).

10. William H. Frey, "Central City White Flight: Racial and Nonracial Causes," *American Sociological Review* 44 (June 1979): 425–48.

11. R. Allen Hays, *The Federal Government and the Urban Housing: Ideology and Change in Public Policy* (Albany: State University of New York Press, 1985), 205–6.

12. Douglas S. Massey and Nancy A. Denton, *American Apartheid: Segregation and the Making of the Underclass* (Cambridge, Mass.: Harvard University Press, 1993), 53.

13. Ibid., 54.

14. Jones, *Great Expectations*, 40.

15. Betty Friedan, *The Feminine Mystique* (New York: Norton, 1963), 255–56.

16. Barbara Ehrenrich and Deidre English, *For Her Own Good: 150 Years of the Experts' Advice to Women* (Garden City, N.Y.: Anchor/Doubleday, 1978), 256; Jo Ann Freeman, *The Politics of Women's Liberation* (New York: McKay 1975), 28–31.

17. For theoretical discussion of neighborhood change, see Thomas C. Schelling, *Micromotives and Macrobehavior* (NY: Norton, 1978): 135-66. Richard L. Morrill, "The Negro Ghetto: Problems and Alternatives," *Geographical Review* 55 (July 1965):339–61.

18. Chafe, *Unfinished Journey*, 216.

19. Kenneth T. Jackson, *Crabgrass Frontier: The Suburbanization of the United States* (New York: Oxford University Press, 1985), 196–99. For a comprehensive discussion of the practices of real estate brokers during the 1940 and 1950s, see Rose Helper, *Racial Policies and Practices of Real Estate Brokers* (Minneapolis: University of Minnesota Press, 1969).

20. Jackson, *Crabgrass Frontier*, 219–30; Arnold R. Hirsch, *Making the Second Ghetto: Race and Housing in Chicago, 1940–1960* (Cambridge: Cambridge University Press, 1983), 100–170.

21. Michael J. White, *Urban Renewal and the Residential Structure of the City* (Chicago: Community and Family Studies Center, 1980), 149–208.

22. St. Clair Drake and Horace Cayton, *The Black Metropolis* (New York: Harcourt, Brace & Co., 1945), 660.

23. Hirsch, *Making the Second Ghetto*, 252–54. See also John F. Bauman, *Public Housing, Race, and Renewal: Urban Planning in Philadelphia, 1920–1974* (Philadelphia: Temple University Press, 1987); Ira Goldstein and William L. Yancey, "Public Housing Projects, Blacks and Public Policy: The Historical Ecology of Public Housing in Philadelphia," in *Housing Desegregation and Federal Policy*, ed. John M. Goering (Chapel Hill: University of North Carolina Press, 1986), 262–89; Adam Bickford and Douglas S. Massey, "Segregation in the Second Ghetto: Racial and Ethnic Segregation in the U.S. Public Housing, 1977," *Social Forces* 69(June 1991): 1011–36.

24. Kenneth B. Clark, *Dark Ghetto: Dilemmas of Social Power* (New York: Harper & Row), 12.

25. Chafe, *Unfinished Journey*, 216.

26. Maya Angelou, *I Know Why the Caged Bird Sings* (New York: Random House, 1969), 214–215.

27. See, for example, Elder *Children of the Great Depression*, Elder argues that parents who experienced "extreme social change" sought new ways to raise children better suited to meet life "in the changed world as parents see it" and were therefor more permissive parents. John K. Kett noted that youth culture appeared to be a commentary on the success or failure of families and other institutions; *Rites of Passage: Adolescence in America, 1790 to the Present* (New York: Basic Books, 1977), Norman Ryder showed how this sizable generation disrupted society; "The Demography of Youth," in *Youth: Transition to Adulthood*, Report of the Panel on the President's Science Advisory Committee (Chicago: University of Chicago Press, 1974). In addition, James Coleman relates the generation's self-awareness to its size, its age distribution, and its affluence; "Youth Culture," in *Youth: Transition to Adulthood*.

28. Bill Davidson, "8,000,000 Teenagers Can't Be Wrong," *Collier's*, January 4, 1957, 13.

29. The growth of the youth culture is described by James Coleman, *The Adolescent Society: The Social Life of the Teenager and Its Impact on Education* (New York: Free Press, 1961). The influence of rock-and-roll on generational consciousness is explored by Jeff Greenfield, *No Peace, No Place: Excavations Along the Generational Fault* (Garden City, N.Y.: Doubleday, 1973).

30. Quoted in James Gilbert, *A Cycle of Outrage: America's Reaction to the Juvenile Delinquent in the 1950s* (New York: Oxford University Press, 1986), 18.

31. Ibid., 74.

32. Kenneth Keniston, "South Change and Youth in America, *Daedalus* 91(Winter 1962), 145–171.

33. *Brown v. Board of Education of Topeka, et. al.*, 347 U. S. 493 (1953).

34. Richard A. Rehberg and Evelyn R. Rosenthall, *Class and Merit in the American High School* (New York: Longman, 1978), 255.

35. This decision is widely considered to have been the first major victory against racial segregation and discrimination in the twentieth century. Thurgood Marshall predicted that within five years, all segregated schools would be abolished, even though the mandate had prescribed no timetable for compliance; However, southern states engaged in a "massive resistance" campaign that was so successful that ten years after the original decision, only about 1 percent of all black students enrolled in the the eleven states of the original Confederacy were attending integrated schools. U.S. Commission on Civil Rights, *Twenty Years After Brown: Equality of Educational Opportunity* (Washington, D.C.: Government Printing Office, 1975), 89–91.

36. Paul H. Jacobson, *American Marriage and Divorce* (New York: Rinehart, 1959), 61, 75.

37. Quoted in Ellen K. Rothman, *Hands and Heart: A History of Courtship in America* (New York: Basic Books 1984), 300.

38. Cited in Gilbert, *Cycle of Outrage*, 12.

39. Quoted in Clark Vincent, *Unmarried Mothers* (New York: Free Press, 1961), 40–41.

40. For the experts' perspective on sex and early marriage, see Harold T. Christensen and Christina F. Gregg, "Changing Sex Mores in America and Scandinavia," in *Sexual Development and Behavior: Selected Readings*, ed. Anna McCreary Juhaz (Homewood, Ill.: Dorsey Press, 1973); Richard Needle, "The Relationship between Sexual Behavior and Ways of Handling Contraceptives among College Students" (Ph.D. diss., University of Maryland, 1973), 26–38.

41. Aaron L. Rutledge, "Marriage Problems and Divorce," in *Children and Youth in the 1960s* (Washington, D.C.: Golden Anniversary White Conference on Children and Youth, 1960), 220.

42. Pitrim Sorokin, *The American Sex Revolution* (Boston: Sargent, 1956).

43. Laurence D. Steinberg and Ellen Greenberger, "The Part-Time Employment of High School Students: A Research Agenda," *Children and Youth Services Review* 2(1980): 159–79.

44. In terms of absolute numbers, the increases in the birthrates of unmarried black adolescents were greater during the 1940s than the 1950s; the problem was not "discovered" until the 1950s. See, for example, Phillips Cutright, "Illegitimacy in the United States: 1920–1968," in *Demographic and Social Aspects of Population Growth*, ed. Charles F. Westoff and Robert Parke, Jr., Commission on Population Growth and the American Future, Research Reports, vol. 1 (Washington, D.C. Government Printing Office 1972), 377–438.

45. Leontine Young, *Out of Wedlock* (New York: McGraw-Hill, 1954), 94.

46. Ibid., 95.

47. Ibid., 121.

48. Andrew Billingsley, *Black Families in White America* (Englewood Cliffs, N.J.: Prentice-Hall, 1968), 78.

49. Drake and Cayton, *Black Metropolis*, 583.

50. Charles S. Johnson, *Shadow of the Plantation* (Chicago: University of Chicago Press, 1934), 67. (My italics.) When Johnson studied the norms in a southern sharecropping community he found that early marriages were not encouraged in these rural communities in the event of an unplanned teenage pregnancy. In that the family was the most efficient unit for raising cotton and food crops, and would be weakened if a young person married and left home, marriage was postponed. And when young couples did marry, they were often expected to live in and become part of the parents' household.

51. Drake and Cayton, *Black Metropolis*, 590.

52. Charles S. Johnson, *Growing Up in the Black Belt: Negro Youth in the Rural South* (Washington, D.C.: American Council on Education, 1941), 229.

53. Hylan Lewis, *Blackways of Kent* (Chapel Hill: University of North Carolina Press, 1955), xxiii.

54. Ibid., 88–89.

55. Josephine Reynolds, "Problems of Forty-four Negro Unmarried Mothers in St. Louis, Missouri, March 1940–March 1941" (Master's thesis, St. Louis University, 1941); Patricia Knapp and Sophie T. Cambria, "The Attitudes of Negro Unmarried Mothers toward Illegitimacy," *Smith College Studies in Social Work* 17(December, 1946):153–254; Hilda Hertz and Sue Warren Little, "Unmarried Negro Mothers in a Southern Urban Community," *Social Forces* 23 (October 1944):73–79.

56. Lewis, *Blackways of Kent,* 86–87.

57. Ibid., 85.

58. Clark, *Dark Ghetto,* 70, 71.

59. Robert W. Roberts, *The Unwed Mother* (New York: Harper & Row, 1966), introduction.

60. Clyde Kiser, Wilson Grabill, and Arthur A. Campbell, *Trends and Variations in Fertility in the United States* (Cambridge, Mass.: Harvard University Press, 1968), ch. 8.

61. See, for example, Bureau of Public Assistance, *Illegitimacy and Its Impact on the Aid to Dependent Children Program* (Washington, D.C.: Government Printing Office, 1960).

62. Department of Labor, Children's Bureau, *Births Out of Wedlock,* CB85–973 (Washington, Government Printing Office, May, 1945), 12.

63. Clark Vincent, *Unmarried Mothers* (New York: Free Press, 1961), 22.

64. Annie Lee Davis, "Attitudes toward Minority Groups: Their Effect on Social Services for Unmarried Mothers" (paper presented at the National Conference on Social Welfare, 1948).

65. *Illegitimacy and Its Impact,* 61–63.

66. David Fanshel, "A Study in Negro Adoption," *Child Welfare* (February 1959): 33.

67. Helen E. Martz, "Illegitimacy and Dependency," Department of Health, Education, and Welfare, Welfare Administration, Bureau of Family Services, September 1963, HEW Indicators (Washington, D.C., Government Printing Office, 1963), xxiv.

68. Rickie Solinger, *Wake Up Little Susie: Single Pregnancy and Race Before Roe v. Wade* (New York: Routledge, 1992), 27.

69. Department of Labor, *Manpower Report to the President and A Report on Manpower Requirements, Resources Utilization, and Training* (Washington, D.C.: U.S. Government Printing Office, 1964), 48.

70. Most of southern states already had eligibility conditions that excluded most unmarried black mothers. See Winifred Bell, *Aid to Dependent Children* (:,) ch. 4, 5.

71. Ibid., 118.

72. Ibid., 68.

73. Ibid., 126–27.

74. Ibid., 101.

75. Ibid., 90.

76. The states: Arizona, Connecticut, Illinois, Louisiana, New Mexico, Rhode Island, Washington. The cities: Baltimore, Chicago, Cincinnati, Cleveland, Denver, Detroit, District of Columbia, Houston, Indianapolis, Kansas City, Los Angeles, Milwaukee, New Orleans, New York, Oakland, San Francisco, St. Louis, and Seattle.

77. Bell, *Aid to Dependent Children,* 87–90.

78. Frances Fox Piven and Richard A. Cloward, *Poor People's Movements: Why They Succeed, How They Fail* (New York: Vintage, 1979), 268.

79. *Facts, Fallacies and Future—A Study of the ADC Program of Cook County, Illinois* (New York: Greenleigh Associates, 1960): 19–20. Out of 619 unmarried mothers in this study, 552 did not want another child, but did not have adequate information on contraception.

80. Pascal K. Whelpton, Arthur Campbell, and John E. Patterson, *Fertility and Family Planning in the United States* (Princeton: Princeton University Press, 1966), 335.

81. Martz, "Illegitimacy and Dependency."

82. Philip Cutright, "Components of Change in the Number of Female Heads Aged 15–44; United States, 1940–1970," *Journal of Marriage and the Family* 36 (November 1974):714–22.

83. Jones, *Great Expectations*, 33.

84. Jeanne Noble, "The Negro Woman's College Education," (New York: Columbia University Press, 1956), 29. For a comparison of educational aspirations among blacks and other groups, see Bernard C. Rosen, "Race, Ethnicity, and the Achievement Syndrome," *American Sociological Review* 24(February 1959):47–60; also Leonard Broom and Norval Glen, *Transformation of the Negro American* (New York: Harper & Row, 1965),172–86; "Current Trends and Events of National Importance in Negro Education," *Journal of Negro Education* 19 (Spring, 1950).

85. Lewis, *Blackways of Kent*, 105–6.

86. William H. Chafe, *The American Woman: Her Changing Social, Economic, and Political Roles, 1920–1970* (New York: Oxford University Press, 1972), 213.

87. Quoted in Steven Mintz and Susan Kellogg, *Domestic Revolutions* (New York: Free Press, 1988), 181.

88. Socioeconomic scores were developed by Otis Duncan from 1950 census data. These scores range from 74 points for professionals to a low of 7 points for domestic servants and nonfarm laborers; see "A Socioeconomic Index for All Occupations," in *Occupations and Social Status*, ed. A. J. Reiss (New York: Free Press, 1961).

89. Reynolds Farley and Walter Allen, *The Color Line and the Quality of Life in America* (New York: Oxford University Press, 1989), 263–66.

90. Although Bane argued that "higher rates of childlessness among blacks are the exception and may be explained by health conditions," she was not factoring in the higher rates of childlessness among well-educated black women. Mary Jo Bane, *Here to Stay: American Families in the Twentieth Century* (New York: Basic Books, 1976), 9.

91. Landon Y. Jones, *The Baby Boom* (,) 32–33.

92. Figures taken from Ronald R. Rindfuss and James A. Sweet, *Postwar Fertility Trends and Differentials in the United States* (New York: Academic Press, 1977), 45.

93. See Linda Gordon, *Pitied but Not Entitled: Single Mothers and the History of Welfare 1890–1935* (New York: Free Press, 1994), for a discussion of these family patterns among black women reformers at the turn of the century (120–21). She noted that more than half of these married women had prominent men as spouses, and their marriages sometimes promoted the wife's leadership positions. Many led lives quite independent of their hus-

bands, and their fertility pattern was related to their independence—43 percent had no children and, more striking, 34 percent of the married women had no children. See also E. Franklin Frazier, *The Negro Family in the United States* (1939; reprint, rev. and abr. (Chicago: University of Chicago Press, 1966), 330–33.

94. Frazier, *Negro Family*, 330.

95. Farley and Allen, *Color Line*, 74.

96. William J. Wilson and Kathryn Neckerman, "Poverty and Family Structure: The Widening Gap between Evidence and Public Policy Issues," in *The Truly Disadvantaged*, 68.

97. See James Sweet and Larry Bumpass, *American Families and Households* (New York: Russell Sage Foundation, 1987); Gerald Jaynes and Robin Williams, *A Common Destiny* (Washington, D.C.: National Academy Press, 1989). These books document both the precipitious decline in the fertility of older, more stable black women and broader social changes that have influenced imbalanced fertility patterns in the black community. These scholars do not attribute these changes to increased irresponsibility in the reproductive behaviors of poor women.

CHAPTER SEVEN

THE "MATRIARCHAL" BLACK FAMILY UNDER SEIGE

Although the scars of emasculation probably penetrated the black man more deeply than the injustices inflicted upon the woman, there has, however, been an overemphasis upon the degree to which the black man has been damaged. . . . They also refuse to place the responsibility on the racist society, but rather insist that it is caused by the so-called domineering wife and/or mother.

Joyce Ladner, Tomorrow's Tomorrow: The Black Woman

The 1950s had witnessed a conservative mood in American politics, with many assuming that the social inequities of the prewar period had been eradicated by Franklin D. Roosevelt's reforms. In 1959 the historian Arthur Schlesinger, Jr., wrote a memorandum entitled "The Shape of National Politics" in which he predicted that the passivity of the Eisenhower period would soon be followed by a "time of affirmation, progressivism, and forward movement."[1]

On February 1, 1960, four black college students set out to integrate a lunch counter in Greensboro, North Carolina. The students refused to leave until they were served; after an hour, the management closed the counter. Even though the students left peacefully, the civil rights movement was launched that day. As it moved forward over the years, Americans would witness many moments of intense drama: the daring feats of the Freedom Riders, a group of black and white young people who traveled to the South in order to help blacks assert their right to vote; Police Commissioner Eugene "Bull" Connor turning firehoses on protesters in Birmingham; and 200,000 participating in the March on Washington, singing "We Shall Overcome" and listening to Martin Luther King's historic speech, "I Have a Dream." The efforts of the civil rights movement were directed at doing away with the traditional Jim Crow practices in the South and securing voting rights for all Americans.

However, when President Johnson spoke at a Howard University commencement on June 4, 1965, he stated that a new administrative policy was needed to address the social and economic aspects of the civil rights problem. At his direction presidential assistants Richard N. Goodwin and Daniel P. Moynihan had drafted the speech; extracted from the Moynihan Report, it gave voice to Johnson's belief that government policymakers should make better use of the social sciences. In a break with tradition, the speech focused on the plight of blacks in the northern ghettos rather than in the South.

Did the Moynihan report say anything original that other social scientists had not already said? What was it about the report that was so alarming? Why was there such a strong negative response from some in the civil rights movement and the academic community? In short, what was it about the Moynihan Report that created so much dissension and controversy? And finally, what factor did all of Moynihan's critics overlook when reacting to the report?

Social Science and the Black Family

Did Moynihan say anything new in his report, compared with what social scientists had been saying about the black family for years before the report appeared? In studying the problems of socialization in the American family, they were asking two questions: Are two parents necessary? and if so, What crucial and indispensable roles do they each play?[2] During the 1950s and 1960s, these questions were being used in most examinations of the African-American family. These questions were driven by the data that indicated that there were increasing numbers of mother-only families in all groups, but especially among African-Americans. Most of these research findings would not come to the public's attention until the contents of the Moynihan report were released to the press.

Abram Kardiner and Lionel Ovesey, two highly regarded psychiatrists, were among the first scholars to apply the psychoanalytic paradigm to the black family. Their book, *The Mark of Oppression*, explored the influence of social environment on the African-American personality, and cited E. Franklin Frazier as having given the "most authoritative analysis of the American Negro family."[3]

Kardiner and Ovesey, like most scholars of the time, traced the structure and organization of the black family to slavery, arguing that the organization of the black family in America had not survived from Africa, but had arisen as an "emergent necessity determined by the exigencies of the new environment." For the purposes of "intraplantation stability," when a slave father was sold he alone was sold, whereas when the slave mother was sold, the children generally went with her, which made the mother the emotional center of the slave family. The authors also contended that the female took the dominant role in the black family during slavery because of her value to whites as a producer of offspring. They described the female-centered family as "most characteristic of the South" and said that "it had a common variant in the form of the grandmother-centered family."[4]

About the problems of the contemporary black family they wrote:

> The Negro family, particularly in the lower classes, suffers a great deal of disorganization. Basic here is the lesser economic opportunity of the Negro male. His inability to meet familial obligations finds its ultimate expression in the large number of broken homes among Negroes as well as in the large numbers of families with female heads. . . . These facts must be contrasted with the basic patriarchal orientation of the white family.[5]

Kardiner and Ovesey went on to discuss the problems that occur within the family system when the father fails in the provider role:

> He cannot be idealized. If the mother can work and does so, the father takes his place as one of the siblings. One cannot retain paternal authority if one ceases to be the source of basic life satisfactions during the normally dependent period of the child.[6]

While social scientists were studying the black family, theoretical formulations were simultaneously being developed on the family structure of the American family. Talcott Parsons, one of the most influential social scientists on the topic of the American family structure, asserting that two-parent families were ideally suited for the temperaments and natural abilities of men and women, co-authored a book with Robert Bales entitled *Family: Socialization and Interaction Process.*[7] A contributing author who examined these questions from a cross-cultural perspective, in an effort to avoid an investigation that was "culture bound," was Morris Zelditch.[8] He conducted a comparative study of fifty-six cultures and found that forty-six reported parental roles that were consistent with the integrative/adaptive typology of parental role differentiation in the American nuclear family. That is, one role was adaptive-instrumental, having to do with management, discipline, and control of children; it was generally allocated to the father. The other was integrative-expressive, involving the handling of mediation, conciliation, and conflict resolution, and was usually taken on by the mother.[9]

In Zelditch's view, two parents were necessary because

> the integrative-expressive leader can't be off on the adaptive-instrumental errands all the time. . . . A stable, secure attitude of members depends, it can be assumed, on a clear structure being given to the situation so that an uncertain responsibility for emotional warmth, for instance, raises significant problems for the stability of the system. And an uncertain managerial re-

sponsibility, an unclear definition of authority for decisions and for getting things done, is also clearly a threat to the stability of the system.[10]

The same year Zelditch's study was published, 1955, Hylan Lewis, an African-American scholar, was pursuing a doctoral degree at the University of Chicago and studying the black subculture in a southern rural town, where "whites and blacks have met daily face to face, often in intimate and close ways, but without any accepted meeting of their respective cultures."[11] His study produced two startling findings: First, as many as half of the children were raised by mothers and maternal relatives "without significant help from the father for major portions of their lives"; second, the mothers were more important in "disciplining and dispensing rewards."[12] In analyzing these findings, he wrote:

> The lesser part played by the male parent in these autobiographies is striking and suggests a lack of appreciation for the father, and even implicit rejection of him. . . . It may also be that what appears to be a lack of a truly confident and aggressive approach to life problems might be related to the lack of the male's influence.[13]

During the late 1950s and early 1960s, studies proliferated identifying so-called aberrant parental role differentiation as the cause for impaired functioning ranging from schizophrenia to gang delinquency among all racial groups, not just blacks.[14]

In the mid-1960s, however, two other scholars would focus specific attention on the black male in his role as father—Elliot Liebow and Thomas Pettigrew. Elliott Liebow was a doctoral student at Catholic University when he wrote his dissertation on streetcorner black men. Working under the direction of Hylan Lewis, he devoted an entire chapter to the topic of fathers, entitled "Fathers without Children."[15] In this participant observation study, Liebow qualified his observations by noting that "the spectrum of the father-child relationship is a broad one, ranging from complete ignorance of the child's existence to continuous, day-by-day contact between father and child." He continued:

> Looking at the spectrum as a whole, the modal father-child relationship for these streetcorner men seems to be one in which the father is separated from the child, acknowledges his paternity, admits to financial responsibility but provides financial support irregularly, if at all, and then only on demand or request. His contacts with the child are infrequent, irregular, and of short duration.[16]

Thomas Pettigrew, a highly regarded social psychologist who had written widely on the African-American personality, also tackled the thorny question of the black family. In his book *A Profile of the Negro American* he examines the relationship between family disorganization and personality.[17] He begins by acknowledging that "both poverty and migration also act to maintain the old slave pattern of a mother-centered family." And like other academics studying the black family during this period, he concedes that employment discrimination is a problem for the black male, who finds it harder to secure steady employment than even the "poorly educated" black female. In discussing the psychological dynamics between black males and females, he states, "Embittered by their experiences with men, many Negro mothers often act to perpetuate the mother-centered pattern by taking a greater interest in their daughters than their sons."[18]

In Pettigrew's view, this preferred treatment accounted for the higher achievement rates of black women. This conclusion was a clear departure from the findings of other scholars on this topic. For example, Jeanne L. Noble, an African American scholar, presented a more convincing argument for why black women pursued higher education:

> She is expected to play the subordinate role of "female." I think it is because she is married to a Negro man. . . . Even though she may have a professional job, the Negro man expects her to be a buffer for him—to work eight hours a day and come home and keep house. I am sure the Negro woman feels incapable of doing this adequately. For this reason she feels that somebody has let her down. She wants college to give her information on how she can do the impossible.[19]

In a book entitled *The Eighth Generation: Cultures and Personalities of New Orleans Negroes*, another pair of psychoanalytically trained scholars, John H. Rohrer and Munro S. Edmonson, observed that black mothers had a preference for their female children. The ideas set forth in this book represented the same kind of limited understanding of the cultural mechanisms operating in the black family that were exemplified by Pettigrew:

> The matriarchs make no bones about their preference for little girls, and while they often manifest real affection for their boy children, they are clearly convinced that all little boys must inexorably and deplorably become men, with all the pathologies of that sex. The matriarchal mother . . . not infrequently attempts to counteract such influences with harsh if erratic punishments, but these frequently mask her own unconscious expectations of her son, and may do a great deal toward shaping him in the image of men she knows and approves or fears and represses.[20]

Kenneth Clark, a social psychologist by training, contributed to the analyses of black families during this period. Like others, he traced the problems of the black family to slavery, noting that the black male was systematically used as a stud and the black female used for purposes of breeding or for the "gratification of the white male." He goes on to say that the postslavery relegation of the black male to "menial and subservient status" has made the female the dominant person in the black family. In Clark's view, the black male could not support his normal desire for psychological dominance:

> He was compelled to base his self-esteem instead on a kind of behavior that tended to support a stereotyped picture of the Negro male—sexual impulsiveness, irresponsibility, verbal bombast, posturing, and compensatory achievement in entertainment and athletics. . . . The pressure to find relief from his intolerable psychological position seems directly related to the continued high incidence of desertions and broken homes in Negro ghettos.[21]

Scholars writing on the black family made class distinctions when scrutinizing black family patterns E. Franklin Frazier targeted the black middle class for harsh analysis, shifting his focus from the black poor to the black middle class, in his book *The Black Bourgeoisie*. Discussing role differentiation between black males and females, he wrote:

> Discrimination [has] caused frustration in Negro men because they are not allowed to play the "masculine role" as defined by American culture. They cannot assert themselves or exercise power as white men do. . . . In the South the middle-class Negro male is not only prevented from playing a masculine role, but generally he must let Negro women assume leadership in any show of militancy. . . . The conservative and conventional middle-class husband presents a pathetic picture. He often sits at home alone, impotent physically and socially.[22]

During the 1950s and early 1960s, although there were disagreements among social scientists from a variety of academic disciplines, they agreed on four salient characteristics of the black family.

1. These families were mother-centered, in ways that could be traced black to slavery; and the resulting problems were being exacerbated by the recent changes in the migration patterns of blacks.
2. Employment discrimination against the black male played a crucial role in perpetuating the dominance of black females in the family.
3. Father absence in black families was contributing to a host of problems in the personalities and behavior of black children, but especially young black males.
4. Within the dynamics of the black family, the more dominant black mothers had a preference for their female children, and, according to the psy-

choanalytically trained
unconscious on the mo

These were some of the
When they were released to
a major factor in the abate
more than a decade. Accord
from researching behavior
racial minorities."[23]

160

The protagonist of *Beulah* w
rescued her employers from
updated version of *Gone*
character of *Beulah* rev
boyfriend, Bill, who
Mammy was
filmed in 191
Congress t
D.C., so
adver
pa

Media Images of Bla

While social scientists v
television was emerging as th
The influential cultural images put forth in telev...
perceptions of race, gender, and American lifestyles. These programs adv...
different images of the American family, based on social class, race, and ethnicity.[24]

WASPs and white ethnics were portrayed as belonging to one of two different types of family—big-city working-class or suburban middle-class. The white fathers in popular situation comedies ranged from William Bendix as the submissive, awkward, working-class father in *The Life of Riley* to Robert Young as the suave and confident middle-class patriarch in *Father Knows Best*.

Mothers, on the other hand, were shown as confined to a domestic life of full-time motherhood, child-rearing, housecleaning, and cooking. This maternal role was most popularly enacted by Donna Reed, whose television family (her pediatrician husband and two children) began appearing in 1958. Working-class marriages were typically depicted as having a high level of domestic squabbling provoked by financial strain, whereas middle-class marriages were characterized as primarily concerned with how to handle the children. White women were portrayed as scatterbrained and wacky, but shrewd enough to get their way with their husbands.

The images constructed to depict black families were very different. Three television shows provided white Americans with a glimpse of black Americans. The sitcom *Beulah* was about a maid working for a white family in suburbia. *Amos 'n' Andy* was a parody on working-class black life in Harlem. While *Amos 'n' Andy* presented an all-black world that rarely even mentioned whites, *Beulah* cast blacks exclusively as servants in a suburban white middle-class family. Both shows were broadcast in the mid-1950s. The third show, and the first to focus on black family life, was *Julia*, starring Diahann Carroll; it was introduced in 1968 in the aftermath of the civil rights movement.

as a bright and resourceful black woman who often
their own ineptness. The show, in some ways an
with the Wind, cast blacks exclusively as servants, and the
ved the Mammy image of black women. She had a slothful
never looked for work, and a giddy girlfriend, Oriole.

originally immortalized in D. W. Griffith's *The Birth of a Nation*,
5. In 1923 the Daughters of the American Confederacy petitioned
erect a commemorative shrine in Mammy's likeness in Washington,
that all Americans could pay tribute to her, and for decades the film and
using industry made frequent use of her image. Even the magazine *Ebony*
ticipated, featuring articles on Lilian Moseley, a television actress who was cast
as Elizabeth McDuffie, the Roosevelt family maid, and Margaret W. Ware, a nursemaid for the Fultz quadruplets.[25] Deborah Gray has claimed that such efforts
"imprinted the image of Mammy on the American psyche more indelibly perhaps
than ever before."[26]

The other major television show to feature blacks, *Amos 'n' Andy*, had been a
popular radio show in the 1930s. The vaudevillian caricatures in the show included
Amos Jones, a hard-working, church-going citizen, married with two children (his
wife and children seldom appeared on camera); Andy Brown, a pudgy, flustered
bachelor who either loafed or chased women; George Stevens, nicknamed Kingfish,
the head of a lodge called The Mystic Knights of the Sea, a fast-talking conniver
who was dominated by his wife, Sapphire, and hounded by his sullen mother-in-
law; Sapphire, a boisterous and pushy wife who was forever overpowering the black
men around her; and Lightnin', the dim-witted janitor of the Mystic Knights
Lodge, who spoke with a high-pitched drawl ("Yazzah") and walked with a lazy
shuffle.

Sapphire, who dominated the show, could hardly have been more different from
Beulah. She personified the emasculating black woman who aggressively usurps the
role of the black male and is totally lacking in such maternal qualities as showing
sensitivity to the needs and feelings of others.

Protests against this show begin almost immediately after its premier. The
NAACP said that it "depicts the Negro in a stereotyped and derogatory manner
. . . [and] strengthens the conclusion among uninformed or prejudiced people that
Negroes and other minorities are inferior, lazy, dumb and dishonest."[27] The
NAACP urged a boycott of the show's sponsor, Blatz beer, but the boycott never
caught on. The television version never attracted the support the radio show had
enjoyed and after two years was canceled. During the early 1960s when the civil
rights movement was in full swing, there were no television shows featuring black
actors, but the cultural images of blacks that had permeated the airwaves in the
1950s had left an indelible impression on the minds of most Americans.

The Moynihan Report

In order to understand the social and political significance of the Moynihan Report, we must first recall some contemporary trends in economic growth. From 1953 to 1960 the gross national product grew at a yearly rate of 2.1 percent; from 1961 to 1963, even when adjusted for inflation, it grew more than twice that rate, 4.5 percent annually. By 1965 unemployment had declined so steadily that only 4 to 5 percent of Americans were unable to find jobs. At the same time, under the Kennedy and Johnson administrations, corporate profits grew by nearly 67 percent. And from 1961 to 1963 consumer prices rose, on the average, only 1.3 percent a year.[28]

Buoyed by this expansion, economists persuaded political leaders to accept a compensatory fiscal policy. Kennedy proposed a $13.5 billion tax cut, which was enacted under Johnson in 1964 and provided a major stimulus to consumer purchasing power. By 1965 the Council on Economic Advisers was exultant, taking credit for the economic growth: "Federal policies have made a major and continuing contribution to the greatest achievements of the American economy during the past four years."[29]

Daniel Patrick Moynihan, a Harvard-trained sociologist who was an assistant secretary of labor under Kennedy and an adviser to Johnson, agreed with the council that economic planning was rapidly "approaching the status of an applied science." Writing in *Daedalus* in 1965, he declared that the question was not whether the federal government could discover means of dealing with the old problems but whether it could find new problems to solve with the new social science tools at its disposal. In March 1965, in collaboration with two members of his staff in the Office of Policy Planning and Research for the Department of Labor, he had completed a confidential report ("for official use only") entitled *The Negro Family: The Case for National Action*. Over a year and a half, Moynihan had been formulating his view that government policymakers should make greater use of the social sciences for the diagnosis and description of social problems.[30]

The Moynihan Report, as it came to be known, first came to public notice when President Johnson used it as the basis for his commencement speech at Howard University in 1965. By presenting a condensation of over three decades of social science research on the "Negro problem," Johnson's remarks created a controversy that would reverberate for years throughout a nation already beleaguered by some of the most menacing racial turmoil in its history.

The basic claims the Moynihan Report made were simple enough:

1. The deterioration of the Negro family is clear from these facts: (a) nearly a quarter of urban Negro marriages are dissolved; (b) nearly one-quarter of

Negro births are now illegitimate; (c) as a consequence, almost one fourth of Negro families are headed by females; and (d) this breakdown of the Negro family has led to a startling increase in welfare dependency. Why should this be so?

2. The "roots of the problem" lie in slavery; in the effects of Reconstruction on the family and particularly on the position of the Negro man; in urbanization, unemployment, and poverty; and in a wage system that often does not provide a family wage. The dimensions of all of these problems are growing because of the high fertility of Negroes. For example, the Negro population and potential labor force will be increasing twice as fast as that of whites between now [1965] and 1970.

3. Because the socioeconomic system has produced an unstable family system for Negroes, there is "the tangle of pathology" in the Negro community [a phrase borrowed from Kenneth Clark's description of Harlem ghetto life]. The elements in this tangle include the following: The matriarchy of the Negro family (because women fare better interpersonally and economically than men, they tend to dominate family life); the failure of youth (Negro children do not learn as much in school as white children and they leave school earlier); higher rates of delinquency and crime among Negroes; the fact that Negroes disproportionately fail the Armed Forced qualification test (and have a poor competitive position in the job market as well); and the alienation of Negro men, whose despair of achieving a stable life results in withdrawal from family-oriented society and higher rates of drug addiction.[31]

"In a society that presumes male leadership in private and public affairs," Moynihan wrote, "the dependence on the mother's income undermines the position of the father." He called for a "national effort to strengthen the Negro family," and urged government support to ensure that "every able-bodied Negro man was working, even if this meant that some jobs had to be redesigned to enable men to fulfill them."[32] Stated another way, this meant establishing male dominance in the black family by reinstating the black man as head of the household, even if this meant decreasing the labor force participation of black women—a position that quickly drew criticism from feminists.[33]

Aftershocks of the Moynihan Report were felt again in 1968, when *Julia*, the first modern TV situation comedy to focus directly on a black family, featured a black single mother, played by Diahann Carroll.[34] (At this time all the white families on television consisted of a husband and wife and their dependent children.)[35] Julia, a widow with a young son, worked as a registered nurse. Except for the fact that she was a single parent, she was indistinguishable from her white counterparts:

She lived in suburbia and faced the same predictable family difficulties. In a period that emphasized the ideals of civil rights and social equality, Julia epitomized racial homogeneity in television.

What Provoked Public Acrimony?

Prominent black leaders—including Martin Luther King, Roy Wilkins, and Whitney Young—had been called in by the White House to read the president's speech before it was delivered at the Howard University commencement. At the time, they had expressed their enthusiasm and "anticipated other civil rights leaders' pleasant surprise" on hearing the speech. Robert Carter, the general counsel for the NAACP, commended the president for having an amazing comprehension of the "the debilitation that results from slum living." A spokesman for the National Urban League commented that many of the ideas in the speech seemed to come from Mr. Whitney Young's book, Too Be Equal. And Martin Luther King stressed that public awareness of problems with black family structure would offer the opportunity "to deal fully rather than haphazardly with the problem as a whole."[35]

Although civil rights leaders had expressed approval of the speech, there was some apprehension about the Moynihan Report in government circles. Indeed, criticism had surfaced within the Department of Labor even before the speech was written. Certain experts felt that Moynihan had not included enough comparisons with whites, to control for economic and educational variables; that data that countered his conclusions had been deleted; and that the conclusions themselves were "overdramatic and not cautious enough."[36] What they made of the report's particulars was not that the data were inaccurate but rather that the selection of data was not in accord with their understanding of the situation.

For example, Dorothy Newman, Elizabeth Herzog, and Hylan Lewis challenged the use of the adjective "alarming" to describe the increases in fatherless homes among African-Americans. What the data had shown, they argued, was a gradual increase between 1949 and 1959 (from 19 to 24 percent) and no net increase at all between 1960 and 1964 (23 percent in the latter year). Thus the total change between 1949 and 1964 was about 5 percentage points, or about one-third of a percentage point per year.[37] The trends in births to unmarried black mothers, as shown in Figure 7.1, were such that such births would not dramatically increase until after 1965.

The president announced in his Howard University speech that he intended to call a White House conference, to which he would invite scholars, experts, and outstanding black leaders and officials of the government at every level. The goal of the conference, he said, would be to "shatter forever not only the barriers of law and public practice but the walls which bound the condition of many" by the

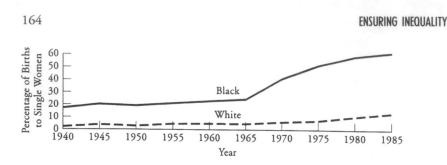

FIGURE 7.1   Trends in percentage of total births delivered to single women by race, 1940–1984. (From Robert D. Grove and Alice M. Hetzel, *Vital Statistics Rates in the United States: 1940–1960*, table 28; National Center for Health Statistics, *Vital Statistics of the United States: 1981*, vol. 1, Natality, table 1–32; *Monthly Vital Statistics Reports*, vol. 33, no. 6, supplement [September 28, 1984], table 17; vol. 34, no. 6, supplement [September 20, 1985], table 17; vol. 35, no. 4, supplement [July 18, 1986], table 18)

color of their skin.[38] A series of preparatory meetings, held in a White House conference room during the month of July, were attended by a distinguished list of social scientists—among them Professors Talcott Parsons, Eric Erikson, Kenneth Clark, Robert Coles, Thomas Pettigrew, Urie Bronfenbrenner, and James Wilson. Civil rights leaders were not invited to attend these meetings; they met informally with the president during the first week in August, but were in no way involved in "planning" the conference.

One can readily understand the uneasiness that was developing among civil rights leaders by the end of the summer. They had been brought into the White House irresolutely, and invited separately from the scholars. In addition, although the Moynihan Report itself had not yet been released to the press, speculation about what it contained was rife in the Washington cocktail circuit. One rumor, for example, was that it presented a complete summary of "the Negro in our society, very broad and very detailed."[39]

Mary McGrory, the *Washington Star* reporter who broke the story of the White House conference-planning activity, noted that in the Howard speech the president had "urged black Americans to forgive and forget and to look frankly at their own failures." She asserted that the president wanted to "hand the civil rights movement back to Negroes and enable them to speak out on the overwhelming problem that faced them—the breakdown of the Negro family structure." It was John D. Pomfret of the *New York Times*, however, who wrote the first story to deal specifically with the contents of the Moynihan Report. He had White House authorization to read and write about the report but not to describe its authorship. Instead he was asked to write about a "White House study group" that was "laying the groundwork for a massive attempt to revive the structure of the Negro family."[40]

Then on August 9, several days before the outbreak of rioting in Watts, *New-*

sweek carried a two-page article summarizing the report's main points. Claiming that the report had "set off a quiet revolution in the basic White House approach to the continuing American dilemma of race," *Newsweek* expressed concern about the touchiness of the issue: "The Negro family problem was scarcely news to social scientists. But its very intimacy has excluded it from the public dialogue on civil rights; it reaches too deep into white prejudices and Negro sensitivities."[41]

Once the report was officially released, anxiety about it escalated in civil rights circles. The attitude of civil rights leaders was perhaps best expressed by William Ryan, who concluded his critique by noting:

> If we are to believe the new ideologues, we must conclude that segregation and discrimination are not the terrible villains we thought they were. Rather, we are told the Negro's condition is due to his "pathology," his values, the way he lives, the kind of family life he leads. The major qualification—the bow to egalitarianism—is that these conditions are said to grow out of the Negro's history of being enslaved and oppressed—generations ago.[41]

This theme was also stressed by St. Clair Drake, who introduced the concepts of direct and indirect victimization:

> Direct victimization might be defined as the operation of sanctions which deny access to power, which limit the franchise, sustain job discrimination, permit unequal pay for similar work, or provide inferior training or no training at all. Indirect victimization is revealed in the consequences which flow from a social structure which decreases "life chances," such as a high morbidity and mortality rates, low longevity rates, a high incidence of psychopathology, or the persistence of personality traits and attitudes which impose disadvantages in competition or excite derogatory and invidious comparisons with other groups.[43]

Stokely Carmichael, who first articulated the ideology of the Black Power movement, offered a more pungent, streetwise critique of Moynihan's analysis: "The reason we are in the bag we are in isn't because of my mama, it's because of what they did to my mama."[44]

During the week of August 16, riots broke out in the Los Angeles ghetto of Watts. Between August 16 and September 1, eleven articles appeared relating the Moynihan Report or the breakdown of the Negro family to the Watts riot. On the last day of the riots, the *Wall Street Journal* ran a background article quoting sociologists, psychologists, and anthropologists (but not the Moynihan Report). Noting that 20 percent of nonwhite homes had no husband present, it identified the "pathology" of the ghetto as having to do not only with family disorganization but with problems of crime, venereal disease, and hopelessness. The article ended with a quote from Herbert Blumer:

> The violence in Watts over the weekend was physical [but] the real violence that brought it out was done to the social fabric of the community long ago—and continues to be done to it here and in practically every other big city in the country.[45]

By far the most influential news story appeared on August 18 in "Inside Report," the syndicated column by Roland Evans and Robert Novak. It purported to give the facts about an intense debate within the Johnson administration on how to handle the Moynihan Report—"a much suppressed, much leaked Labor Department document which strips away usual equivocations and exposes the ugly truth about the big city Negro's plight." Secretary of Labor Willard Wirtz was said to have opposed the release of the report because it would become grist for the mills of racist propaganda. Other officials were said to believe it "would stir up trouble by defining insoluble problems." The writers implied that Moynihan had "leaked" his report over Wirtz's head to the president's press secretary, Bill Moyers, who was "fascinated" by it and presumably influenced the president to use it in the Howard University speech.[46] This extensive media coverage led many people to see the problems defined in Moynihan Report as the government's explanation for the riots.

The most serious fallacy in the report was that Moynihan apparently presumed that black mothers were increasingly single by choice, which led him to look for ways to break up a "matriarchal culture." Christopher Jencks, however, a sociologist on the faculty of Harvard at that time, could find little evidence that poor blacks preferred matriarchal families; on the contrary, he wrote, "there is considerable reason to suppose that they eagerly adopt the more patriarchal middle-class norm whenever they can."[47]

Others criticized the report for a flawed social science base, statistical errors, ideological rationalizations, and dangerous political implications. By the spring of 1966, however, the attacks were being directed not at Moynihan but at those who had planned the White House conference. Moynihan formed an uneasy truce with civil rights leaders, but his credibility was further eroded in civil rights circles when he later served in the Nixon administration and once advocated "benign neglect" as a response to urban problems.[48]

Class and Gender in the Civil Rights Movement

As the furor about the report began to die down, it seemed clear that *none* of its critics had considered on obvious question: If women were so dominant in the black family and community, why were so few of them leaders in the civil rights movement or key participants in the Moynihan controversy?

When Lee Rainwater and William Y. Yancey compiled a list of approximately 60 persons who had been publicly involved in the controversy, only nine were black men and only two were black women, Dorothy Height and Pauli Murray.[49] Murray, a lawyer member of the NAACP and later one of the founders of NOW, rejected Moynihan's thesis about a black matriarchy; but Height, president of the National Council of Negro Women, did not seem to challenge it when she declared:

> If the Negro woman has a major underlying concern, it is the status of the Negro man, and his position in the community and his need for feeling himself an important person, free and able to make his contribution in the whole society in order that he may strengthen his home.[50]

With this perspective on black male and female relationships, it is not surprising that Height was the only black woman invited to attend the planning sessions for the White House conference.[51]

The lack of leadership roles for black women was not unique to the White House planning sessions but was generally true for all black organizations. Thus Ella Baker, of the Southern Christian Leadership Conference (SCLC), could say: "There would never be any role for me in a leadership capacity with SCLC. Why? First, I'm a woman. Also, I'm not a minister. And second . . . my penchant for speaking honestly . . . would not be well tolerated.[52]

One of the major recommendations of the Moynihan Report was that black men should retreat to an "utterly masculine world . . . a world away from women, a world run by strong men of unquestioned authority."[53] It was clear to many black women that black men had created this sort of environment within the civil rights movement, for black women were not being invited to have a voice in a dispute over their own roles.

The selection of Dorothy Height as the spokesperson for black women during the apex of the civil rights movement was especially puzzling because her organization, the National Council of Negro Women (NCNW), had come under considerable criticism from welfare activists. The NCNW, founded by Mary McLeod Bethune in 1935, had historically been quite effective in lobbying against efforts to perpetuate racial inequities. Its stated purpose was "to harness woman power to fight oppressive and demoralizing poverty, unemployment and racism, hunger and malnutrition, unfair housing and unresponsive social services" and to promote movement "toward self-reliance."[54]

As strategies for achieving equality shifted during the 1960s, the NCNW was perceived as being out of touch with the prevailing political and social climate. In an interview, a woman who attended a meeting organized by the NCNW in a rural southern community described the class tensions between women in the NCNW and others in the movement:

> We went to the meeting, and I just couldn't stand it, you know. 'Cause it was just some bunch of little biddies sittin' there, what I call these "highly elites" you know. And they didn't know what in the world was going on in the community, but they was there, you know, talking about flowers and beautification programs and all this other kind of stuff, which you know wasn't even hittin' nowhere what we was talking about. So, I went back to the hotel and went to packing my few clothes.[55]

Although the male-dominated scholarship on the black family had traced the "matriarchal" black family to slavery, the same scholars failed to note that there was a black patriarchal ethos that could be traced to the Reconstruction period. In the public sphere in the South, black men had historically functioned as the most powerful leaders of black communities, and this was most clearly evident in the role of the black clergy. The dominance of male leaders in the civil rights movement was simply an extension of this legacy. Whereas black women may have had more equality with black men within the private sphere compared to white women within theirs, the patriarchal ethos in the public sphere was comparable to that found in the white community. Although the civil rights movement was divided along ideological lines, there was agreement on one major point—the importance of maintaining male leadership in the struggle for black freedom.

It was common knowledge among those active in the civil rights movement that Martin Luther King had problems with black women he considered strong or overbearing, and he was conspicuously not alone in having this dilemma.[56] And a striking example of the pervasiveness of male dominance within the movement could be seen in the 1963 March on Washington, which culminated in King's famous "I Have a Dream" speech: even though black women had outnumbered black men in the freedom marches and civil rights activities in the South, the leaders of the march failed to include any women speakers on the original program.[57] Privately, King himself was probably in agreement with the black power advocates and black nationalist groups who championed male dominance and the need to establish a conventional sexual division of labor within the black household.[58]

Although Dorothy Height did not challenge Moynihan's thesis, other black women have rejected it.[58] For example, Pauli Murray wrote in a letter to *Newsweek*:

> Since our current emphasis is on better education to get better jobs for all Americans it is bitterly ironic that Negro women should be censured for their

efforts to overcome a handicap not of their making and for trying to meet the standards of the country as a whole.[60]

Joyce Ladner, a black sociologist and poverty researcher, presented some powerful criticisms:

> Although the scars of emasculation probably penetrated the black man more deeply than the injustices inflicted upon the woman, there has, however, been an overemphasis upon the degree to which the black man has been damaged. . . . They also refuse to place the responsibility on the racist society, but rather insist that it is caused by the so-called domineering wife and/or mother. Few will accept the theory that much of the damage is done outside the male-female relationship and that it is within the home that his failure is reinforced because it is there that he is reminded of his inability to function as a productive member of the society and to his fullest capacity in his home.[61]

And Alice Walker spoke for millions of black women when she wrote, "Our plainer gifts, our labors of fidelity and love, have been knocked down our throats."[62]

The Transformation of the Civil Rights Movement

As reactions to the Moynihan Report abated, events accelerated the transformation of the civil rights movement into a struggle against poverty and exploitation in northern ghettos. Even the moderate black leadership had perceived the Moynihan controversy as a major setback in their pursuit of racial equality. Now militant young blacks were rejecting the movement's original emphasis on nonviolence and integration; for them, the Moynihan debate further clarified the ideological direction the movement should take.

The political framework for this next phase was conceptualized by Stokely Carmichael and Charles Hamilton in the idea of black power: "The concept of black power rests on a fundamental premise: *Before a group can enter the open society, it must first close ranks* . . . solidarity is necessary before a group can operate effectively from a bargaining position of strength in a pluralistic society.[63] Even the harshest black critics of the new nationalism, like Kenneth Clark, denouncing "its programmatic emptiness and its pragmatic futility," conceded that Black Power held a "tremendous psychological appeal" for the black masses.[64]

During the early 1960s, many in the civil rights movement had begun to shift their emphasis to economic problems. They organized demonstrations, boycotts, and picket lines in an effort to attack racial discrimination in employment; they staged rent strikes to protest substandard housing conditions and unscrupulous landlords; and they denounced destructive urban renewal endeavors. The hymn "We Shall Overcome" reverberated throughout the nation, and in a three-month period during the summer of 1963, the Justice Department counted 1,412 separate demonstrations.[65]

These organized exhibitions escalated into mass rioting between 1964 and 1968. There were twenty-one major riots and civil disorders in 1966 and eighty-three major disturbances in 1967. July 1967, for example, was a month of riots: in Milwaukee four persons died, and in Detroit, forty-three; and there were serious disturbances in over thirty cities across the country.[66] As July ended, a Civil Disturbance Task Force was established in the Pentagon, and the president established a "riot commission." In February 1968 the commission called for a "massive and sustained commitment to action" to end poverty and racial discrimination. Only days before, in his State of the Union message, the president had announced legislative proposals for programs to train and hire the hard-core unemployed and to rebuild the cities.[67]

Abandoning the "unsuitable homes" assault on black welfare recipients that was common during the 1950s, welfare agencies became more considerate in dealing with those who applied for assistance. Discontinuation rates began to drop, especially discontinuations for "failure to comply with departmental regulations," an administrative category that could include such things as failure to locate a father or negligence in showing up for an interview. As a result of these modifications, and the government's "commitment to action," the number of families applying for AFDC benefits rose abruptly, from 588,000 in 1960 to 788,000 in 1963 to 903,000 in 1966—up by more than half over 1960. In 1968, when the rioting finally reached a peak, applications had doubled since 1960 to 1,088,000—and they exceeded one million in each year thereafter.

A study that compared twenty-three riot cities with twenty nonriot cities of similar size found that the riot cities had larger welfare budget increases in the year following their riot.[68] Many of the black poor had evidently come to believe that a society that denied them jobs and a living wage at least owed them a maintenance income. A national welfare movement had unquestionably emerged.[69]

The NWRO and Gender Politics

The favorable political and economic climate throughout the nation coincided with the rise of various welfare rights leaders, whose efforts eventually led to the birth of the National Welfare Rights Organization (NWRO) in 1966.[70] One of these leaders was George Wiley, a former chemistry professor at Syracuse University who had resigned his position to become active in the civil rights movement. When James Farmer resigned as the director of the Congress on Racial Equality (CORE) in late 1965, Wiley—as associate director—became one of the two contenders for the top position. After being defeated in a bitter contest with Floyd McKissick, he left CORE to become one of the founders and the first executive director of the NWRO.

Another person destined for national prominence was Johnnie Tillmon of Watts, California—a single mother with six children to support. In the late 1950s, after a period of poor health and financial difficulty, she had been forced to go on welfare. She found it a dehumanizing experience, and decided that people needed better opportunities to move out of poverty. Surveying the needs of poor women in her Watts housing project, she found that all but one of the 600 women wanted training and jobs rather than welfare.[71] By late 1963 she had started Aid to Needy Children, one of the first welfare rights organizations in the country. She became the first chairperson of the NWRO.

In the early 1960s another group dedicated to getting money for poor women and children, the Alameda County Welfare Rights Organization, was being launched in California. Its director, Timothy Sampson, was a white social worker who had been trained as a professional organizer by Saul Alinsky.

Though Tillmon and Sampson fundamentally agreed on the nature of the problems facing poor women in California, it soon became clear that they had different views on strategy and tactics. Sampson, as a well-trained organizer, saw the need to coordinate the growing number of welfare rights groups in the state and proposed a statewide confederation. Tillmon, on the other hand, questioned the right of a white male who had never received welfare to assume leadership in a movement of welfare mothers. Believing that Sampson was organizing in order to control the movement, Tillmon decided to challenge his authority in a public meeting. Even though Sampson was the chosen representative of the newly formed Alameda Co. WRO, he resigned as a result of this incident. Ironically, he would later be hired by George Wiley as the NWRO's associate director, where he would wield more power than many of the organization's grassroots women leaders.

In January 1966, when Wiley was leaving CORE, he had attended a meeting in Syracuse—a "Poor People's War Council on Poverty"—at which he met Richard Cloward, who, along with Frances Fox Piven, had been developing a strategy for creating "political power for welfare recipients and other poor people."[72] While other leaders had rejected the Cloward and Piven strategy of mobilizing around the welfare issue, Wiley was immediately attracted to its central focus on an economic concern.

During his years in the civil rights movement, Wiley's interest in racial justice had begun to focus increasingly on the needs of poor blacks, whom he believed had not shared equally in the gains of the movement. But unlike many young black leaders in the movement, Wiley was an "integrationist who believed that whites could play an important role in the movement."[73] In addition, he had a white wife—a touchy predicament for a black male to be in during the 1960s, especially if he were a civil rights leader. Thus when he set out to organize the NWRO with a commitment to cooperate with whites, he was sharply criticized by many black leaders.

Not only were all the poor urged to join the movement, but all racial and ethnic groups within the poverty population were embraced. The NWRO stated this principle of racial inclusiveness in its constitution, by-laws, and publications, and in the speeches of its leaders. Wiley often pointed out that poverty was not confined to blacks, noting that a majority of the poor were white. He viewed the single economic issue of poverty as a "really important link between blacks and whites."[74]

Wiley extended these political and ideological principles into the hiring practices of the NWRO. The staff in the national headquarters was already integrated, and as Wiley increased his own staff the ratio of whites to blacks tipped in favor of whites. For example, with the exception of Wiley himself, who was executive director, the top administrative positions were held by whites. The second highest position in the organization was held by Timothy Sampson, the professional organizer from California. In addition, the office and field staff were "very heavily white."[75] With the exception of Hulbert James in New York City, all the field organizers were white. Before long black staff members were accusing Wiley of showing favoritism toward the white staff, and blacks within the NWRO membership charged that blacks were assigned the menial tasks, relegated to lower-ranking positions, and excluded from the inner circle of policymakers. Black staff members were talking of ways to remove Wiley from leadership of the organization.

The outcome of this conflict was a reapportionment of power within the national office. Observers were bewildered when Wiley and the executive committee reassigned all the top posts to black men, and none to welfare women. Timothy Sampson, the associate director, was replaced by Hulbert James, and blacks were given all the top paid leadership positions. Two black welfare mothers, Joyce Burson and Jackie Post, were given trivial staff assignments. Whites who were relieved of their responsibilities moved over into Wiley's personal "shadow staff"—an unofficial policymaking group that was predominantly white. This policymaking group was totally separate from the national office and its staff, which was by now almost entirely black.

Another upheaval in the national organization occurred when Faith Evans, a black man receiving welfare as an AFDC father, joined the executive committee. Evans's personal experiences—as a child growing up in poverty, and as an NWRO organizer in the state of New York—had made him a firm believer in the potential abilities of welfare women. He was confident that they could run the NWRO with only limited external support. As a result, he fought to make women the de facto policymakers in NWRO, and this led to a confrontation with Wiley, who was convinced that a movement run by women with few skills and little training could never achieve its goals without considerable support from outsiders.

These opposing views led to an organizational crisis in late November 1972. According to Kotz and Kotz, "it started out as just another executive board meeting, with the members badgering Wiley with questions and criticism, but the arguments soon became an indictment: Wiley had usurped for himself the policy-making role of the board."[76] With this charge out on the table, it became clear that chronic and bitter disagreements had split the board into irreconcilable factions. Something had to give.

The first move came when Evans announced his resignation. He admitted that he had been responsible for some of the conflict because he had urged the women to get rid of George Wiley and run the organization for themselves. He added that he still believed such a change would lead to a more functional recipient movement, but he acknowledged his failure to get across a plan for the future of the organization. In response, Wiley approached Evans and asked him to take over the organization. But Evans refused, stating that the executive committee had chosen Johnnie Tillmon as its executive director, and he believed that the choice was properly theirs and not Wiley's. He once again indicated that he deplored the fact that Wiley, like other black leaders, had little faith in the ability of poor black women to run their own organizations.

Wiley submitted his formal resignation on December 15, 1972. Johnnie Tillmon replaced him as executive director, and Evans became her associate director. In January 1973 the new leaders issued the following press release:

> NWRO feels that it is time to utilize the capabilities of women who have been associated with the welfare movement. Approximately 98 percent of the organization's membership is comprised of women. NWRO views the major welfare problems as women's issues and itself as strictly a women's organization. They are willing to cooperate fully with men in activities but will maintain responsibility for NWRO policies and programs.[77]

With Johnnie Tillmon at its helm, the organization shifted its emphasis to showing solidarity with women in general and black women in particular. At its 1973 annual convention, the NWRO singled out eight women and their organizations to receive awards. Dorothy Height and the NCNW was one of them. In an interview with the journal *Social Policy* in 1973, Height disavowed her initial reaction to the Moynihan Report, saying that she had "never accepted the Moynihan thesis which sees the black family as disorganized and malfunctioning" and claiming that the "myth of the black matriarchy has to be dispelled."[78] As the NWRO struggled to find new sources of support in 1973, the NCNW responded with a $500 donation to the Tillmon Half-a-Chance Campaign.[79] Financial contributions such as these were erratic, however, and the NWRO eventually closed its doors in 1975.

Some observers of the NWRO have argued that its demise was probably inevitable given the actions of national leaders in Washington and renewed public hostility toward welfare. But it is also clear that the organization was brought down by internal conflicts based on race, class, and gender that resulted in loss of fiscal and human resources.

During the nine turbulent years of its existence, the NWRO had a beneficial effect on the lives of the poor, especially those families receiving AFDC. The organized efforts of the NWRO protest movement succeeded in transferring millions of dollars in public subsidies to the poor. Legal assistance agencies, such as the Center for Social Welfare Policy and Law, worked with the NWRO to change the man-in-the-house rule and establish the right to have a third party accompany a welfare mother at appeals or termination hearings. In a review of the book *Passion for Equality* for the *New York Times* in 1977, Roger Wilkins declared that the NWRO had "left indelible marks on America's political system."[80]

Conclusion

Although the Moynihan Report contained nothing that other social scientists had not already communicated, it quickly became the subject of intense public controversy. One reason for this was that the riots in Watts occurred within a week after its release, and extensive media coverage linked these two events in the minds of most people. Among blacks, however, the report was controversial because civil rights leaders saw it as evidence that the Johnson administration was trying to shift its efforts away from combating racial segregation and discrimination in favor of dealing with the "pathology" of the black family.

In the black community, the controversy around the Moynihan Report exposed the historic tension between black men and women in the public sphere. Most glaringly, there was no female leadership in any of the major civil rights organizations. Dorothy Height, the president of the NCNW, a moderate organization founded in 1935 by Mary McLeod Bethune, was the only black woman invited to attend the planning sessions for the White House conference pursuant to the report, even though other black women had made impassioned responses to it. The leaders of the March on Washington had also failed to include women speakers on their original program, even though black women outnumbered black men in the civil rights movement. One of Moynihan's recommendations to remedy the emasculation of black males by black females was for black men to retreat to an "utterly masculine world . . . a world away from women, a world run by strong men of unquestioned authority." In the minds of many black women, black men had created precisely this kind of environment in the civil rights movement.

During the mid-1960s various civil rights activists and groups began to abandon the movement's original emphasis on nonviolence. Between 1964 and 1968 there were twenty-one major riots and disturbances, and eighty-three serious civil disorders in 1967 alone. A Civil Disturbance Task Force was set up in the Pentagon, and the president appointed a "riot commission." In 1968, the year that the rioting reached a peak, this commission called for a "massive and sustained commitment to action" to end poverty and racial discrimination. In the same year, AFDC applications had doubled over the number filed in 1960, and cities in which riots had occurred were increasing their welfare budgets. Beginning in the mid-1960s, the NWRO began to coordinate efforts across the country to mobilize the rights of welfare recipients.

George Wiley, the first executive director of the NWRO, adopting a political empowerment strategy developed by Frances Fox Piven and Richard Cloward, tried to focus on the needs of poor blacks, whom he believed had not benefited equally from the achievements of the movement. Unlike many younger black leaders in the movement, Wiley was an integrationist, and his leadership emphasized coalition-building with whites. Like many other black leaders, however, he took a paternalistic view of the abilities of poor women and effectively excluded them from leadership roles in the NWRO—although 90 percent of its members were women. In 1972 there was a "takeover" of the national office by black women; Wiley was forced into resigning, and Johnnie Tillmon replaced him as executive director. The organization survived only until 1975. It collapsed in part because of a conservative tide in the political environment, but also because of internal conflicts based on race, class, and gender.

While it was active, however, the NWRO had a beneficial effect on the lives of the poor. The organized efforts of the NWRO protest movement succeeded in transferring millions of dollars in public subsidies to poor families; and its collaboration with other agencies helped expand clients' welfare eligibility rights and ensure that their benefits would not arbitrarily be terminated. More broadly, the NWRO movement demonstrated that massive organized protests by citizens can mobilize a government redistribution of economic resources. It also launched a new series of debates on the individual's right to public welfare in a democratic society, and helped reduce the stigma attached to receiving it. Finally, it reached out to women who had been effectively excluded from many traditional social movement organizations and had not been touched by the central ideas of the feminist movement.

Notes

1. Arthur Schlesinger, Jr., *A Thousand Days* (Boston: Houghton Mifflin 1965), 17–18.

2. For example, see H. E. Barnes and O. M. Ruedi, *The American Way of Life* (New York: Prentice-Hall, 1951); Ernest W. Burgess and H. J. Locke, *The Family* (New York: American, 1950); Erik H. Erikson, *Childhood and Society* (New York: Norton, 1950); Talcott Parsons, *The Social System* (Glencoe, Ill.: Free Press, 1951); R. M. Williams, *American Society* (New York: Knopf, 1951).

3. Abram Kardiner and Lionel Ovesey, *The Mark of Oppression* (New York: Norton, 1951), 58.

4. Ibid., 59. Other scholars who studied mother-centered families in the Caribbean during this period included Edith Clarke, *My Mother Who Fathered Me* (London: George Allen, 1957); Raymond T. Smith, *The Negro Family in British Guiana* (London: Routledge, 1956); and M. G. Smith, *West Indian Family Structure* (Seattle: University of Washington Press, 1962).

5. Kardiner and Ovesey, *The Mark of Oppression*, 59–60.

6. Ibid., 381–82.

7. Talcott Parsons and Robert W. Bales, *Family: Socialization and Interaction Process* (New York: Free Press, 1955). What is more interesting is that a model so supposedly well suited for the temperaments and abilities of men and women would be so quickly abandoned after the 1960s, especially by those who had the economic resources to preserve it. Social scientists in the 1980s would argue that this family model emerged in the nineteenth century and represented only a minority of families, who were largely middle-class and nonrural. It took time for the this model to emerge and to extend its dominion over other classes. For example, see Carl Degler, *At Odds* (New York: Oxford University Press, 1980); Mary Ryan, *Cradle of the Middle Class* (Cambridge: Cambridge University Press, 1981); Michelle Barrett and Mary McIntosh, *The Anti-social Family* (London: Verso, 1982); Barrie Thorne, *Rethinking the Family* (New York: Longmans, 1982).

8. Morris Zelditch, Jr., "Role Differentiation in the Nuclear Family: A Comparative Study," in Parsons and Bales, *Family*, 307–51.

9. Zelditch made a distinction between patrilineal and matrilineal society, and many matrilineal societies did not fit into his typology. They included: the Arapesh and the Mundugomor (South Sea Islanders); the Cheyenne and the Arapaho; the Nuer and the Malinowski (Trobriand Islands); the Tchambuli and the Manus, and the Marquesas (New Guinea). For Zelditch's explanation of why these societies did not fit, see "Role Differentiation," 321–33.

10. Ibid., 312.

11. Hylan Lewis, *Blackways of Kent* (Chapel Hill: University of North Carolina Press, 1955), xxiii. Upon completion of his dissertation, Hylan Lewis accepted a faculty appointment at Howard University and later chaired the family session at the White House Conference on the Moynihan Report.

12. Ibid., 100.

13. Ibid., 102–3.

14. Murray A. Straus, "Conjugal Power Structure and Adolescent Personality," *Journal of Marriage and the Family* 24 (February 1962): 17–25. Walter B. Miller, "Lower Class Culture as a Generating Milieu of Gang Delinquency," *Journal of Social Issues* 14 (Third Quarter, 1958):5–19; David B. Lynn and William L. Sawrey, "The Effects of Father-Absence on Norwegian Boys and Girls," *Journal of Abnormal and Social Psychology* 59 (September 1959):258–62; R. V. Burton and J.W.M. Whiting, "The Absent Father and Cross-Sex Identity," *Merrill-Palmer Quarterly* 7(1961):85–95; Melvin L. Kohn and John A. Klausen, "Parental Authority Behavior and Schizophrenia," *American Journal of Orthopsychiatry* 27(April, 1956):297–313.

15. Elliot Liebow, *Tally's Corner: A Study of Negro Streetcorner Men* (Boston: Little, Brown, 1967). Hylan Lewis was the director of the research project, funded by the National Institute of Mental Health.

16. Ibid., 78–79.

17. Thomas F. Pettigrew, *A Profile of the Negro American* (New York: D. Van Nostrand, 1964).

18. Ibid., 15–16.

19. Jeanne L. Noble, "The Negro Woman's College Education (New York: Columbia University Press, 1956), 98.

20. John H. Rohrer and Munro S. Edmonson, eds., *The Eighth Generation: Cultures and Personalities of New Orleans Negroes* (New York: Harper, 1960), 161–62.

21. Kenneth B. Clark, *Dark Ghetto: Dilemmas of Social Power* (New York: Harper & Row, 1965), 70.

22. E. Franklin Frazier, *The Black Bourgeoisie* (New York: Collier-Macmillan, 1957), 182.

23. William J. Wilson, *The Truly Disadvantaged* (Chicago: University of Chicago Press, 1987) 4.

24. See Muriel G. Cantor and Joel M. Cantor, *Prime-Time Television: Content and Control,* 2d. ed. (Newbury Park, Calif.: Sage, 1992); E. Barnouw, *A History of Broadcasting in the United States,* 3 vols. (New York: Oxford University Press, 1966–70); Harry Castleman and Walter J. Podrazik, *Watching TV: Four Decades of American Television* (New York: McGraw-Hill, 1982); Herbert J. Gans, *Popular Culture and High Culture* (New York: Basic Books, 1974); E. Taylor, *Prime Time Families: Television Culture in Postwar America* (Berkeley: University of California Press, 1989); Horace Newcomb, *TV: The Most Popular Art* (Garden City, N.Y.: Doubleday, 1974), ch. 2.

25. "Secrets of a Movie Maid," *Ebony,* November 1949, 52; "FDR Was My Boss," *Ebony,* April 1952, 64; "Nursemaid to the Quadruplets," *Ebony* June 1948, 36.

26. For a detailed analysis of how Mammy has been venerated, see Deborah Gray White, *Arn't I a Woman: Female Slaves in the Plantation South* (New York: Norton, 1985), 165–67. Gray notes that Mammy was becoming a national symbol of perfect domesticity at the very time millions of black women were leaving the South in search of northern employment.

What she omits is that after World War II, black women were searching for employment that was not in the domestic sphere and the efforts of whites to enshrine Mammy may have been an attempt to keep them in their place.

27. Quoted in Castleman and Podrazik, *Watching TV*, 57–59.

28. For a description of the social and economic status of blacks during this period, see Talcott Parsons and Kenneth Clark, ed., *The Negro American* (Boston: Houghton Mifflin 1966); Hugh D. Graham, *The Civil Rights Era: Origins and Development of National Policy* (New York: Oxford University Press, 1990); Michael Katz, *The Undeserving Poor: From the War on Poverty to the War on Welfare* (New York: Pantheon, 1989); Charles V. Hamilton and Dona C. Hamilton, "Social Policies, Civil Rights and Poverty," in *Fighting Poverty: What Works and What Doesn't*, ed. Sheldon H. Danziger and Daniel H. Weinberg (Cambridge Mass.: Harvard University Press, 1986).

29. Council on Economic Advisers, *Economic Report of the President, 1965* (Washington, D.C.: Government Printing Office, 1965), 61–62.

30. Lee Rainwater and William Y. Yancy, *The Moynihan Report and the Politics of Controversy* (Cambridge, Mass.: MIT Press, 1967), 23–25.

31. Ibid., 5–6,

32. a feminist critic, summarized women's objections to this statement: "The assumption that Moynihan makes that leadership is necessarily male in our society is not correct. Rather the leadership should be dealt to the qualified person without regard to their sex. We must develop a sense of partnership between male and female. The question is not how do you upgrade the male and how do you downgrade the woman"; quoted in Rainwater and Yancey, *Moynihan Report*, 187.

33. Carl Ginsburg argues that this report continues to exert influence in the media and the public sphere; *Race and Media: The Enduring Life of the Moynihan Report* (New York: Institute for Media Analysis, 1989).

34. Bonnie Franklin would be the first white female to portray a single parent on a television sitcom when she played Ann Romano, the divorced mother of two teenage daughters, in *One Day at a Time,* which aired in the mid-1970s.

35. Quoted in Rainwater and Yancy, *Moynihan Report*, 188–89, 200.

36. Quoted in ibid., 168.

37. Ibid., 181.

38. Quoted in ibid., 3.

39. Ibid., 191.

40. Quoted in ibid., 136–47.

41. Quoted in ibid., 139–40.

42. Quoted in ibid., 464.

43. Quoted in ibid., 159.

44. Stokely Carmichael, "Notes and Comments," in *Black Nationalism in America*, ed., John H. Bracey, Jr., August Meier, and Elliott Rudwick (Indianapolis, Ind.: Bobbs Merrill, 1970), 472. Stokely Carmichael is best remembered for his outrageous observation in a 1964 SNCC staff meeting that the best position for women in the organization was "prone."

45. Quoted in Rainwater and Yancy, *Moynihan Report* 140.

46. Column quoted in full in Rainwater and Yancy, *Moynihan Report*, 375–77.

47. Quoted in ibid., 444.

48. Charles E. Lindbloom and David K. Cohen, *Usable Knowledge: Social Science and Social Problem Solving* (New Haven: Yale University Press, 1979): 58.

49. Rainwater and Yancy, *Moynihan Report* viii. Pauli Murray was a graduate of Howard University Law School and experienced "Male condescension . . . never far from the surface." Upon graduating, she found her opportunities even more limited than those of her male classmates. Pauli Murray, "Black Women, Racism and the Legal Process in Historical Perspective," November 1979. (Washington, D.C.: National Archives for Black Women in History): 9–11.

50. Quoted in ibid., 80.

51. Why weren't black women who were influential and active in the civil rights movement interviewed by Rainwater and Yancy or invited to the planning meetings for the White House Conference?—for example: Ella Baker, an influential associate of Martin Luther King, Jr., and the person who spearheaded and organized the student civil rights movement; Daisy Bates, the person responsible for integrating Central High School, who went on to become president of the Little Rock chapter of the NAACP; Rosa Parks, the activist who is credited with starting the civil rights movement when she refused to give her bus seat to a white man and was arrested; Fannie Lou Hamer, an activist in the freedom marches, the Mississippi Freedom Democratic Party, the National Women's Political Caucus, and the Freedom Farm cooperative; or young black women attorneys and activists such as Eleanor Holmes Norton and Marian Wright Edelman.

52. Ella Baker, interview, Civil Rights Documentation Project, Moorland-Spingarn Collection, Howard University, 34–35.

53. Quoted in Rainwater and Yancy, *Moynihan Report* 88.

54. "An Interview with Dorothy I. Height," *Social Policy* 4 (September–October 1973): 35.

55. Unita Blackwell interview, "Civil Rights Documentation Project," Moorland-Spingarn Collection, Howard University 28.

56. Andrew Young analyzed this discomfort on King's part and traced it to his relationship with his mother: "We had a hard time with domineering women in SCLC, because Martin's mother, quiet as she was, was really a strong, domineering force in the family. She was never publicly saying anything but she ran Daddy King, and she ran the church and she ran Martin, and Martin's problem in the early days of the movement was directly related to his need to be free of that strong matriarchal influence"; quoted in Nick Kotz and Mary Kotz, *A Passion for Equality: George Wiley and the Movement* (New York: Norton, 1977), 252.

57. Gloster Current, a planner for the agenda, has admitted that as an "afterthought" a hasty tribute was put together for black women freedom fighters; Jacqueline Jones, *Labor of Love, Labor of Sorrow: Black Women's Work and the Family from Slavery to the Present* (New York: Basic Books, 1985), 282. This incident was also reported in Anna Arnold Hedgeman, *The Trumpet Sounds: A Memoir of Negro Leadership* (New York: Holt, Rinehart and Winston, 1964), 178–180. It was Ella Baker who observed that there were more women;

see Gerda Lerner, ed., *Black Women in White America: A Documentary History* (New York: Pantheon, 1972), 351.

58. For perspectives that document the philosophy of black male dominance during the 1960s, see Bobby Seale, *Seize the Time: The Story of the Black Panther Party and Huey Newton* (New York: Random House, 1968); Eldridge Cleaver, *Soul on Ice* (New York: McGraw-Hill, 1968); E. U. Essien-Udom, *Black Nationalism: A Search for an Identity in America* (Chicago: University of Chicago Press, 1962); Imamu Amiri Baraka, ed., *African Congress: A Documentary of the First Modern Pan-African Congress* (New York: Morrow, 1972); Elaine Brown, *A Taste of Power: A Black Woman's Story* (New York: Pantheon, 1992).

59. For black women's perspective on the report, see Nathan and Julia Hare, "Black Women 1970," *Trans-action* 8(November–December 1970): 65–68.; Patricia Bell Scott, "Debunking Sapphire: Toward a Non-racist and Non-sexist Social Science," in *But Some of Us Are Brave*, ed. Gloria T. Hull, Patricia B. Scott, and Barbara Smith, 85–92; Barbara A. Sizemore, "Sexism and the Black Male," *Black Scholar* 4(March–April, 1983): 2–11; Angela Davis, "Reflections on the Black Women's Role in the Community of Slaves," *Black Scholar* (December 1971): 23–28

60. Quoted in Rainwater and Yancy, *Moynihan Report*, 185.

61. Joyce Ladner, *Tomorrow's Tomorrow: The Black Woman* (New York: Doubleday, 1972), 43.

62. Alice Walker, *In Search of Our Mother's Gardens*, (New York: Harcourt, Brace, 1984), 62.

63. Stokely Carmichael and Charles V. Hamilton, *Black Power and the Politics of Liberation in America* (New York: Vintage, 1967), 44.

64. Kenneth Clark, "The Present Dilemma of the Negro," in *Conflict and Competition: Studies in Recent Black Protest*, ed. August Meier and Francis L. Broderick (1965; reprint, Indianapolis: Bobbs-Merrill, 1971): 618.

65. William Brink and Louis Harris, *The Negro Revolution in America* (New York: Simon and Schuster, 1964), 46.

66. Francis Fox Piven and Richard A. Cloward, *Poor People's Movements: Why They Succeed, How They Fail* (New York: Vintage, 1977), 272–73. The cities: Cambridge, Maryland; Lansing, Kalamazoo, Saginaw, and Grand Rapids, Michigan; Philadelphia; Providence; Phoenix; Portland, Oregon; Wichita; South Bend, Indiana; Memphis, Tennessee; Wilmington, Delaware; San Francisco, San Bernardino, Long Beach, Fresno, and Marin City, California; Rochester, Mt. Vernon, Poughkeepsie, Peekskill, and Nyack, New York; Hartford, Connecticut; Englewood, Paterson, Elizabeth, New Brunswick, Jersey City, Palmyra, and Passaic, New Jersey.

67. Piven and Cloward, *Poor People's Movements*, 272–73.

68. Michael Betz, "Riots and Welfare: Are They Related?" *Social Policy* 21 (1974): 345.

69. For an analysis of how the threat of urban disorder influenced the welfare policy agenda, see Jill Quadagno, *The Color of Welfare: How Racism Undermined the War on Poverty* (New York: Oxford University Press, 1994); especially ch. 9.

70. This discussion summarizes the following historical interpretations of the NWRO: Kotz and Kotz, *Passion for Equality*, 282–83; Piven and Cloward, *Poor People's Movements*

(New York: Vintage Books, 1977): ch. 5; Guida West, *The National Welfare Rights Movement: The Social Protest of Poor Women* (New York: Praeger, 1981); Gilbert Y. Steiner, *The State of Welfare* (Washington, D.C.: Brookings Institution, 1971); Lawrence Neil Bailis, *Bread or Justice: Grassroots Organization in the Welfare Rights Movement* (Lexington, Mass.: Heath, 1970); Susan Hanley Hertz, *The Welfare Mothers Movement: A Decade of Change for Poor Women* (Washington, D.C.: University Press of America, 1981); William Howard Whitaker, "The Determinants of Social Movement Success: A Study of the National Welfare Rights Organization" (Ph.D. diss., Brandeis University, 1970).

71. West, *National Welfare Rights Movement*, 92.

72. Kotz and Kotz, *Passion for Equality*, 182; Piven and Cloward, *Poor People's Movements*, ch. 5.

73. August Meier and Elliott Rudwick, *CORE: A Study in the Civil Rights Movement, 1942–1968* (New York: Oxford University Press, 1973), 406–7.

74. Hobart A. Burch, "Conversations with George Wiley," *Journal of Social Issues* (November December 1970): 5.

75. Ironically, this was the same Sampson who had been forced out of the California WRO leadership and charged by Tillmon with trying to take control.

76. Kotz and Kotz, *Passion for Equality*, 290.

77. Quoted in West, *National Welfare Rights Movement*, 122.

78. "Interview with Dorothy I. Height," 35.

79. Michele Wallace, "Black Women United: Sororities, Alliances, and Pressure Groups," *Ms.*, (January 1979), 45–48, 87–91.

80. Roger Wilkins, review of Kotz and Kotz, *Passion for Equality*, *New York Times*, September 14, 1977.

CHAPTER EIGHT

FAMILY COMPOSITION AND THE "UNDERCLASS" DEBATE

The increase in out-of-wedlock childbearing may or may not mean that people are more willing to have babies they cannot care for properly. . . . The practice has been spreading to all levels of American society. We may, in other words, be seeing a change in the content of middle-class morality rather than the growth of an underclass that repudiates or ignores that morality.

Christopher Jencks, "What Is the Underclass—and Is It Growing?"

In June 1976, the year of the Bicentennial celebration, Vernon Jordan, Jr., gave the keynote address at the National Conference on Social Welfare. His remarks expressed the sentiments of many African-Americans:

> The social programs, the civil rights advances, and the national commitments to economic progress and racial equality that characterized the 1960s have faded away. And in their place have come economic stagnation, continued racial divisiveness, and abandonment of national consensus on minority rights. Indeed, in a few short years we have gone all the way from "We shall overcome" to "We don't care."[1]

In that same year, the Department of Commerce released a report indicating that the wealthiest fifth of American families received about 40 percent of all income, whereas the poorest fifth received about 5 percent. Not surprisingly, the majority of the poorest families were headed by black women.[2]

Of the nation's 25 million blacks, 7.5 million had incomes below the poverty line. Further, three out of ten blacks lived in poverty, whereas the figure for whites was one of ten. Unemployment among blacks was twice as high as among whites, and 43 percent of all AFDC recipients were black. Only one in every twenty-five white households obtained food stamps, while one in every five black households did.[3]

This government document was one of the first to report that America's War on Poverty, launched in the mid-1960s, had not done much to help the poorest Americans.[4] But one significant factor had been altered by the War on Poverty—the public image of the poor. Beth Hess has described the old image as follows:

> When poverty became a national issue in the early 1960s, the image of America's poor still bore a resemblance to portraits of the Great Depression: grim-faced farmers, prematurely old women surrounded by children, elderly white folk, perhaps a dignified black or two.[5]

By the mid-1980s, the public's stereotype of the poor had undergone a radical change: It now featured unmarried black mothers, typically living in deteriorating urban slums, and having one baby after another in order to increase their welfare payments.

Why, after all the social programs and advances for women and people of color during the 1960s, did poverty intensify for mother-only black families during the 1970s and 1980s? During this period when poverty among single black mothers was intensifying, how did the government conduct an assault on their fertility? How did the government's complicity in the unlawful sterilization of an estimated 100,000 to 200,000 black women come to the public's attention?

The Decline of the Liberal Agenda

Vernon Jordan, in his bicentennial speech, referred to an "abandonment of national consensus on minority rights." This statement immediately raises a question: Was there ever a "national consensus" on minority issues, or was the progressive agenda set forth during the 1960s initiated by a minority of Americans? In any case, had public commitment to the economic progress of the nation's poor faded away by the mid-1970s?

In 1967 a prescient speech was made by Robert C. Wood, a social scientist from MIT serving as undersecretary of the Department of Housing and Urban Development (HUD). He noted that over the years a common bond or "union" had evolved between "the central city poor, more and more Negro, and the educated, economically secure, mostly white, Protestant suburbanites." And although these individuals shared a concern with social justice, their combined numbers were not great and their attitudes were fundamentally different from those of the majority. The typical representative of that majority, the average working American, had little interest in social justice or community issues and was preoccupied with protecting his job, his family, and his home.[6]

In *The Emerging Republican Majority*, published in January 1969, Kevin Phillips argued that two national demographic movements would soon convert the historic Democratic majority, which had lasted from the Great Depression to the 1960s, into a natural Republican majority. One of these movements was geographical—a population shift out of the Northeast and the Middle West into the Sunbelt, which stretched from Florida across Texas through the growing Southwest to southern California. The other was sociological—the arrival of new members into the middle class—most of them immigrants, who were also moving out of the cities into the suburbs. There was a major difference, however, between these new suburbanites and the ones Robert Wood had described: They were not committed to a liberal agenda.[7]

By the late 1970s patterns of race and ethnicity were undergoing a transformation, as Phillips had predicted. The roots of this transformation can be traced to the Immigration Reform Act of 1965, which abolished national origin quotas and promoted unforeseen changes in the composition of the immigrant population and the competition for fewer jobs with lower wages.

The number of European immigrants declined steadily, until by 1976 more than half of all immigrants came from seven countries in Asia and Latin America. These figures did not include additional millions of undocumented immigrants, chiefly from Mexico and Latin America. As the national birthrate plummeted, immigration accounted for an increasingly large proportion of the total population growth. For example, in 1940 immigration had accounted for 6 percent of the increase, but by 1976 it accounted for nearly 25 percent.[8]

In 1979 the Census Bureau estimated that more than 12 million persons of Hispanic descent were living in the United States: 7.2 million from Mexico, 1.8 million from Puerto Rico, 700,000 from Cuba, 900,000 from Central and South America, and 1.4 million from other regions of the world. The Hispanic population was not only overwhelmingly urban, it was also relatively young; its median age was twenty-two years, compared with thirty years for non-Hispanic Americans. Compared to other immigrant groups, it was also a relatively penurious population with low levels of educational attainment. Nearly one out of four of Spanish-speaking families lived below the poverty line. The economic well-being of this population, however, varied somewhat according to country of origin. For example, while 17 percent of Cubans lived in poverty, 22 percent of Mexican families and 39 percent of Puerto Rican families did.[9]

The issue that would create the strongest backlash against immigrants in general, and poor immigrants in particular, was that many would increasingly have undocumented status. According to annual estimates by the Immigration and Naturalization Service (INS), the number of undocumented immigrants who succeeded in entering the United States each year increased from 110,000 in 1965 to more than a million by 1977. By the late 1970s, no fewer than 7 million were estimated to be residing in the United States.[10] The preliminary report of the Domestic Committee on Illegal Aliens described these immigrants as "an invisible subculture outside the boundaries of law and legitimate institutions."[11] The declining productivity and stagnation of the national economy after 1973 would further compound the consequences of the changing American population mix, as the new immigrants competed with native minorities for fewer jobs with lower wages.

Black Women and the Illusion of Progress

During the 1960s and early 1970s, heavy pressure from women's groups had helped win several federal legislative victories. Title VII of the Civil Rights Act of 1964 had outlawed discrimination in hiring and employment on account of gender, race, or national origin. In 1970 the Office of Federal Contract Compliance issued guidelines banning gender discrimination by federal contractors. In 1971 and 1972 the House and the Senate passed the Equal Rights Amendment (ERA) to the Constitution by a vote of 354 to 23 and 84 to 8, respectively. The ERA stated simply that "equality of rights under the law shall not be denied or abridged by the United States or by any State on account of sex." To become part of the Constitution, the amendment would have to be ratified by two-thirds of the states (thirty-eight) within seven years.

A major breakthrough came in 1972, when Congress passed the Equal Pay Act, which prohibited sexual discrimination in federally supported education programs, and also expanded the jurisdiction of the Equal Employment Opportunity Commission to include local government agencies and educational institutions. By the mid-1970s affirmative action programs were helping women even more than they were helping members of racial minorities, and this was happening during years in which the number of women workers was increasing dramatically. From 1965 to 1975, about 10 million women entered the labor force, compared with 7 million men. In 1975 nearly half of all American women held jobs.

In the late 1960s, black women as a group began to approach parity with white women in terms of their wages. Whereas in 1960 the median earnings of black women were 75 to 80 percent of the median for white women, six years after the passage of Title VII the median earnings of northern black women had increased to about 95 percent of the white women's median. The increase in the earnings of southern black women, however, was much smaller—from 45 to 55 percent of white women's earnings.[12]

Although Congress was empowered during the 1960s and 1970s to pass legislation that assisted virtually all working women, black women at the bottom of the economic ladder made very little progress. In an effort to explain this phenomenon, social scientists in the 1970s devised intricate statistical techniques for measuring social mobility. One of these was the OCG Scale, which described occupational changes in a generation by cross-tabulating certain facts about sons (e.g., jobs, income, or educational attainment) and the same facts about their fathers at a similar age. This statistical technique was applied to a population sample in 1973, and the results were reported in a government publication entitled *Social Indicators, 1976*. The scale not only revealed that occupational status was inherited for the total male civilian labor force, but since marriages almost always occurred within class lines, the economic status of the parents was "transferred to daughters almost to the same extent that it would have been if they had married their brothers."[13] This analysis demonstrated that for women, the selection of a marital partner was a more important predictor of future economic well-being than occupational choice. This reason alone goes far toward explaining why both poor and middle-income black women are at a distinct economic disadvantage when compared to white women, and why the greatest economic vulnerability is experienced by the poorest black women.

In the early 1970s a Louis Harris–Virginia Slims poll asked women about their interest in gaining more social and economic equality for women. When asked whether they favored "efforts to strengthen or change women's status in society," 62 percent of the black women participating in the poll agreed, compared to only 45 percent of white women. Even more surprisingly, 67 percent of black women expressed "sympathy with the efforts of women's liberation groups," compared with only 35 percent of white women.[14]

Given these more forceful attitudes, why were black women more reluctant than white women to actually participate in the women's movement?[15] In a *New York Times Magazine* article entitled "What the Black Woman Thinks about Women's Lib," Ida Lewis reflected the sentiments of many black women:

> Women's Liberation is basically a family quarrel between white women and white men. And on general principle it's not good to get involved in family disputes. Outsiders always get shafted when the dust settles. . . . Suppose the Lib movement succeeds. It will follow since white power is the order of the day that white women will be the first hired, which will still leave black men and women outside.[16]

The Feminization of Poverty

Michael Harrington's *The Other America* is generally recognized as providing the initial impetus for the rediscovery of poverty by federal officials and the emergence of Great Society programs. Inspired by John Kenneth Galbraith's *The Affluent Society*, Harrington asserted that a fifth of the population, or approximately 40 million Americans, were poor. He maintained that there was a "social blindness" in American society that kept this population invisible, and that the most familiar example of this blindness was the common opinion that "the poor are that way because they are afraid of work." Harrington argued that most of the poor would never have a chance to work their way out of the "other America" because "they are caught in a vicious circle" and "live in a culture of poverty."[17]

Besides serving as a catalyst for many Great Society programs, Harrington's classic book may have also spurred a resurgence in poverty research. The number of articles on poverty published annually in five prestigious sociology journals increased from three in 1965 to an average of ten a year in the early 1970s.[81] Beginning in 1966, a journal entitled *Poverty and Human Resources Abstract* focused on studies of poverty, and conferences with poverty as the central theme proliferated.[19]

Although interest in poverty was on the decline by the mid-1970s, *Social Indicators, 1976*, a scholarly volume published by the Department of Commerce, presented statistics disaggregated by race, age, gender, and income. Although real personal income, after being adjusted for a fourfold increase in consumer prices, had doubled from the late 1930s to the late 1970s, the income distribution figures showed that the economic impact of the civil rights movement on the poorest African Americans had been minuscule. In fact, the inequality was greater than it had been forty years earlier. The wealthiest fifth of American families received about 40 percent of all income, whereas the poorest fifth received about 5 percent. Not surprisingly, the majority of the poorest families were headed by black women, who were increasingly overrepresented on the welfare rolls.[20]

In the late 1970s black workers were finding it harder to get jobs than at any time since the Great Depression, and the unemployment rate among blacks was twice that among whites. Whereas the unemployment rate for black adults was 13 to 14 percent, the rate among black teenagers was a staggering 40 percent. These escalating unemployment rates for blacks were related to the movement of the economy away from manufacturing and toward services industries, a trend that was occurring most dramatically within formerly industrial urban centers. One economist observed that central cities were changing "from centers of goods processing to information processing."[21]

In 1977 the proportion of AFDC recipients who were black was 43 percent, whereas the figure for whites was 42.5 percent: Although whites outnumbered blacks in the population by ten to one, a slightly greater number of blacks than whites were receiving welfare.[22] One year earlier, a study released by the Urban Institute had identified the major factor driving the growth of welfare dependency among blacks: "[M]ore than half of all AFDC assistance in 1975 was paid to women who were or had been teenaged mothers."[23] Although some research had been conducted on black adolescents during the 1960s, the baby boom among black adolescents and its relationship to poverty and welfare dependence among black families had gone virtually unnoticed until this report was released.

In 1978 two scholars drew public attention to urban poverty as one of society's most menacing problems. William J. Wilson observed the development of "a deepening schism . . . in the black community, with the black poor falling further and further behind middle- and upper-income blacks." He concluded that "class has become more important than race in determining black life chances."[24] And Diana Pearce, who is generally credited with introducing the concept of gender into the poverty debates, focused on the plight of women in poverty. She emphasized two factors that contributed to it: low wages and the meager benefits provided by the welfare system. She described the institutionalized marginality of women in the labor force and clarified the role of the welfare system in perpetuating this condition. She noted that it is difficult for women to make a permanent change in status from welfare recipient to worker because welfare policies and tax rates actually create disincentives to work. As she put it, "Employers have no reason to raise wages, for there is no scarcity of low-wage workers and much disincentive for those who are on welfare to seek employment."[25]

From 1960 to 1980, three major changes occurred among the poor. The first was a demographic shift. In 1960 the majority of poor blacks were living in rural areas; by 1980 the number of poor blacks living in urban areas had increased by 74 percent, whereas the increase for whites was only 42 percent. Second, the proportion of blacks within the total population of the poor increased from one-quarter to almost one-third. Finally, women became a larger fraction of the poor during this period. Even in 1960 the poor had been mostly women and children, but at that time the majority of poor individuals lived in families with a male as the designated head of the household; by 1980, however, fewer than one-third of poor households had this status.[26]

In brief, economists who have evaluated the general growth in poverty rates and father-absent families during this period have identified several factors that influenced these trends:

1. the stagnation of the economy after 1973;
2. a sharp increase in the incidence of divorce and separation;
3. an increase in independent living by unmarried mothers, primarily adolescent mothers;
4 the greater increase in labor market participation of married women, which may have improved the economic situation of two-parent families;
5. the disproportionate growth of low-wage jobs and the declining value of the minimum wage;
6. shifts in occupational structure and the mismatch between better jobs and the education of the urban poor.[27]

Table 8.1 Distribution of Poor Whites and Poor Blacks Living in the
Fifty Largest Cities, by Poverty Rate in the Census Tract of Residence,
1970 and 1980 (Percentage)

Percentage in Poverty in the Census Tract	Poor Whites		Poor Blacks	
	1970	1980	1970	1980
Under 20	64	66	20	16
20–29	18	17	26	21
30–39	10	9	27	27
40 and over	8	8	27	36

SOURCE: David T. Ellwood, *Poor Support: Poverty in the American Family* (New York: Basic Books, 1988), p. 202.

Not only did the economic situation worsen for poor black single-parent families during the 1970s, but the poverty concentration level in black neighborhoods deepened. Table 8.1 shows the proportion of whites and blacks living in census tracts with varying poverty rates. The differences are striking. In 1980, two-thirds of poor whites living in central cities lived in neighborhoods in which the poverty rate was less than 20 percent, and only 8 percent lived in the highest poverty areas. In contrast, only 16 percent of poor blacks in central cities lived in neighborhoods with a poverty rate under 20 percent, and over one-third lived in neighborhoods with a rate over 40 percent. What this means is that black mother-only families were more disadvantaged than white mother-only families: They were more likely to be confined to the most impoverished, drug-infested, crime-ridden neighborhoods in the inner cities.

The Government's Assault on Black Fertility

When President Eisenhower was asked at a news conference in 1959 about his views on the federal government's role in family planning, he replied:

I cannot imagine anything more emphatically a subject that is not a proper political or government activity or function or responsibility. This government has not, and will not as long as I am here, have a positive political doctrine in its program that has to do with this problem of birth control.[28]

Eisenhower's hands-off policy on birth control did not last. During the Johnson administration, HEW began allocating federal funds to dispense family planning services, and these funds were targeted to poor communities.[29] The change in federal policy was justified on the ground that several studies during the 1950s and

1960s had indicated that many poor women were having unwanted children because they were having difficulty securing contraceptives.

Two major investigations into the fertility patterns of blacks conducted in the 1960s had predicted that black birthrates would decline and the racial difference in fertility would disappear. By the 1970s the anticipated racial convergence had not occurred.[30] The federal government's efforts were intensified in 1972 after the Commission on Population Growth and the American Future, appointed by President Nixon, concluded that "No substantial benefit would result from continued growth of the nation's population."[31] Although the commissioner's report did not say which segments of the population would be targeted, it was clear that lowering the birthrates of poor women, and particularly women of color, would have the highest priority.

When the federal government embarked on its mission to provide comprehensive family planning services to poor and minority communities, it had not studied the history of the birth control movement in the United States. Had it done so, it might have understood why so many black women were suspicious of the cause. In 1939, for example, the Birth Control Federation of America (the successor to the American Birth Control League) had planned a "Negro Project" directed at the "mass of Negroes, particularly in the South," because it considered that segment of the population "least fit, and least able to rear children properly." The federation recruited black ministers to provide leadership in the birth control campaign in black communities. In a letter to a colleague, Margaret Sanger wrote, "We do not want word to get out . . . that we want to exterminate the Negro population and the minister is the man who can straighten out that idea if it ever occurs to any of their more rebellious members."[32]

The population targeted in this campaign did not come to the public's attention until July 1973, when a black couple named Mr. and Mrs. Lonnie Relf complained to the Southern Poverty Law Center that in two of their daughters—Mary Alice, twelve years old, and Minnie Lee, fourteen years old—had been surgically sterilized without their knowledge or consent. These adolescents had first been injected regularly with an experimental drug called Depo-Provera, to prevent conception. When federal authorities learned that this drug had been linked with cancer in laboratory animals, they ordered the injections be discontinued. With the drug no longer available, the authorities in Montgomery, Alabama, had ordered the sterilization procedure. Katie Relf, aged seventeen, a sister of the sterilized girls and a welfare recipient, had escaped this surgery only because she had physically resisted.[33]

The Southern Poverty Law Center filed suit on behalf of the Relf sisters. During the course of the trial, Mrs. Relf, who was unable to read, revealed that she had "consented" to the operation by putting her X on a document. Since the content of the document had not been discussed with her, she had assumed that it simply authorized continued use of the Depo-Provera injections, not the surgical sterilization of her daughters.

Shortly after this scandal was reported in the media, other cases came to light. Mrs. Marietta Williams, a black welfare recipient from Aiken, South Carolina, related that when she was prepared to deliver her third child, her white physician, Clovis H. Pierce, refused to attend unless she consented to being sterilized. When interviewed, Dr. Pierce stated that his policy was to require sterilization after a woman on welfare had delivered three children, and that he did this to reduce welfare costs for tax-paying citizens. An investigation into the Aiken County hospital records showed that of thirty-four deliveries paid for by Medicaid in 1972, a total of eighteen had included sterilization; all eighteen involved black women, and all were performed by the same physician, Dr. Pierce. In the preceding eighteen months, Pierce had been paid Medicaid fees by the hospital totaling $60,000 of taxpayers' funds.[34]

Other stories soon came to light. For example, it was learned that the Relf children were not alone in Montgomery, Alabama; eleven other young teenage girls had been sterilized there, and ten of them were black. It was then revealed that from April 1972 to July 1973 government-sponsored birth control clinics (3,260 nationwide) had sterilized at least eighty more children, the vast majority of whom were black and Southern.

In 1973 a black woman from North Carolina, Nia Ruth Cox, filed a suit against a doctor who had surgically sterilized her after telling her that the results would be "temporary" and would "wear off." This lawsuit was leveled at a state government that had diligently practiced eugenics. Under the auspices of the Eugenics Commission of North Carolina, 7,686 sterilizations had been performed since 1933 and about 5,000 of the sterilized persons had been black. These operations were justified by the commission as measures to prevent the reproduction of "mentally deficient persons."[35]

By mid-July 1973 an investigation of these practices, led by Edward M. Kennedy, was underway in the Senate. At first officials in HEW announced that in 1972 alone at least 16,000 women and 8,000 men had been sterilized by the federal government, and that 365 of them were under the age of 21.[36] But these figures were soon revised upward by Carl Shultz, director of HEW's Population Affairs Office, who estimated that in 1972 between 100,000 and 200,000 sterilizations had been funded by the federal government.[37] The widely publicized Kennedy hearings brought national attention to the government's complicity in these unlawful activities.[38]

Some strong reactions followed. For example, the Women's Coalition of Jackson, Mississippi, an organization composed of both black and white women, stated, "We feel that it is clear that the [Relf] girls were sterilized not for their own good but for the convenience of the social welfare system." Eva Clayton, a veteran champion of civil rights, put it more bluntly: "Whether by accident or design, family planning as it is now conceived is directed mainly toward reducing population growth among the poor, and primarily the black poor. The implication in this direction is genocide."[39]

Public response to the facts uncovered in the hearings led to the adoption in September of 1973 of new HEW regulations to prevent forced sterilization. However, by the end of October the Health Research Group in Washington, D.C., released a study that found that many of these practices continued. This report stated:

> Doctors in some cities are cavalierly subjecting women, most of them poor and black to surgical sterilization without explaining either potential hazards or alternate methods of birth control. . . . Many women were being subjected to sterilization methods that posed a higher degree of medical risk than other methods in use. "Informed consent" forms demanded of women by some hospitals were a farce in many cases. Doctors in some hospitals were "selling" irreversible sterilization operations to many women who had few children and were under psychological stress and might not be making rational decisions.[40]

The Emergence of the New Right

As poverty and welfare dependence proliferated, lower-middle-class and blue-collar constituencies mobilized to reverse the gains of the civil rights movement. One of the earliest efforts came in California in 1978, when citizens concerned about stagnating incomes managed to pass a statewide initiative, Proposition 13, that would severely restrict the growth of property taxes. Others states hastily passed similar laws.[41]

What was different about this new movement was that conservatism had historically been associated with prosperous Americans who limited their ideological concerns to economic issues; they were probusiness and antilabor. But in the rhetoric of the New Right, welfare issues were linked to issues that were not economic but cultural. According to Richard Viguerie, one of the four men who framed the ideology of the New Right, "We talk about issues that people care about, like gun control, abortion, taxes, and crime. Yes, they're emotional issues, but that's better than talking about capital formation."[42] According to the New Right, the proliferation of welfare recipients, out-of-wedlock births, and families without fathers showed that society was on the brink of a moral breakdown.

These ideas were not new; they had emerged at least a decade earlier in commentary on the social disorganization of blacks and the causal relationship between culture and behavior. What was different about the ideology of the New Right was that it placed the blame for these problems on the civil rights movement and the nascent feminist movement. This represented a major shift in conservative philosophy, which Barbara Ehrenreich characterized as follows: "Capitalism itself is moral, even 'Christian,' and works in the interest of the average 'middle American.' It is the attempts to interfere with it—from affirmative action to social welfare programs—which lead to trouble."[43]

The New Right's views on poverty and welfare dependency were strengthened by the work of two influential and conservative economists, who also happened to be African-American. The first was Thomas Sowell. In *Race and Economics* he compared the history of African-Americans with that of West Indians; the latter, he found, were more prosperous and better-educated and had a "more stable and patriarchal family life." In his historical analysis, he argued that although West Indians had also experienced slavery, since whites had made up only 10 percent of the population they had to permit some economic autonomy and self sufficiency among the slaves. Thus "the West Indian setting permitted and fostered more self-reliance, more economic experience, and more defiance of whites." The American slavery experience, on the other hand, undermined the former slave's self-reliance, which suffered a further damage with the mass migration of blacks from the rural South to the urban North. Unlike the nineteenth- and early twentieth-century migrants, the migrant blacks had flocked to cities that were losing entry-level jobs. Lacking skills and the self-confidence to compete with whites, they took what was available; according to Sowell, this was welfare, which only reinforced dependency.[44]

The second economist, Glen Loury, writing on the relationship between race, poverty, and welfare dependency, moved even further to the right. He argued not only that the black community should shift its focus away from government support, but also that black people had placed too much emphasis on race:

> For too many blacks, dedication to the cause of reform has been allowed to supplant the demand for individual accountability; race, and the historic crimes associated with it, has become the single lens through which to view social experience; the infinite potential of real human beings has been surrendered on the altar of protest.[45]

By the early 1980s several influential books on the subject of poverty and welfare dependence were expounding this New Right philosophy. Lawrence Mead, in *Beyond Entitlement*, argued that "the main problem with the welfare state is not its size, but its permissiveness."[46] In *The End of Equality*, Mickey Kaus asserted that "only work works" in breaking the cycle of poverty.[47] And Charles Murray, in

Losing Ground, argued that the poor had not changed, only the "rules had changed" with the expansion of social programs in the 1960s. The poor had not taken part in changing the rules, they had merely responded to more permissive expectations.[48] Since the poor were merely acting like pampered children in accepting the more indulgent policies, the most effective course of action would be to discipline them with punitive policies. Although many of the New Right arguments were not articulated in published form until the early 1980s, they had already been used by politicians to justify reductions in welfare programs that began in the 1970s.

Backlash: The Work Requirement and Benefit Reductions

A major source of income in America for poor mother-only families is the public transfer of funds. The two major programs in this area are AFDC and Survivors Insurance (SI). Welfare, as AFDC is usually called, is available to poor single mothers, and the average benefit level is rather low. Survivors Insurance is provided only to widowed mothers and is somewhat more generous. When Sheila Kammerman and Alfred Kahn analyzed family policies in fourteen industrialized countries, they found that the United States is unique in relying so heavily on welfare, in proportion to to assist mother-only families.[49]

In his 1986 State of the Union Address, President Reagan blamed welfare for the "breakdown of the family," stating that the "welfare culture" was responsible not only for female and child poverty but also for "child abandonment, horrible crimes, and deteriorating schools."[50] In the hope of initiating federal policies that would have more popularity among voters, the Reagan administration set itself three goals for reducing welfare costs: first, to eliminate or substantially reduce the federal role in AFDC and turn over more welfare responsibility to the states; second, to require all able-bodied mothers with no children under a specified age to register for work; and third, to eliminate the use of AFDC as a supplement to low wages.

During the Reagan administration Congress passed legislation that effectively reduced the welfare benefits by several methods:

1. basing the welfare grant on the applicant's income during the prior, rather than the current, month;
2. lowering the age of eligibility for a child from twenty-one to eighteen;
3. offering AFDC benefits to women pregnant with their first child only at the third trimester of pregnancy;
4. prohibiting AFDC payments to strikers and their families;
5. including a stepparent's income in the determination of eligibility for AFDC;

6. limiting benefit levels in the states by restricting them to 150 percent of the state's definition of "need."

In 1981 the Congress passed the Omnibus Budget Reconciliation Act, which had a particularly debilitating impact on poor women who had to rely on AFDC benefits to supplement what they could earn from a job. The Act terminated the right of AFDC recipients who were working to receive such benefits as cash supplements, food stamps, and Medicaid insurance, and made them ineligible for numerous other programs. Previously, in adding up employment income that would be counted against their welfare grant, women could disregard the first $30 plus one-third of their gross earnings, as well as their taxes, work expenses, and child care expenses. Now, under the new policy, the amount that could be claimed for work expenses was limited to $75 per month, and the period in which it was possible to disregard income from work was limited to the first four months of employment. Furthermore, funds to cover child care expenses were limited to a maximum of $160 per month per child—far less than the average national cost for child care.[51]

One of the crowning achievements for those trying to reform the welfare system came in 1988 when Congress passed a bill requiring all AFDC mothers to work. The idea of work for AFDC mothers had first appeared in the Work Incentives Program in 1967 and the infamous Talmadge amendments of 1971, which required mothers with school-age children to register for work and training. Sponsored by Senator Daniel Moynihan, who declared that it would "turn the welfare program upside down," the bill also appropriated over a billion dollars in federal funds to induce states to furnish "transitional" day care for the children of the working mothers and to provide Medicaid coverage for a year if the mother found work.[52]

The Reagan administration was successful in achieving its goal of reducing welfare benefits to single mothers and their children. The real value of welfare benefits, including the cash grant plus food stamps, for a family of four with no other income fell from $10,133 in 1972 to $8,374 in 1980 and to $7,657 in 1992. These figures represent a loss of 26 percent between 1972 and 1992. According to David Ellwood, the only social program that was not cut back during the Reagan years was Medicaid. In fact, Medicaid's eligibility categories were expanded, not, in Ellwood's view, because of any concern for poor single mothers, but in order to increase benefits for the elderly and the disabled.[53]

As welfare benefits plummeted, so did the quality of life for African-Americans in poverty. Between the early 1970s and the late 1980s the percentage of black families that had two parents fell from 63.4 to 40.6; the labor force participation rates of black high school dropouts also fell by 25 percentage points; and the percentage of newborn children whose mothers were unmarried increased from 35.1 to 62.6.[54]

From Matriarchs to Welfare Queens

During the 1960s black women were portrayed in the media as tough and efficient and as playing crucial roles in their families, though they were often disparaged for taking over the role of black fathers. By the late 1970s, however, the image of black women had been completely reconstructed in the media. In 1977 *Time* magazine announced the emergence of a menacing underclass in America's urban centers and described the values of this population as "often at odds with those of the majority—even the majority of the poor."[55] According to *Time*, the underclass produced a disproportionate number of juvenile delinquents, school dropouts, drug addicts, and welfare mothers. In the early 1980s, the *New Yorker* published a series of articles on the underclass by Ken Auletta, in which he defined the underclass as a group that suffers from "behavioral as well as income deficiencies" and "operates outside the mainstream of commonly accepted values." In describing members of this underclass he focused on street criminals, hustlers, drug addicts, and welfare mothers.[56] Although Auletta was not the first to use the term *underclass*, he is generally credited with shifting attention to the behavioral dimension; previously other social scientists had focused on particular geographical or residential areas and whether certain groups were in the "occupational mainstream."[57]

In 1983 and 1984 the *Chicago Tribune* ran a series, later published as a book, entitled *The American Millstone: An Examination of the Nation's Permanent Underclass*. To describe a segment of an underclass that is "mostly black and poor and hopelessly trapped" in the urban centers of the nation, it presented narratives that featured criminals, drug addicts, and welfare mothers. Two of the stories described welfare mothers. The first was Freddie Hopkins, a nineteen-year-old mother of two daughters, aged one and two.

> Freddie had never been married and the father of her daughters was a 21-year-old who had fathered at least eight other children in their North Lawndale neighborhood. Hopkins was taking birth control pills, but she still became pregnant. "Everybody else I knew was havin' babies, so I just went along." The young man was elated. "He say: 'Freddie! You pregnant with my baby?' And I say, 'No, I not.' I just didn't want to believe it. He put his head to my belly and listened and he say, 'Man, I done got me a son.'" Freddie had been a student at Marshall High School, but when her child was born she dropped out and with a child to support she applied for her

own welfare case. . . . In welfare culture, Freddie had become a woman, she was getting her own check.[58]

Another narrative featured Rosemary Gordon, twenty-five, the oldest of four children, whose father had died when she was eight.

> Rosemary was raised, at various times in her youth by each of her grand-mothers. When she was 17, Gordon dropped out of high school pregnant with her first child, a girl she named Samaria, who was now 8. Shortly after Samaria was born, Gordon joined mother and maternal grandmother on the welfare rolls. Two more children followed—Antwoin, now 3 and Laketa, now 1. Gordon attributes the birth of her first three children to the fact that she did not take birth control pills according to schedule. According to Gordon, all of her children have the same father, a man who has been married to someone else for eight years. Gordon, who was only seven months preg-nant at the time, remembers feeling labor pains one morning shortly after she awoke. But she did not tell anyone. She went about her normal routine, "Then I went to the bathroom, and as I stood up, he just slid out." Roosevelt McGee was born in a toilet. Gordon recalls she looked up to find her mother standing in the bathroom doorway—gasping, with her hand up over her mouth. "Girl!" the mother said. "You done had the baby in the bathroom!"[59]

No one could argue that these two stories were not a fair representation of the lives of most black welfare mothers. In fact all the narratives in the series were chosen to highlight the most vile and offensive aspects of life in the nation's poor inner cities. And the phrase in the book's title, "permanent underclass," suggested that the problems in the lives of these poor people may never be solved, because nothing society can do will *really* make a difference.

In 1986 a similar series appeared in the *Washington Post*, written by Leon Dash, a veteran journalist who conducted seventeen months of intensive interviews in the black community of Washington Highlands, talking with adults who had be-come parents while still teenagers.[60] In one story, Dash was conducting an interview with Charmaine Ford when they were interrupted by a tapping on the apartment door:

> There stood one of Charmaine's neighbors, a six-year-old girl, her cheeks stained with tears, crying so hard that her pigtails shook. . . . Sobbing, the girl said that she had been taking care of her seven-month-old sister since her mother had left early that morning. It was then eight-thirty in the eve-ning. The weeping girl said her mother had telephoned, but only to say that she was spending the night out. Before hanging up, the mother told the girl

to fix a bottle of formula for the baby. Confused, unsure how to make the formula, the girl had panicked.[61]

The images presented in these newspaper stories were powerfully reinforced by a Bill Moyers television special entitled *The Vanishing Family: Crisis in Black America,* which was broadcast on January 26, 1986. One part of the program was an interview with Timothy, a young man of about twenty who had fathered six children by several different women who were all receiving welfare. When asked why he felt no responsibility to support them, he said, "That's on them . . . I ain't gonna let no woman stand in the way of my pleasures."

In view of this sustained media coverage, it is not surprising that the 1990 General Social Survey (GSS) from the University of Chicago's National Opinion Research Center found that 78 percent of white Americans believed that blacks prefer living on welfare. Such reports may explain why the derogatory term "welfare queen" is applied to black, but never white, women who receive welfare. As president, one of Ronald Reagan's favorite anecdotes was the story of a welfare queen living in Chicago with "80 names, 30 addresses, 12 social security cards and a tax free income of over $150,000."[62] Clearly, the "queen" epithet expresses attitudes that are not simply antiwelfare but racist, for it has been used against black professional women as well. The law professor Lani Guinier, President Clinton's first choice for civil rights enforcement chief, was labeled a "quota queen" in a *Wall Street Journal* headline during her confirmation fight.[63] Surgeon General Dr. Jocelyn Elders was frequently called a "condom queen" in the press when she argued that young people be educated to use condoms in the fight against AIDS.

Declining Age Structure and the Reproduction of Poverty

The popular news media seldom asked questions about what had happened in poor black communities to create its current level of social isolation from mainstream values and behavior. Had things always been this bad? If not, what could explain the dramatic changes that had occurred in recent years? Scholars who had observed the disintegration of ghetto communities over the years offered various answers. William J. Wilson stated:

> In the earlier years, the black middle and working classes were confined by restrictive covenants to communities also inhabited by the lower class, and their very presence provided stability to inner city neighborhoods and reinforced and perpetuated mainstream patterns of behavior. This is not the situation of the 1980s. Today's ghetto neighborhoods are populated almost exclusively by the most disadvantaged segments of the black urban community. . . . Included in this group are individuals who lack training or skills

and either experience long term unemployment or are not part of the labor force, individuals engaged in street criminal activities and other forms of aberrant behavior, and families who experience long-term spells of poverty and/or welfare dependency.[64]

What this analysis overlooks is a crucial change in the age structure of African-Americans. While the birthrate among older, better-educated, and married black couples has declined sharply, the birthrate among black women in younger age cohorts has risen and recently stabilized. As a consequence, there has been a disproportionate increase in the number of births to unmarried black women. As the fertility gap between poor blacks and upwardly mobile blacks has widened, so has the difference in values and behaviors between socially isolated black neighborhoods and more stable black communities. Media attention is rarely given to the stable communities, however, and the behaviors of the poor are often generalized to apply to the majority of African-Americans.

Linda Burton's comprehensive explanation of how multigenerational patterns of early childbearing create age-condensed families enhances our understanding of why recent research conducted on "shared parenting" contradicts the findings of earlier studies.[65] For example, in the 1970s Sheppard Kellam and his colleagues found that children raised by single mothers and grandmothers did nearly as well as children raised by two parents.[66] But a recent study conducted by Lindsay Chase-Lansdale and her associates found that the quality of parenting was lower in multigenerational families than in single-mother families.[67] Although Chase-Lansdale's study focused on the diffusion of parental responsibility between mother and grandmother and the Kellam research evaluated mental health outcomes in children, it seems clear that in age-condensed families the role conflict between mother and grandmother would be exacerbated by the fact that they are closer in age. And a young single mother's lack of emotional maturity would contribute to higher levels of stress, anxiety, and depression as she undertakes the parental role.

The stress experienced by residents of ghetto neighborhoods is increased by their high incidence of crime and victimization. Wilson reported that in 1980 the Robert Taylor Homes public housing project, which housed just one-half of 1 percent of Chicago's population, was the site of "11 percent of the city's murders, 9 percent of its rapes, and 10 percent of its aggravated assaults." He adds that over a nine-week period the following year at Cabrini-Green, another Chicago housing project, "10 Cabrini-Green residents were murdered [and] 35 were wounded by gunshots, including random sniping."[68]

Some of the ambivalence concerning marriage and family among African-Americans has be attributed to the child-rearing patterns found among single black mothers living in poor neighborhoods. According to Phyllis Harrison-Ross and

Barbara Wyden, the prolonged absence of men in some of these lower-income, single-mother households is a contributing factor in the maladaptive child-rearing patterns that are found there. On the one hand, the black mothers urge their sons to "Hurry and grow up and take care of me the way your father never did. Be the man of the house." The other part of the double message is "You better grow up gentle and obedient and do everything I tell you."[69] As a result of receiving these mixed messages from their mothers, young black men develop a cool style that can be described as "emotionless, smooth, fearless, and aloof." This results in a marked lack of emotional intimacy between black males and females, preventing them from establishing "strong, committed, and authentic relationships."[70]

Yet another explanation for the proliferation of age-condensed mother-only families is delineated in Elijah Anderson's vivid descriptions of the "sexual games" young men and women played in the poverty neighborhood he studied. In Anderson's participant observation study, the young women dream of marriage, and the young men exploit their fantasies in order to gain sexual favors. The games he describes are not surprising, since poverty researchers have known for years that the poor hold the same ideal norms and values as the middle class.[71] For example, Lee Rainwater argued that when circumstances militate against their achieving the middle-class ideal, the poor develop a set of alternative norms to guide their social behavior.[72]

In the 1980s poverty researchers noted that the set of adaptive norms for blacks residing in inner-city neighborhoods was changing. Although there was an increase in the schooling of white and black teenagers and little increase in the incidence of out-of-wedlock births, "the labor market involvement of black women who had either dropped out of high school or had an out-of-wedlock birth had declined by the 1980s, while their reliance on AFDC had become much greater."[73] The increasing reliance on welfare by young black mothers corresponded with the erosion of opportunities for young black males. For example, in 1970 only 9 percent of young black males between the ages of twenty and twenty-four were neither employed nor in school, but by 1990 that figure had risen to 28 percent for black males.[74]

In the words of one counselor who appeared on Bill Moyer's television special, *The Vanishing Family*, these young people are "on a trip without a road map." The road map that is usually provided to young people consists of parents who are mature and caring and have access to an opportunity structure that allows them to serve as role models for their children. Not surprisingly, many young people in ghetto communities—where everyone is affected by danger and insecurity—have single mothers who experience high levels of stress, anxiety, and depression, all of which lead to inconsistent parenting. In such conditions, it is difficult for mothers to provide the kind of discipline and affection that children and adolescents desperately need.[75] And in too many cases fathers are not on the scene to insist, by word or example, that their sons accept responsibility for the children they conceive. Thus while the young women may dream of marriage, the reality is that AFDC has replaced a husband as the primary means of financial support in the poorest black neighborhoods.

Never-Married Black Mothers: The Truly Disadvantaged

When Christopher Jencks examined the family formation patterns of a group he classified as the "reproductive underclass," he found that even though teenage motherhood was on the decline, there were increasing numbers of unmarried mothers. The proportion of all children born to unmarried mothers was rising, among both whites and blacks. Jencks concluded by noting that the practice of having children independent of marriage may be spreading to all levels of American society.[76]

During the late 1980s, some important changes were noted among the marital status of single mothers. Whereas divorced or separated mothers began to level off, the number of never-married mothers continued to grow. Figure 8.1 compares the increases in the number of black and white never-married mothers from 1970 to 1990. Even though blacks comprise only about 12 percent of the nation's population, the number of never-married black mothers is greater than the number of white never-married mothers, and these figures are continuing to increase. By 1993, 58 percent of black mother-only families were comprised of never-married mothers and that figure for whites was 22 percent. Not surprisingly, in that same year, 50 percent of all mother-only families that fell below the poverty line were African-Americans.[77]

In the late 1980s the overall percentage of children in mother-only families began to level off, and women who had never married replaced women who were divorced or separated as the group most vulnerable to persistent poverty. By 1993, approximately 50 percent of all black mother-only families, 30 percent of all white families, and 25 percent of all nonwhite Hispanic families would fall below the poverty line.[78] It was becoming clear that whereas the marriage rate had declined modestly for white women, it had declined substantially for black women, with the poorest among them being the most likely never to marry. And the increasing separation of marriage and childbearing among all groups was most pronounced among African-Americans.[79]

There were some marked changes in the proportion by race of children under eighteen living in both one-parent and two-parent families between 1989 and 1993. In all racial groups, the proportion of children living with either never-married or divorced mothers increased, but the larger increase was with never-

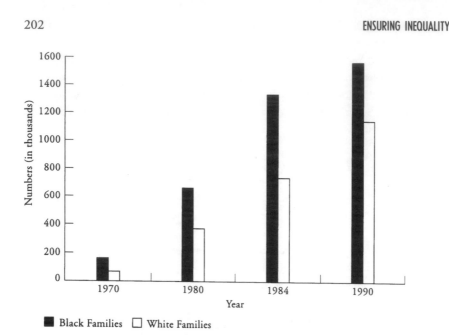

FIGURE 8.1   Number of families headed by never-married mothers, 1970, 1980, 1984, 1990. (From Department of Commerce, Bureau of the Census, *Household and Family Characteristics*, Current Population Reports [1984], ser. P-20, no. 398; Current Population Reports [1990], ser. P-20, no. 447 [Washington, D.C.: Government Printing Office, 1984, 1990], tables D and H)

married mothers. In all racial groups there were decreases in the proportion children living with widowed mothers; among separated mothers there were decreases for blacks and Hispanics, but increases for white mothers.[80]

Figure 8.2 categorizes recent census data on the living arrangements of black children by the marital status of the mothers. What this table confirms is not only that the greatest increases were in the proportion of children living with never-married mothers, but 58 percent, 39 percent, and 22 percent of all mother-only African-American, Hispanic, and white families, respectively, are headed by a never-married mother. These figures are particularly alarming in view of the fact that these mothers experience a greater vulnerability to long-term poverty.

In an effort to understand further how the mother's marital status relates to more persistent poverty, my colleagues and I analyzed the differences between never-married and ever-married (divorced, separated, widowed) mothers residing in Chicago poverty neighborhoods.[81] The most striking differences between these two groups are that a much higher proportion of the ever-married mothers had never received welfare assistance when they were children—67.4 percent compared with 48.8 precent of never-married mothers. Conversely, never-married mothers

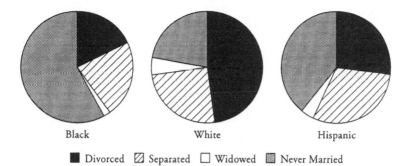

Black   White   Hispanic

■ Divorced ☒ Separated ☐ Widowed ▨ Never Married

FIGURE 8.2   Percentage of children living with mother only, by marital status and race, 1993. (From Department of Commerce, Bureau of the Census, *Population Characteristics*, Current Population Reports [1984], ser. P-20, no. 398; Current Population Reports, ser. P-20, no. 447 [Washington, D.C.: Government Printing Office, 1993], 40, 44, 48)

had received welfare while growing up at almost two and a half times the rate for ever-married mothers.[82] In addition, a higher percentage of ever-married mothers grew up with a father in the household or came from two-parent families.

Table 8.2 utilizes recent data to compare divorced, separated, widowed, and never-married African-American mothers on such characteristics as age, education, employment status, area of residence, and whether or not they reside in public housing. Predictably, the never-married mothers are the youngest and most likely not to have completed high school. More problematic, however, are the disproportionate number of never-married-mothers who live in the central cities and have four or more children. In addition, 61 percent are not working, compared with 39 and 50 percent of the divorced and separated mothers, respectively.

The characteristics associated with black never-married mothers are as follows:

1. They have the weakest attachment to the labor force.
2. They are more likely to be on welfare and therefore to have the lowest median income.
3. They have the highest proportion of teenaged parents.
4. They are more likely to live in public housing or in neighborhoods with the highest concentration of poverty, and therefore likely to experience greater social isolation than divorced or separated mothers.[83]

These are the traits generally associated with the so-called underclass.

What this analysis begins to demonstrate is how the marital status of the mother affects the reproduction of poverty. The black mothers residing in the poorest neighborhoods experience the highest levels of social isolation because these communities have the highest proportion of male unemployment and its conse-

Table 8.2 Living Arrangements of Black Children under 18 Years,
by Marital Status and Selected Characteristics of Mother: March 1993

	Divorced	Separated	Widowed	Never Married
Number of siblings in household	100	100	100	100
None	24	13	27	26
One	32	32	29	30
Two	22	27	23	21
Three	11	14	4	12
Four	4	7	16	7
Five or more	6	6	1	4
Age of head	100	100	100	100
15–19	0	1	0	6
20–24	1	6	1	22
25–30	7	19	3	26
30–34	25	25	7	14
35 and over	67	49	89	22
Education of head	100	100	100	100
Under 12 years	21	29	18	36
High school only	43	43	47	43
Some college (no degree or associate degree)	28	23	23	18
College or more	8	5	12	3
Employment status of head	100	100	100	100
Full-time	52	38	30	30
Part-time	9	12	12	9
Nonworking	39	50	58	61
Area of residence	100	100	100	100
Central cities	61	55	53	64
Outside central cities	25	27	21	23
Outside metropolitan areas	14	18	26	13
Percent of black female-headed families residing in public housing	24	34	2	35

SOURCE: Dept. of Commerce, Census Bureau, *Population Characteristics*, Current
Population Reports, series P-20, March 1993, table 6 (Washington, 1993), p. 44.

quence—father-absent, welfare-dependent families. If we extend the logic of
intergenerational continuity to marriage and welfare patterns, we can predict that
poor mothers reared on welfare without fathers in the home will be influenced by
these environmental conditions: When they reach adulthood, they will be more
likely to perceive public assistance as a more attainable means of support than
marriage.

And this perception would be accurate. With limited community resources like jobs and quality education, the poorest mothers have had sustained exposure to behaviors that have not only become normative but are reinforced by the constraints imposed by the ghetto environment. Poor mothers who try to pursue mainstream values such as marriage and a job but are thwarted would predictably modify their behavior over time. Such modifications are clearly evident in the fact that the youngest black mothers have the highest reliance on welfare and the weakest attachment to the labor force.

Conclusion

During the 1970s the economic situation for poor black single-parent families grew worse, and poverty became increasingly concentrated in black neighborhoods. In 1976, the year of the Bicentennial celebration, a report released by the Department of Commerce indicated that the wealthiest fifth of American families received about 40 percent of all income, whereas the poorest fifth received about 5 percent. Not surprisingly, the black mother-only families were overrepresented in the poorest fifth. Despite the Great Society's poverty programs and the various advances for women made in the 1960s, poor black families have experienced a relapse.

Economists who have evaluated the general growth in poverty rates and father-absent families during this period have identified several factors in the relapse:

1. The stagnation of the economy after 1973;
2. An increase in marital dissolution;
3. An increase in independent living by adolescent mothers;
4. The increase in labor market participation of married women may have improved the economic situation of two-parent families;
5. Shifts in occupational structure and the mismatch between the better jobs and the education of the urban poor.

As the poverty rates among single black mothers increased, the government embarked on a campaign to reduce the fertility of blacks. These efforts did not attract nationwide interest until the summer of 1973, when the Southern Poverty Law Center filed suit on behalf of the Relf sisters, two black teenagers who had been surgically sterilized without their knowledge or consent. Once this story broke, others began to appear in quick succession. By mid-July of 1973 an investigation was under way in the Senate, led by Edward M. Kennedy. Final estimates were that federal government funds had paid for between 100,000 and 200,000 sterilizations in 1972. The Kennedy hearings received national media coverage and by September of 1973 HEW adopted regulations to prevent forced sterilization.

As black poverty and welfare dependence spread, various lower middle-class and blue-collar constituencies began to attach the gains of the civil rights movement. Whereas conservatism in America had historically been focused on economic issues, the conservative rhetoric of the New Right linked welfare to various cultural issues such as abortion, school prayer, pornography, and "family values." It claimed that the increase in welfare recipients, out-of-wedlock births, and families without fathers showed that society was on the brink of a moral breakdown. These problems were hardly new; what was new was the attempt to blame them on the civil rights and feminist movements.

The philosophy of the New Right lay behind many of the Reagan administration's legislative proposals to reduce welfare benefits. An early effort was included in the Omnibus Budget Reconciliation Act of 1981. Under this Act, AFDC recipients who were working could no longer receive cash supplements, food stamps, and Medicaid insurance. Recipients were likewise declared ineligible for numerous other programs. In 1988 Congress passed a bill requiring all AFDC mothers to work. Sponsored by Senator Daniel Moynihan, this legislation also appropriated over a billion dollars in federal funds to induce states to furnish "transitional" day care for the children of the working mothers and to offer Medicaid coverage for a year if the mother found work.

Beginning in the late 1970s the image of black women presented in the media underwent a dramatic change; the tough and efficient matriarch was replaced by hapless mother on welfare. In the early 1980s national interest in a "permanent underclass" was stirred by a series of articles in the *New Yorker*, reports in the *Chicago Tribune* and the *Washington Post*, and a Bill Moyers television special. Given the sustained media coverage of the worst aspects of life in urban ghettos, it is not surprising that the 1990 GSS found that 78 percent of white Americans believed that blacks preferred living on welfare. It became common to hear black welfare recipients disparaged as "welfare queens," a phrase never used against white women. Even black professional women were targeted: The law professor Lani Guinier was called "the quota queen" and Dr. Joycelyn Elders, the Surgeon General, "the condom queen."

Due to the sharp decline in the births to better-educated, married black couples, younger black women were having a disproportionate share of all new births, and this accelerated changes in the age structure of African-Americans. The disproportionate increase in the number of births to unmarried black women contributed to their ever-greater proportion among all the new births occurring outside marriage. As the poorest African-Americans have become more isolated in urban ghettos and the difference in fertility between poor and upwardly mobile blacks have widened, so have the differences in values and behavior between poor and affluent blacks.

In the 1980s, poverty researchers noted that the adaptive norms for blacks residing in inner city neighborhoods were changing. Despite an increase in the schooling of both white and black teenagers and little increase in the incidence of out-of-wedlock births, fewer black women who were high-school dropouts or un-wed mothers had jobs, and more of them relied on AFDC for support. The increasing reliance on welfare by young black mothers corresponded to the erosion of opportunities for young black males.

In the late 1980s, as the overall percentage of children in mother-only families began to level off, mothers who had never married, rather than those who were divorced or separated, became the most vulnerable to persistent poverty. Policy analysts were concerned to find that whereas the marriage rate had declined modestly for white women, it had declined substantially for black women, and that it was the poorest black women who were more likely never to marry. By 1993 the largest proportion of black children living in single-parent households were living with a never married mother.

This situation is troublesome because never-married mothers have the characteristics associated with an urban "underclass": they have the weakest attachment to the labor force, are more likely to be on welfare, having the lowest median income, they have the highest proportion of teenaged parents, and they are more likely to live in public housing or neighborhoods with the highest poverty concentration, and therefore likely to experience more social isolation.

Notes

1. Vernon E. Jordan, Jr., "Blacks and the Bicentennial," speech given at the annual National Conference on Social Welfare June 13, 1976, published in the *Social Welfare Forum* (New York: Columbia University Press, 1977), 77.

2. Office of Federal Statistical Policy and Standards, Department of Commerce, *Social Indicators, 1976* (Washington, D.C: Government Printing Office, 1977). The January 1978 issue of *Annals of the American Academy of Political and Social Science* was devoted to an analysis of the volume.

3. The official poverty line index was formulated by the Social Security Administration in 1964. In times of economic growth, some economists have argued, this index neglects the rising real incomes of the nonpoor, thereby overlooking the a greater gap between the standard of living of the poor and the nonpoor. See, for example, Joan Huber, "Political Implications of Poverty Definitions," in *The Sociology of American Poverty*, ed. Joan Huber and H. Paul Chalfant (Cambridge, Mass.: Schenkman, 1974); W. Korpi, "Approaches to the Study of the Poverty in the United States: Critical Notes from a European Perspective," in *Poverty and Public Policy: An Evaluation of Social Science Research*, ed. Vincent T. Covello (Cambridge, Mass.: Schenkman, 1980).

4. The War on Poverty did not end poverty in America, and it was not designed to

do so. Only $800 was appropriated for its first year of operation, and the programs were not designed to redistribute wealth or fundamentally restructure the economy. See S. M. Miller and Martin Rein, "The War on Poverty: Perspectives and Prospects," in *Poverty as a Public Issue*, ed. Ben Seligman (New York: Free Press, 1965), 272–320.

5. Beth B. Hess, "New Faces of Poverty," *American Demographics* (May 1983): 26.

6. Robert C. Woods. A copy of his speech was obtained from the Department of Health and Human Services.

7. Kevin Phillips, *The Emerging Republican Majority* (New Rochelle, N.Y.: Arlington House, 1969).

8. For an appraisal of race and ethnicity during the 1970s, see Andrew M. Greeley, *Ethnicity in the United States* (New York: Wiley, 1974); Thomas Sowell, "Ethnicity in a Changing America," *Daedalus*, 107(Winter 1978) 213–38; William L. Yancey Eugene D. Erickson, Richard N. Juliani, "Emergent Ethnicity: A Review and Reformation," *American Sociological Review* 41(June 1976) 391–403; For an evaluation of the impact of the 1965 Immigration Reform Act, see Elliott Abrams and Frankin S. Abrams, "Immigration Policy—Who Gets in and Why?" *Public Interest*, 38(Winter 1975): 3–29.

9. Census Bureau, *Current Population Reports*, series P-20, *Persons of Spanish Origin in the United States March, 1977*: (Washington, D.C.: Government Printing Office, 1977).

10. For a discussion with the INS commissioner on the basis of these estimates and their accuracy, see "Why the Tide of Illegal Aliens Keeps Rising," an interview with Leone J. Castillo, *U.S. News & World Report*, February 20, 1978, 33–35.

11. Domestic Council Committee on Illegal Aliens, *Preliminary Report* (Washington, D.C.: Government Printing Office, 1976), 2.

12. Albert W. Niemi, Jr., "The Impact of Recent Civil Rights Laws: Relative Improvement in Occupational Structure, Earnings and Income by Non-whites, 1960–1970," *American Journal of Economics and Sociology* 33 (April 1974): 137–44.

13. William H. Sewell, "Social Mobility and Social Participation," *Annals* 435 (January 1978): 230. See also Robert M. Hauser and David Featherman, *The Process of Stratification: Trends and Analyses* (New York: Academic Press, 1977); Richard F. Curtis and Elton F. Jackson, *Inequality in American Communities* (New York: Academic Press, 1977).

14. Jo Freeman, *The Politics of Women's Liberation* (New York: Longman, 1975), 38.

15. If the readership of *Ms.* magazine was any indicator, the race and class composition of the movement was asymmetrical. An analysis of 200,000 subscribers to *Ms.* in 1973 found that nine out of ten were college-educated and two out of three who worked full-time held either professional, technical, or managerial positions.

16. Quoted in Toni Morrison, "What the Black Woman Thinks about Women's Lib," *New York Times Magazine*, August 22, 1971, 15.

17. Michael Harrington, *The Other America: Poverty in the United States* (1962; New York: Collier, 1993), 14–15.

18. Harold R. Kerbo, "Characteristics of the Poor: A Continuuing Focus in Social Research," *Sociology and Social Research* 65 (April 1981): 323–31.

19. The word *poverty* was dropped from the title in 1975, when interest in poverty was waning.

20. Department of Commerce, *Social Indicators, 1976.*

21. John D. Kasarda, "Jobs, Migration, and Emerging Urban Mismatches," in *Urban Change and Poverty*, ed. Michael G. H. McGeary and Laurence E. Lynn, (Washington, D.C.: Natonal Academy Press, 1988), 174–75.

22. "Aid to Families with Dependent Children, 1977," in *Recipient Characteristics Study*, U. S. Department of Health and Human Services, Social Security Administration, Office of Policy (Washington, D.C.: Governmental Printing office, 1980).

23. Kristin Moore and Steven B. Caldwell, "Out-of-Wedlock Pregnancy and Child-bearing," Working paper no. 999–02, Urban Institute, 1976.

24. William J. Wilson, *The Declining Significance of Race: Blacks and Changing American Institutions* (Chicago: University of Chicago Press, 1978), 152, 150.

25. Diana Pearce, "The Feminization of Poverty: Women, Work and Welfare," *Urban and Social Change Review* 11 (Winter-Summer 1978): 35.

26. Census Bureau, *Current Population Reports*, series P-60, *Characteristics of the Population Below the Poverty Level, 1982*, (Washington, D.C.: Government Printing Office, 1984); Martha S. Hill, "The Changing Nature of Poverty," *Annals of the American Academy of Political and Social Science*, 479 (May 1985): 31–47.

27. For explanations of the movement of married women into the labor force, see William Butz and Michael Ward, "The Emergence of Countercyclical U.S. Fertility," *American Economic Review* 69 (June 1970): 318–328; Valerie Kincade Oppenheimer, *The Female Labor Force in the United States*, Population Monograph Series no. 5 (Berkeley: Institute of International Studies, 1970); Hill, " Changing Nature of Poverty," 38–39. For interpretations of how the labor force participation of women influenced marriage rates, see Samuel H. Preston and Alan Thomas Richards,"The Influence of Women's Work Opportunities on Marriage Rates," *Demography* 12 (May 1975): 209–22; Alan Friedman, "The United States Marriage Market," *Journal of Political Economy* 82(March–April 1974): S34–S53; Andrew Cherlin, "Postponing Marriage: The Influence of Young Women's Work Expectations," *Journal of Marriage and the Family* 42 (May 1980): 355–65; For clarification of the transformation of the economy, see Frank Levy, *Dollars and Dreams: The Changing American Income Distribution* (New York: Russell Sage Foundation, 1987); Sar A. Levitan and Isaac Shapiro, *Working but Poor: America's Contradiction* (Baltimore: Johns Hopkins University Press, 1987). There are several good essays in Michael G. H. McGeary and Laurence E. Lynn, eds., *Urban Change and Poverty* (Washington, D.C.: National Academy Press, 1988).

28. Quoted in Charles B. Nam and Susan O. Gustavus, *Population: The Dynamic Aspects of Demographic Change* (Boston: Houghton Mifflin, 1976), 135.

29. This penchant for targeting the poor had historical antecedents, which can be found in an article written by Margaret Sanger in the American Birth Control League's journal in 1919; she identifies the major objective of birth control as "more children from the fit, less from the unfit." It should be noted that by 1922 Sanger had dropped her ties with the eugenic movement and then stated that "birth control is essentially an education for women." Margaret Sanger, *The Pivot of Civilization* (New York: Brentano, 1922), 254. An excellent discussion can be found in Linda Gordon, *Women's Body, Women's Right: Birth Control in America* (New York: Penguin, 1976): 280–82.

30. Norman B. Ryder and Charles Westoff, *Reproduction in the United States: 1965* (Princeton: Princeton University Press, 1971), 114–130.

31. Quote from the commission's report in Nam and Gustavus, *Population*, 142.

32. Quoted in Gordon, *Woman's Body, Woman's Right* 332–33.

33. For details of the Relf family case, see *Poverty Law Report* (Montgomery, Ala.: Southern Poverty Law Center, September 1973).

34. Sam Nesbit, administrator of the Aiken County hospital, approved the reasoning and the practice of Dr. Pierce. See Nancy Hicks, *New York Times*, August 1, 1973.

35. Harold X, "Forced Sterilization Pervades South," *Muhammad Speaks*, October 10, 1975, 2.

36. For the coverage of the Kennedy hearings, see the *Christian Science Monitor*, July 13, 1973,

37. Angela Davis points out that during Hitler's Germany 250,000 sterilizations were carried out under the Nazis' Hereditary Law, and she asks, "Is it possible that the record of the Nazis, throughout the years of their reign, may have almost equaled the U.S. government funded sterilizations in the space of a single year?"; *Women, Race and Class* (New York: Random House, 1981), 218.

38. See Jack Slater, "Sterilization: Newest Threat to the Poor," *Ebony*, October 1973, 150-56. This article was one of the features having the greatest impact in the black community.

39. Quoted in Herbert Aptheker, "Sterilization, Experimentation and Imperialism," *Political Affairs* 52(January, 1974): 40–41.

40. Quoted in Aptheker, "Sterilization, Experimentation and Imperialism," 41.

41. Thomas Edsall and Mary Edsall argue that the New Right coalition "articulated a public philosophy directed at drawing into the Republican party citizens with the kinds of economic, racial, and social concerns that could be addressed in terms of a free market doctrine"; *Chain Reaction: The Impact of Race, Rights, and Taxes on American Politics* (New York: Norton, 1991), 138.

42. Quoted in Connie Paige, *The Right-to-Lifers: Who They Are, How They Operate, Where They Get Their Money* (New York: Summit, 1983), 135.

43. Fred Block, Richard A. Cloward, Barbara Ehrenreich, and Frances Fox Piven, *The Mean Season: The Attack on the Welfare State* (New York: Random House, 1987), 164.

44. Thomas Sowell, *Race and Economics* (New York: Longman, 1975), 33.

45. Glen Loury, "Race and Poverty: The Problem of Dependency in a Pluralistic Society," paper presented at the Working Seminar on the Family and American Welfare Policy, American Enterprise Institute, Washington, D.C., November 1986.

46. Lawrence Mead, *Beyond Entitlement: The Social Obligation of Citizenship* (New York: Free Press, 1985), 3.

47. Mickey Kaus, *The End of Equality*, (New York: Basic Books, 1992,) chap. 9. See also "Welfare and Work: A Symposium," *New Republic*, October 6, 1986, 23.

48. Charles Murray, *Losing Ground: American Social Policy 1950–1980* (New York: Basic Books, 1984). For more on similar arguments advanced for the New Right philosophy, see George Gilder, *Wealth and Poverty* (New York: Bantam, 1982); Kaus, *End of Equality*.

49. Sheila Kamerman and Alfred Kahn, eds., *Family Policy: Government and Families in Fourteen Countries* (New York: Columbia University Press, 1978).

50. President Ronald Reagan's State of the Union Address, *New York Times* 6 (January 12, 1986); A26.

51. For a description of the changes and an analysis of their impact, see U.S. Congress, Congressional Budget Office, *Major Legislative Changes in Human Resource Programs since January 1981*, staff memorandum, August 1983; John L. Palmer and Isabel V. Sawhill, *The Reagan Experiment* (Washington, D.C.: Urban Institute, 1982), chap. 12; Rosemary C. Sarri, "The Impact of Federal Policy Change on Low-Income Working Women," in *Women, Households, and the Economy*, ed. Lourdes Beneria and Catherine R. Stimpson (New Brunswick: Rutgers University Press, 1987).

52. Jason DeParle, "Using Books instead of Brooms to Escape Welfare," *New York Times*, September 9, 1991, A-1. According to this article, in 1991 about 510,000 welfare families were participating in this program—33 percent in basic education, 11 percent in postsecondary school, 16 percent in learning a technical skill, 15 percent in other miscellaneous education, 11 percent in job search, and 4 percent in an actual work setting. For a rigorous evaluation of these workfare programs, see Judith M. Gueron and Edward Pauly, *From Welfare to Work* (New York: Russell Sage Foundation, 1991).

53. David T. Ellwood, *Poor Support: Poverty in the American Family* (New York: Basic Books, 1988), 106.

54. Jill Quadagno, *The Color of Welfare* (New York: Oxford University Press, 1994), 176.

55. *Time* 110 (August 29, 1977): 14–27.

56. Ken Auletta, "The Underclass: Part ," *New Yorker*, November 1981), 105. See also special issue, *Time* 110 (August 29, 1977): 14–27.

57. Other social scientists described this population as residing in particular geographical and residential areas. Isabel Sawhill described it as "people who live in neighborhoods where welfare dependency, female-headed families, male joblessness, and dropping out of high school are all common occurrences"; *Challenge to Leadership: Economic and Social Issues for the Next Decade* (Washington, D.C.: Urban Institute, 1988). William J. Wilson likewise depicts the underclass as poor people, mostly black, who live in urban ghettos and who are "outside the mainstream of the American occupational system"; *The Truly Disadvantaged: The Inner City, the Underclass, and Public Policy* (Chicago: University of Chicago Press, 1987), 8. See also Frank Levy for a definition based on persistent poverty; "How Big is the American Underclass?" working paper 0090–1, Urban Institute, 1977. See also Erol R. Ricketts and Isabel Sawhill for a definition based on geographic and behavioral criteria; "Defining and Measuring the Underclass," *Journal of Policy Analysis and Management* 7 (Winter 1988). Mary Jo Bane and Paul A. Jargowsky have done descriptive work on the underclass based on a spatial concentration of poverty definition; "Urban Poverty: Basic Questions Concerning Prevalence, Growth, and Dynamics," in *Inner-city Poverty in the U.S.*, ed. Michael McGeary and Laurence Lynn (Washington, D.C.: National Academy Press, 1990). See also Martha Van Haitsma, "A Contextual Definition of the Underclass," *Focus* 12 (Spring Summer 1989), 27–32; Sara McLanahan and Irwin Garfinkel, "Single Mothers,

the Underclass, and Social Policy," *Annals of the American Acadmey of Political and Social Science* 501 (January, 1989): 92–104.

58. *Chicago Tribune* staff, *The American Millstone: An Examination of the Nation's Permanent Underclass* (New York: Contemporary Books, 1986): 91–93.

59. *Chicago Tribune* staff, *American Millstone*, 123–125.

60. Leon Dash, *When Children Want Children* (New York: Morrow, 1989).

61. Dash, *When Children Want Children*, 37.

62. Edsall and Edsall, *Chain Reaction*, 148.

63. Ellen Joan Pollock, "Jilted by the President, Not-quite Nominee Try to Pick up the Pieces, " *Wall Street Journal* CCXXI, 122, Eastern Edition, 1, 14.

64. William J. Wilson, "Cycles of Deprivation and the Underclass Debate," *Social Service Review* 59 (December 1985): 242.

65. Linda Burton, "Teenage Childbearing as an Alternative Life-Course Strategy in Multigenerational Black Families" *Human Nature* 2 (1990): 123–43.

66. Sheppard G. Kellam, Margaret E. Ensminger, and R. J. Turner, "Family Structure and the Mental Health of Children," *Archives of General Psychiatry* 34 (1977): 1012–22.

67. P. Lindsay Chase-Lansdale, Jean Brooks-Gunn, and E. S. Zamsky, "Young African-American Multigenerational Families in Poverty: Quality of Other and Grandmothering," *Child Development*, 65 (April, 1994): 373–94.

68. William J. Wilson, "The Urban Underclass," in *Minority Report: What Has Happened to Blacks, Hispanics, American Indians, and Other Minorities*, ed. Leslie W. Dunbar (New York: Pantheon, 1984), 84.

69. Phyllis Harrison-Ross and Barbara Wyden, *The Black Child: A Parent's Guide* (New York: Peter Wyden, 1973), 237.

70. Richard Majors and Janet Mancini Billson, *Cool Pose: The Dilemmas of Black Manhood in America* (Lexington, Mass.: Lexington, 1992), 43. For a superb discussion on black speech patterns that bolster this "cool pose," see Thomas Kochman, "Toward an Ethnography of Black American Speech Behavior," In *Rappin' and Stylin' Out: Communication in Urban Black America*, ed. Thomas Kochman (Urbana: University of Illinois Press, 1972), 241–65. Another excellent essay in this volume is Claudia Kernan-Mitchell, "Signifying, Loud-Talking, and Marking," 315–36.

71. Elijah Anderson, *Streetwise: Race, Class, and Change in a Urban Community* (Chicago: University of Chicago Press, 1990).

72. Lee Rainwater, "Crucible of Identity: The Negro Lower Class Family" *Daedalus* 95 (Winter, 1966): 172–216.

73. Greg J. Duncan and Saul D. Hoffman, "Teenage Underclass Behavior and Subsequent Poverty: Have the Rules Changed?" in *The Urban Underclass*, ed. Christopher Jencks and Paul E. Peterson (Washington, D.C.: Brookings Institution, 1991), 15.

74. Finis Welch, "The Employment of Black Men," *Journal of Labor Economics* 8 (January 1990):526–74.

75. Oprah Winfrey's company bought the rights to Alex Kotlowitz's non-fiction book about a black single mother, *There Are No Children Here* (New York: Doubleday, 1991), and produced a dramatization for ABC television. The next day Orlando Patterson, a pro-

fessor at Harvard University, blasted Oprah in *New York Times* for her failure to report that in the book, the mother, LaJoe Rivers, shamefully neglected the needs of her two sons. He further stated, "Her child-rearing method alternated beween seductive overindulgence and maternal abuse—a ghetto pattern that contributes to youths' predatory, 'cool pose' sexuality and to the poisoned relations between the sexes." Patterson places the blame unfairly on the single mother without mentioning the environmental conditions that contribute to her parenting patterns. *New York Times*, OP-ED, November 30, 1993.

76. Christopher Jencks, "What is the Underclass and is it Growing?" *Focus* 12 (Spring-Summer, 1989): 14–27.

77. Department of Commerce, Census Bureau, *The Black Population in the United States: March 1993, 1994*. Current Population Reports, series P-20, no. 480 (Washington: Government Printing Office, 1994), 40, 44, 48.

78. Ibid. 40, 44, 48.

79. For analyses that have compared white and black marriage patterns, see Neil G. Bennett, David E. Bloom, and Patricia H. Craig, "The Divergence of Black and White Marriage Patterns," *American Journal of Sociology* 95 (November 1989): 692–722; Willard C. Rodgers and Arland Thornton, "Changing Patterns of First Marriage in the United States," *Demography* 22 (May 1985): 265–79; R. Schoen and J. R. Kluegel, "The Widening Gap in the Black and White Marriage Rates: The Impact of Population Composition and Differential Marriage Propensities," *American Sociological Review* 51 53 (December, 1988): 465–81; Arthur J. Norton and Jeanne E. Moorman, "Current Trends in Marriage and Divorce among American Women," *Journal of Marriage and the Family* 49 (February 1987): 3–14.

80. The increases in the proportion of children living in households with never-married mothers were as follows: 9.2 percent per thousand white children, 26.2 percent per thousand Hispanic children, and 39.7 percent per thousand African-American children; Department of Commerce, Census Bureau, *Household and Family Characteristics, March 1993*. Current Population Reports, series P-20, table 6 (Washington, D.C.: Government Printing Office, 1993), 40, 44, 48.

81. For more information on the research design and the sampling procedures and techniques, see Donna L. Franklin, Susan E. Smith, and William McMiller, "Correlates of Marital Status among African American Mothers in Chicago Neighborhoods of Concentrated Poverty," *Journal of Marriage and the Family* 57 (February 1995): 141–52.

82. When Susan Smith analyzed data from the National Longitudinal Survey of Youth—a random sample of girls of all races and ethnicities who were followed from age 14 to 28, she likewise found that the strongest indicator that a girl would live in a poor household at age 28 was having a nonmarital birth. Other powerful indicators were family structure, having a teen birth, and being African-American; "Public Policy and Economic Hardship: Determining where Individual Delusions Confront Structural Barriers," Ph.D. diss. University of Chicago, 1996. Frank Furstenberg and Jean Brooks-Gunn conducted a longitudinal analysis of teen mothers and found that those who were married at the time of the five-year follow-up study were more likely to have succeeded economically than those who never married; "Causes and Consequences of Teenage Pregnancy and Childbearing,"

in *Women's Life Cycle and Economic Insecurity* ed. M. N. Ozawa (New York: Praeger, 1988), 71–100.

83. For a study demonstrating the never-married mother's vulnerability to longer-term welfare receipt when compared with separated and divorced mothers, see Mary J. Bane and David T. Ellwood, "The Dynamics of Dependence: The Routes to Self-Sufficiency" report prepared for the assistant secretary for planning and evaluation, Department of Health and Human Services, 1983. For a comprehensive analysis of single black mothers living in poverty areas and their vulnerability to persistent poverty, see McLanahan and Garfinkel, "Single Mothers, the Underclass, and Social Policy."

CHAPTER NINE

WHERE DO WE GO FROM HERE?

The President keeps repeating the "dignity of work" idea. What dignity? Wages are the measure of dignity that society puts on a job. Wages and nothing else. There is no dignity in starvation. The problem is that our economic policies deny the dignity and satisfaction of self-sufficiency to millions of people—the millions who suffer in underpaid dirty jobs and still don't have enough to survive.   **Johnnie Tillmon,**

For several decades, the question of weakening marital ties among poor African-Americans has been central in discussions of the persistence of welfare dependence. The poorest and most economically unstable of these families have been described as having "behavioral deficiencies" in that many of them operate outside of mainstream values. For example, an evaluation survey completed in 1996 by the Jobs Opportunities and Basic Skills Training Program (JOBS) found that 84 percent of the AFDC mothers in Fulton County, Georgia, were never married to the biological fathers of their children. In addition, only 2 percent of the children's biological fathers lived in the same household, and only one-fifth of the children whose fathers lived outside of the household had seen their fathers at least once a week in the twelve months prior to the survey.[1]

The "situational" and "cultural" paradigms that have been utilized to explain this phenomenon are limited in that they cannot explain the differential effect societal changes have had on the family structure of black families over time. In addition, these paradigms do not make conceptual allowances for the feedback loops and patterns of interaction that could possibly link the mediating role of institutions, social networks, and kinship supports.

In the historical evolution of the African-American family structure from slavery to the present time, one can trace at least five cumulative factors contributing to its transformation over time: slavery; the northern migration (especially the loss of communal institutions); welfare policies; declining job opportunities for black men;

and isolation in neighborhoods of concentrated poverty. These distinct historical anomalies have been combined with the effects of changing societal values in America that have contributed to greater independence and autonomy for all women, more changes in traditional gender roles within the family and workplace, and more relaxed attitudes toward out-of-wedlock childbearing and single parenting. These overall changes have placed the traditional nuclear family under much greater strain and have predictably had the most devastating impact on African-American families.

The growth of single-mother families has stimulated much debate between liberals and conservatives over what, if anything, should be done to alleviate the economic insecurity of such families. Although a national opinion poll found that Americans overwhelmingly think it is better for children if one parent stays home, the electorate has clearly demonstrated an unwillingness to compensate mothers on welfare for doing so.[2] This reluctance was most clearly reflected in the passage of the Family Support Act (FSA) in 1988 and its nucleus, JOBS, a program that requires eligible recipients of AFDC to participate in education, job training, work experience, and/or job-search activities. The arguments presented in the legislative debates that led to the passage of the Act were driven by two convictions: First, single mothers were not a legitimate or conventional family form, and second, welfare mothers will be responsive only to coercion by the government.

The old debate on the consequences of family structure for black children, for the African-American community, and for the nation as a whole has been reopened. Some of the questions most often debated today include: What is it about growing up in a mother-only family that contributes to educational and economic disadvantage? To offset these outcomes, what changes should policymakers be thinking about? What are the real issues in welfare reform? Should we end welfare as we have known it? Are most black mothers on welfare willing to work? What can we do about the most disadvantaged mothers and their children? Finally, what can be done to break this cycle of poverty?

Family Values and Father-Absent Families

The different positions taken by social scientists on the issue of father-absent families reflect the differing values they attach to the traditional family roles of women; these values often determine whether they see single motherhood as a cause or a consequence of poverty. Some examples follow.

William J. Wilson has argued that the rise in nonmarriage and marital disruption has been caused chiefly by the declining ability of poor black men to support their families, or at least to make a substantial financial contribution to the household. In his perspective, the growth of mother-only families represents social dislocation rather than an increase in options for women.[3] Although Wilson has been viewed as a liberal in the social science community, this argument creates an ironic link with him and conservatives.[4] The criticisms leveled against his viewpoint have been both methodological and ideological. First, a more rigorous analysis of the data has found that the unemployment of black men explains only a small portion of the decline in marriage rates. Second, he has been criticized for framing the analysis exclusively around the interests of poor black men with domestic arrangements that have a patriarchal emphasis, thereby overlooking the interests of poor black women who may remain single.[5]

Mainstream feminists contend that the growth of father-absent families is a sign of forward movement in the struggle for women's equality. They note that the increase in demand for women workers and rising wage rates after World War II drew an ever-increasing number of women into the paid labor force, which in turn expanded women's roles and made it easier for them to support themselves outside of marriage. It is for these reasons, they argue, that women today marry less often, divorce more, and form mother-only families at a faster rate than they did in the past.[6]

Another group, whose members classify themselves as socialist-feminists, have challenged the analyses of both Wilson and the mainstream feminists. Emphasizing class and gender constraints, they argue that unmarried mothers, especially those who were poor before having children, are seldom more autonomous than married women because they are held back by their role as domestic laborers and by sexual and racial stratification in the labor market, which assigns them to low-paying or unpaid jobs. In contrast, they continue, middle-class mothers are more likely to be able to earn a living wage and move toward independence because they can hire poor women to work for them as housekeepers and day care providers.[7]

Another group of social scientists have pointed out that all poor blacks, men and women alike, share problems overlooked by Wilson and all the feminists. Both black men and black women have difficulty securing employment, they say, because they lack the necessary skills, do not have the appropriate connections, or are victims of racial discrimination. Thus only when the economy is booming and labor is scarce do blacks have an opportunity to get jobs that pay a living wage.[8]

Another dimension has been added to these debates by "profamily" feminists, who insist that other writers have ignored the potential costs to children of women's growing independence.[9] Thus Sylvia Hewlett has argued that in the absence of social policies and institutions that support women in their dual roles as child care providers and breadwinners, the struggle for independence and social equality has been a catastrophe for most women. Contending that we pay a high price for our failure to provide support structures for today's families, she quotes Albert Shanker, the former president of the American Federation of Teachers:

The nation goes on year after year spending excessive time, money, and effort on the problems of juvenile delinquency and crime. We are looking in the wrong place for solutions to problems resulting from a generation of children growing up without proper supervision.[10]

The costs to children of women's growing independence has also been documented recently by Sara McLanahan and Gary Sandefur, who have reopened an old debate over the consequences of family structure for children. They conclude:

Children who grow up in a household with only one biological parent are worse off, on average, than children who grow up in a household with both of their biological parents, regardless of the parents' race or educational background, regardless of whether the parents are married when the child is born, and regardless of whether the resident parent remarries.[11]

Children from father-absent families are more likely to drop out of school and generally obtain fewer years of education than those from two-parent families. Offspring from these families also have lower earnings in young adulthood, and they are more likely to be poor and receive welfare when they become adults. Thus the intergenerational continuity of economic and material deprivation is perpetuated. Growing up in a household with one parent is perhaps a more convincing explanation for the educational and economic disadvantages blacks experience vis-à-vis whites than the genetic and biological arguments set forth by Richard Hernstein and Charles Murray, the conservative authors of *The Bell Curve*.

Findings such as these have once again raised the question of the importance of the father's role in the family. Deborah Prothrow-Stith, a leading specialist on crime and violence among black juveniles, has effectively argued that a father offers an essential role model, especially for young black men.[12] Mercer Sullivan, in his study of poor neighborhoods in New York, maintains that the absence of fathers, especially in black areas, deprives the community of those safeguards that informally but often effectively control boys on the street.[13] These viewpoints have been echoed by single African-American mothers who are employed but living below the poverty line. In a recent survey they revealed that the parenting of young black males, without assistance from their fathers, was particularly stressful.[14]

Even with the mounting evidence against the desirability of single parenting, the majority of feminists still view the critics of single-mother families as measuring such domestic arrangements against unchanging patriarchal standards. An organization has even been formed, Single Mothers by Choice, which provides resource materials and professionally led support groups for single mothers and their children. This organization's membership is 90 percent white women.[15]

Feminists rarely make the distinction between the differential effect the decision to become a single mother has on women based on their economic rsources. Once exposed to the grim realities faced by poor mothers, many change their minds. For example, Donna Shalala, a feminist and the secretary of Health and Human Services, recently broke rank with her more strident sisters and raised strong objection to mothers having children outside of marriage.[16] Academic feminists who have studied the lives of poor women, however, have argued that the United States should have followed the lead of the European welfare states in making support for women and children universal like Social Security, rather than a need-based, stigmatizing form of public assistance.[17]

Moving beyond the polemics of the debate, the reality is that the growth of the drug trade and the prison industry (one-third of all black men between the ages of twenty and twenty-nine are in the criminal justice system) coupled with declining job opportunities for black males have drastically reduced the pool of marriageable males for black women, especially in the poorest and most isolated black communities. And the inclining fertility rates of unmarried women have clearly demonstrated that women of childbearing age, especially poor African-Americans, are unwilling to forego their prerogative to become mothers, even if there is not an available supply of marriageable males.

All available evidence shows that children minimally need one caregiver, with assistance from a supportive adult, to care attentively for them.[18] Furthermore, the evaluation of the developmental outcomes of children who were from deprived economic backgrounds and grew up successfully suggests that they all had the common denominator of one adult who gave them inordinate attention.[19] Policymakers will have more of an impact on the lives of poor African-American children when they accept the irreversibility of the high levels of nonmarriage of their mothers as a starting point for thinking about changes in public policy. If the mother is drug-free, motivated to be a good mother, and considered to be fit to rear her child, resources should be directed at fortifying the mother-child dyad by strengthening her parenting skills.

Ending Welfare as We Know It

Public welfare is part and parcel of contemporary American society. Since the passage of the Social Security Act in 1935, the federal government has been responsible for public welfare. And welfare programs for single mothers have been the most important source of income for nonworking poor mothers. The United States, however, remains one of the few industrialized countries that does not provide universal child allowances and that requires poor single mothers to demonstrate need in order to qualify for public welfare. Robert Reich, Clinton's secretary of labor, in noting that one of the most expensive forms of federal assistance is the $200 billion per year to corporations in the form of tax breaks and subsidies, has correctly assessed the nation's priorities.[20]

Debates over welfare policy in the United States, unlike Western European countries, have generally revealed a tension between two different approaches: the income approach, which emphasizes the behavior of the individual in response to the structure of welfare benefits; and the employment approach, which focuses on the behavior of the bureaucracy in providing job-related services. Yet these two approaches are inextricably linked, for the application of one always influences the outcome of the other. In the 1980s, as Reaganomics pushed the poor further down the economic ladder, it became fashionable on both sides of the political spectrum to emphasize the reliance of poor black women on welfare, and to try to remedy this dependence by requiring that they go to work.

Although partisan and ideological debates over welfare reform continue in Congress, there does seem to be one area of common ground: the moral value of work. The concern with attacking poverty at its roots has become narrowly focused on black welfare mothers, who are set up as examples of promiscuous sexual behavior and a weakened commitment to work and responsible living. The position of "moral renewal" was summarized in the clearest possible terms by Bill Archer (R-Texas), chairman of the House Ways and Means Committee: "This bill [comprehensive welfare measure] will reverse the decades-long federal policy of rewarding unacceptable and self-destructive behavior. We will no longer reward them for doing the wrong thing."[21]

Many other recent events bear witness to a renewed assault on welfare mothers. First, the Republican speaker of the house, Newt Gingrich, has recommended that children living in urban ghettos, where they are ensnared in an environmental quagmire of drugs, poverty, and ignorance, should be taken from their mothers and placed in orphanages (rather than removing both mothers and children from these environments and resettling them in habitable neighborhoods). Second, there has been a resurgence of special investigations of welfare fraud, reminiscent of the "suitable homes" investigations of the 1960s. Since June 1994 a team of eight special investigators from the district attorney's office have been working on a state-authorized pilot study of welfare fraud in Orange County, California. They have probed deeply into the lives of 450 randomly selected welfare recipients, none of whom are suspected of any wrongdoing. In some cases investigators have followed recipients to see if they have jobs that have not been reported to welfare officials, and they have made surprise visits to recipients' homes, asking to search rooms for signs that a recipient of AFDC has fewer children than reported.[22]

It is hard to miss the implication that unmarried black mothers are not to be valued or trained as parents and homemakers, despite a general agreement that competent, attentive parents are critical to the safety, education, and development of poor children. Ruth Rosen in a recent commentary has pointed out the mixed messages Democrats and Republicans are sending to mothers: "Poor moms are supposed to leave their children, find a job and go out to work. Well-paid professional working mothers—like prosecutor Marcia Clark—should quit, stay home, and care for their children."[23] Herbert Gans, a veteran poverty researcher, has argued that the issues have less to do with the availability of economic resources and more to do with the national will: "If all the externalities, good and bad, associated with spending by and for (or against) the poor were added together, they would show that the country can afford far better antipoverty programs than it now provides."[24]

While the work ethic continues to be touted as the American way, the duplicity of Congress is reflected in two major factors that continue to undermine work for poor black mothers: AFDC policies, and the social isolation in urban ghettos. First, AFDC policies have undermined participation in the labor force by requiring poor welfare mothers pay a far higher marginal tax on their earnings than would be considered tolerable for the richest Americans. (The recent extension of the earned income tax credit does increase somewhat the financial attractiveness of work over welfare by supplementing earnings directly with cash.)[25] Many would be worse off working full-time, because they would lose nearly a dollar in benefits for each dollar earned, including the loss of Medicaid benefits.[26] Second, thirty years after the fight began to end racial segregation, many black mothers living in poverty continue to be isolated in urban ghettos. The rates of racial concentration in thirty metropolitan cities remained virtually unchanged from 1970 to 1990.[27] Not only has the segregation of blacks undermined the political support necessary for jobs and services to reach the ghetto, but as the conditions of life there have declined over time, blacks have adapted socially and culturally to an environment of deprivation.

With a stated commitment to breaking the cycle of welfare dependence among recipients, Republicans and Democrats have presented various proposals. Republicans propose to cut the earned income tax credit, job training, child care, and other programs intended to encourage a transition from welfare to work. In short, they want to eliminate welfare entirely, which will presumably force people to work. Democrats, on the other hand, have focused on "making work pay" by providing an expanded earned income tax credit, a higher minimum wage, and modest investments in vocational skills. This policy is directed at decreasing the long-term attractiveness of AFDC as an alternative to work.

What both liberals and conservatives are doing is promising to transform AFDC into a transitional assistance program while restricting welfare outlays, each with a different set of inducements: Republicans concentrate on sticks, while Democrats give some attention to carrots. Both groups are making these proposals at a time in American history when low-skill jobs are disappearing and wages declining. For example, a study released in 1995 by the Manhattan Borough President found that at any given time about 50,000 jobs, of all types (not just entry level), are available in New York City. If they were all filled by welfare recipients, 300,000 more jobs would be needed for the remaining adults on welfare, and an additional 200,000 jobs would be needed for other unemployed New Yorkers.[28]

Thus while the welfare discussion has shifted to the problematic behaviors of nonworking black mothers, the opportunities for all low-wage workers have been deteriorating, and the black poor have increasingly been isolated in neighborhoods of concentrated poverty.[29] In the words of Jill Quadagno, "The equal opportunity welfare state was replaced by a welfare state that encouraged racial isolation and the concentration of the black poor in inner cities."[30]

In today's conservative climate, no attention is being paid to the operation of forces that deny access to jobs, sustain discrimination in housing, or provide inferior education or no education at all to ghetto residents. As public attention to these issues has evaporated, so have federal funds. New low-income housing starts financed by HUD dropped from 183,000 in 1980 to only 28,000 in 1985. Housing assistance subsided from more than 50 million dollars in 1977 to less than 9 million in 1988.[31] Perhaps more important, as conditions in the ghetto have continued to deteriorate, society has justified the isolation of poor blacks by blaming them for these conditions and their byproducts: drugs, crime, violence, poverty, and the proliferation of father-absent families.

Are Black Welfare Mothers Willing to Work?

When the late Johnnie Tillmon surveyed the needs of poor women in her Watts housing project in 1963, she found that all but one of six hundred women wanted training and jobs rather than welfare. The group figured out that it would cost only $1,000 for a woman to get one year of schooling and one year of job training or apprenticeship; Tillmon said "we could see her in two or three years completely off the welfare rolls." One woman wanted to be a mortician, so the group arranged with a local undertaker to guarantee a job at the end of the training period. All they lacked was $1,000 to pay for the training, but, according to Tillmon, they "could not get that out of the welfare department."[32]

One of the few rigorous studies to examine whether black welfare mothers preferred welfare to work was conducted in the early 1970s by Leonard Goodwin, a research associate in the Brookings Governmental Studies program.[33] He developed a framework for understanding and measuring the work orientations of welfare mothers and surveyed more than 4,000 persons living in Baltimore. What is important about this study is that it compared the responses of mothers who lived both inside and outside the ghetto, though still within the city limits of Baltimore.

The Goodwin study found that all the groups of women—whether inside or outside the ghetto, whether long-term or short-term welfare recipients—gave equally high ratings to the work ethic. There were significant differences, however, in what they believed about the effectiveness of their efforts. Long-term welfare recipients lacked confidence in their ability to achieve job success. Even black mothers who did not live in ghetto neighborhoods were more uncertain about their abilities to succeed in a job than white women who lived in similar neighborhoods. The difference Goodwin found between blacks who resided in the ghetto neighborhoods and those who did not was that the blacks who had moved out had more often stayed in their jobs and stayed married in spite of whatever obstacles they had to confront. Predictably, the welfare mothers found welfare more acceptable than the other women, but they did not believe that this acceptance eroded their motivation to work. More important, all the women seemed willing to get further training and to work if they had "adequate" incomes.

Goodwin summarized the findings of his study by noting that although the task of helping persons move out of poverty is generally perceived in economic terms, the responses from blacks who lived outside of ghetto neighborhoods clearly suggest that there is a "great deal of psychological stress associated with social mobility." In addition, he proposed that public policies that focus on eliminating poverty should include incentives for husbands and wives to stay together as a family unit.[34]

Manpower Demonstration Research Corporation recently conducted an analysis of African-American women's attitudes toward employment.[35] The 790 respondents had participated in the JOBS evaluation in Fulton County, Georgia, which was designed to provide a descriptive measure of the effectiveness of two alternative approaches to welfare-to-work programs: a human capital approach, which emphasizes education and training activities, and a labor force attachment approach, which emphasizes quick entry into the job market through job-search strategies. Ninety-six percent of the respondents were African-Americans, and all were mothers whose youngest child was between the ages of three and five at the time of the study. Although none of the mothers were teenagers at the time of the study, 40 percent had been 19 or younger at the birth of their oldest child living in the household.

Study participants were asked to respond to a series of questions regarding their attitudes toward employment and welfare. Using an eleven-point scale ranging from zero (not at all true) to ten (completely true) respondents were asked to indicate how true each statement was for them. One in ten women responded that it was "completely true" that the money she made at her job was not "worth the hassle." More than one-third of the mothers thought it was "completely true" that it would be better to have a low-paying job than to be on welfare. And about one-third responded "completely true" to the statement "It's wrong to stay on welfare if you can get a job, even a job you don't like." Only 6 percent of mothers felt it was "completely true" that it is unfair to make people on welfare get a job if they do not want to work.

There were subgroups of women who were less likely to believe that mothers should be employed. Women with a stronger belief that mothers should not work outside the home were significantly more likely to be on welfare longer and to reside in public housing. These mothers likewise had more negative psychological well-being levels—which included higher levels of depressive symptoms—perceived more barriers to working, and were more likely to have an external locus of control and less social support. Women who reported more barriers to employment were less likely to have worked during a quarter of the months of the child's life and tended to have children who were developing less well.

Another study that endeavored to control for neighborhood effects compared black mothers living in crime-ridden public housing projects in Chicago with participants in the Gautreaux Program, which resettled 3,500 black families from the same projects into better housing in white middle-class suburbs. Although researchers expected that the efforts of the new suburbanites to find work might be constrained by the long-term effects of poverty, poor education, and welfare dependency, they found that 13 percent more of them held down jobs than the city-dwellers. Among those who had never worked before, 46 percent of suburban participants found jobs, as opposed to only 30 percent of their urban counterparts. There were also problems reported in the suburbs. For example, about half the women said that they had experienced some racial harassment from the police, neighbors, or others during their first year in the suburbs, but most of them believed that these problems had tended to subside over time.[36]

The Step Up program in Chicago is one of the few projects that set out to train former welfare recipients in jobs that would enable them to earn a living wage. Building on the idea of "adequate" wages, this program used federal housing rehabilitation money to train former welfare recipients in construction jobs.[37] When the Chicago Housing Authority (CHA) held a jobs call in the fall of 1992, some 1,200 residents, many of them high-school dropouts and welfare recipients who had never worked before, showed up to apply for 300 training slots. To be hired, they had to pass a drug test, be able to read at sixth-grade level, and show that they were on a public housing lease. The CHA promised the participants that they would not lose their Medicaid benefits and that their rents would not be raised. The trainees received no other public assistance while in the program.

To make the program possible, the HUD established a new job category to satisfy federal restrictions of who can work on federal job sites. It also had to persuade trade unions to cooperate with housing authorities, both in training residents and by offering union membership to those who qualified. The trainees went to work late in 1992. They were paid $13.52 an hour to paint, plaster, scrape, scrub, sweep, hang doors, and lay tile to make abandoned public housing units, stripped by vandals and gang members, ready for occupancy again. During the sixteen months of the program they renovated 1,551 apartments in half-a-dozen housing projects.

Vincent Lane, the chairman of the CHA, said he had decided to pay the trainees middle-class wages because he felt he needed to extend them "as big a carrot as possible" to change their way of thinking: "Five dollars an hour is no incentive. They need to know what it tastes like to be able to put some money in the bank, to get beyond just surviving." But even with the very high wage as an inducement, a third of the trainees never adjusted to the rigors of work: sixty-four were discharged for poor attendance, eight for showing up for work drunk or high on drugs, nine for misconduct (usually fighting on the job), and one for taking a coworker on a joy ride in the middle of the day. According to the *New York Times*, some of them continued to "call up begging in vain to get their jobs back."

Of the original 298 participants, 50 finished the program and were hired by the CHA as workers to remove lead from the projects at $19 an hour, as clerks with pay comparable to Step Up's, or as truck drivers at about $18 an hour. Eighteen entered training for union carpentry apprenticeship, which requires four years to complete.

The program administrators insisted that even the trainees who dropped out had learned a valuable lesson about life in the real world. One trainee, Melinda Powell, had been on welfare for fourteen years before enrolling in Step Up in 1992. Now, in 1995, she is a tax-paying, card-carrying member of the Laborers' Union Local No. 1, making $19 an hour and worrying about things like retirement savings and bank fees. She can imagine helping her children go to college.

Welfare-to-work programs are likewise finding that fewer women than anticipated are staying on the jobs. For example, an agency that dispatches homemakers to assist the elderly and disabled residents confined to their homes hired more than eighty women over a period of seventeen months. According to Deborah Washam, the program administrator, fewer than twenty-five remained on the job. She predicts that many more will quit over "perceived slights to their dignity." A welfare-to-work program in Kansas City has also faced unanticipated challenges. Since the program began in April 1995, 542 of the 1,162 job openings certified for participation have been filled by welfare recipients, but only 217 of those hired remain at work. What is important about this program is that the participants selected had the highest qualifications from the 7,726 families eligible for the program.[38]

The high rates of attrition in these welfare-to-work programs calls into question how much taxpayers are willing to pay to reduce welfare dependency among poor mothers. Five-year evaluation studies were conducted and completed in 1995 on four welfare-to-work programs: one each in Virginia and Arkansas, and one each in Baltimore and San Diego.[39] Of the four programs, two produced substantial budgetary savings but only small financial benefits for enrollees; the other two produced financial gains for enrollees but no net benefits for budgets. The greatest expense has been the child care funding, which more than doubled from 1991 to 1994. Despite the initial costs, even conservatives may find that their emphasis on shared responsibility requires them to consider supporting such programs. In a Heritage Foundation book advocating a conservative strategy for welfare reform, Stuart Butler and Anna Kondratas have written that although the cost-saving potential for work–welfare should not be overstated, "it is important for society to send a clear message, and workfare sends it: Good welfare policy must involve reciprocal obligations."[40]

Helping the Most Disadvantaged Mothers

The five-year study completed in 1995 found that several welfare-to-work programs "did not produce a sizable impact on the more disadvantaged," who made up "a significant percentage of the program caseload."[41] This study has documented the handicaps that many black mothers on welfare have experienced, handicaps that have been exacerbated by the isolation in neighborhoods of concentrated poverty.

Employers have expressed dissatisfaction with even the most qualified with problems that include absenteeism, lack of discipline about work hours, poor reading and communication skills, and open resentment when given directions. Overcoming years of dependency on entitlement programs without restrictions or limits is the challenge facing these programs. One administrator puts it this way, "I don't think they have had much exposure to structure in their lives. As single mothers, they have been on their own and think of themselves as authority figures."[42] The workers that are the most daunting to employ are the welfare veterans. The success or failure of welfare-to-work programs will rest on their ability to instill in these mothers a sense of the "dignity" of work.

The remaking of welfare will not work unless it addresses the needs of four distinct types of African American women on welfare:[43]

1. Young unmarried mothers who started their parenting careers as teenagers, live in age-condensed families with a multigenerational pattern of welfare dependence, and reside in either public housing or a neighborhood of concentrated poverty (these are the mothers whose children are doing less well developmentally);
2. Young mothers who may also have become parents as teenagers but whose

own parents have both worked outside the home and who have seldom or never relied on welfare;

3. Mothers who are temporarily poor owing to job loss, divorce or separation, or poor health;
4. Older black women who may have worked all of their lives in back-breaking low-wage jobs and are now virtually disabled and thus poor candidates for work.

Women in the first category are the most vulnerable to persistent poverty and will have the hardest time making the transition from welfare to work. Besides being given basic education, they will have to be socialized to the culture of work. Many of them have been reared in families where no one has ever held a permanent job, and thus have never observed firsthand the amount of discipline and the household routines that are needed to juggle the dual responsibilities of motherhood and employment.[44] They will also have greater difficulty understanding the expectations of their employers—that it is important not only to get to work, but to get to work on time. A "culture" has been created in these mothers over time, a set of attitudes, values, and behaviors. A lot of individualized psychosocial support will be needed either from paraprofessionals or professionals, in that these women have more depressive symptoms and generally do not score as high on tests that measure psychological well-being. In addition, their children, who are doing less well developmentally, will need more specialized attention. From a service perspective, this means increasing benefits and using support services to help young mothers care for children and households, as well as for themselves, as they are introduced to a new way of life.

Women in the second category, who have a much greater potential capacity to move away from welfare, also need increased benefits and support services to help them care for children and households. They need less help with basic education and more assistance with skill development and job training.

For women in the third category, AFDC should continue to be a temporary safety net, providing adequate benefits and modest transitional assistance. And for those in the fourth, AFDC should provide a transition to the Supplemental Security Income program and appropriate intensive or maintenance services.

Age-specific differences in the mothers should also be taken into consideration. First, should the mothers who are under eighteen years of age and/or have not completed high school be allowed to establish their own households? In the 1970s Sheppard Kellam and his colleagues found that children raised by single mothers with grandmothers did nearly as well as children raised by two parents.[45] However, a recent study conducted by Lindsay Chase-Lansdale and her associates described greater role conflict between mothers and daughters in low-income multigenerational families than in single-mother families, which lowered the quality of parenting.[46] During the years between these two studies, the proliferation of age-condensed multigenerational families, which has reduced the interval between the ages of the teenaged mothers and the grandmothers, has contributed to this increased role conflict. If changes in federal or state policies prevent teenaged mothers from having their own welfare grant if they establish an independent household, they will then go without not only parental moral support but help with child care and other assistance they need to stay in school. What is needed is the development of comprehensive mentoring programs in which these mothers are assigned to mentors and their progress is carefully monitored. (Programs of this nature are currently operating in many cities and are discussed later).

Second, what can be done to prevent further pregnancies among the youngest mothers who are most vulnerable to persistent poverty? States are required by law to develop a family planning program for AFDC parents and their dependent children that is designed to prevent or reduce the incidence of births to single mothers. One of the reasons these provisions have not been enforced is that the poorest communities have the least family planning resources. One evaluation study conducted in Los Angeles found that there were no private subsidized family planning clinics in South Central Los Angeles, one of the most impoverished Latino and black areas in the city.[47] Increased access to and utilization of family planning services is imperative if these young are to defer childbearing.

Under current economic conditions, welfare reform will inevitably increase the supply of less-skilled female workers, who must compete with male workers in a labor market that has a declining capacity to absorb them both. What this means is that AFDC mothers will not be going to work any time soon. Even if some do, the most disadvantaged mothers will not be going to work without taxpayers making major investments in the development of human capital. It is time to abandon the misleading notion that welfare reform can be the principal weapon in the fight against poverty.

Breaking the Cycle of Poverty

Although welfare reform is essential, without a commitment to improving the quality of life of poor black families, reform remains an elusive goal. Five other strategies are critically important—and are significant in that they endeavor to link the macro and micro dimensions of the problem:

1. social interventions provided by community-based family service agencies;
2. an expanded network of traditional government social services;

3. the development of more innovative foster care programs;
4. economic policies to create more jobs that would pay enough to offer a way out of poverty;
5. "self-help" efforts, which must include the participation of more affluent blacks who are willing to establish and maintain links with the poorest blacks.

Because the family plays a critical role in nurturing individual growth and protecting its members in times of adversity, all three approaches should be aimed at strengthening the family, even if there is no father in the home.

Social Interventions for Low-Income Mothers Historically, much of the attention given to low-income single parents has focused on structural forces rather than individual agency. One study examined social interventions with poor women of color and found that there were four psychological changes that were crucial in moving these women from despair to action: an increase in "self-efficacy," or a sense of competence; the development of a group consciousness, the reduction of self-blame, and the assumption of personal responsibility for change.[48] Approaches have been developed to specifically combat the effects of isolation and helplessness on low-income mothers and to enhance their coping skills for living in urban poverty. These interventions have included social support mobilization and a survival skills program.[49]

These types of interventions are particularly important in view of the research findings cited earlier, that found an association between mothers' psychological well-being and their willingness to work outside the home. Mothers with higher levels of depressive symptons had fewer social supports, were on welfare longer, and were more likely to reside in public housing.

Social interventions with families living in poverty are critically important as well. Building on the four types of African-American women on welfare, there are additionally four distinctive types of black families that utilize the services of family service agencies (Table 9.1). These categories have been constructed based the family's level of competence and functioning and are not just limited to black families living in poverty.[50]

Level I families are the most vulnerable and are struggling with basic survival issues. These families are age-condensed have experienced multigenerational welfare dependency, and are organized around a matrifocal family system. Studies of the single mothers in these families have demonstrated that they have higher levels of depressive symptoms, perceive more barriers to working, and have a more external locus of control, fewer social supports, and children who are doing less well developmentally.[51] If adult men are in these families they are only there on a peripheral basis. In addition, the mothers in these families have initiated childbearing

Table 9.1   African-American Family Assessment and Intervention

Level	Description	Intervention Strategy	Intervention Techniques
I	Age-condensed; multigenerational; adolescent childbearing and welfare dependency; matrifocal; never-married mothers	Focus on strengths, not problems; mobilize available supports to bolster executive capacity	Family preservation; case management; Gather resources from extended family and community agencies; professional acts as convener, advocate, teacher, role model
II	Weak attachment to the labor force; no multigenerational welfare dependency; matrifocal; probably divorced or separated	Focus on strengths; develop coalition of those in charge against those needing control; increase clarity of expectation	Ecosystems oriented; set limits; clear communication; social learning: written contracts, behavioral reinforcers, and task assignments
III	Two-parent family structure; may be divorced or separated; labor force participation; may be temporarily unemployed; no history of welfare dependency	Focus on problems; clarify the "ideal" family structure in conformity with family expectations; generational clarity	Defend family and individual boundaries; balance triangles; rebuild alliances; develop generational boundaries; task assignments; communication skills
IV	Two-parent family structure, father or step-father in the home; patriarchal or egalitarian marital dyad; strong labor force participation	Focus on problems; clarification and resolution of legacies and historical trauma; insight; focus on yearnings	Focus on cognition, affect, communication, interpersonal relationships, and structural issues in the family

Adapted from J. S. Weltner, "Matchmaking: Choosing the Appropriate Therapy for Families at Various Levels of Pathology," in *Handbook of adolescents and family therapy*, eds. M. P. Mirkin and S. L. Koman (New York: Gardner Press, 1985), p. 49.

during their adolescent years. With a condensed age structure, these families generally lack an organizational structure that can ensure that their basic survival needs are met. In these families, gradual and negotiated transitions from child-daughter to mature daughter capable of mothering her own child do not take place. Rather, role transitions are abrupt and conflictual, without the socializing influence of an adult male as well as other supports that would make for a smoother transition.

While Level II black families are somewhat more stable than those in Level I, and may not have experienced multigenerational welfare dependency, they still have a weak attachment to the labor force. The family system remains matrifocal, but single mothers are more likely to be either divorced or separated than never-married. While some of these mothers may initiate childbearing as teenagers, there may also be exceptions. (At Level I and II, family members rarely discuss their own feelings or comment on the feelings of others.) Structural interventions in these families should enable adults in the household to develop a coalition strong enough to demonstrate sufficient authority for the family to gain control of intimidating or destructive behaviors. Weltner emphasizes that the focus of intervention in such situations must be to "develop a coalition of those in charge against those needing control."[52]

Families in Level III have stronger labor force participation and work and marriage histories than families in the first two levels. These families have strong working- and middle-class values. If the mother is currently single, she has been married, and there is no history of welfare dependency. Within the marital dyad, the family structure is either patriarchal or egalitarian.

Level IV families are the most competent and highly functioning black families. There is a clear two-parent family structure, and there is generally a father or stepfather in the home. If the mother is currently single, her children have strong relationships with grandfathers, uncles, and other strong adult male role models. If the husband is a professional and the wife is a homemaker, the family structure is probably more patriarchal. If both spouses are professionals, the marriage is probably egalitarian. These families have fairly clear structural boundaries. Within these families, the quality of family life becomes the focus of interventions.

Level III and IV families both have a rich blend of coping mechanisms, and work with these families would involve changing ingrained patterns. Interventions would involve reshaping current patterns of behavior within the family, to develop differentiation and individuation of family members from each other and more flexibility within the emotional system.

Expanded Network of Services Because infant mortality rates are highest in black neighborhoods with concentrated poverty, the government should commit itself to the goal of giving all pregnant women access to prenatal care and information on early childhood nutrition.

One program that provided these services achieved remarkable results. The Infant and Health Development Program provided an intensive array of services to nearly one thousand premature, low-weight infants in eight U. S. cities. The infants were randomly assigned to treatment and control groups. The infants and parents in the experimental groups were given three services: trained counselors made bi-weekly home visits to parents; infants were seen at child development centers five days a week after they reached their first birthday; parents attended a parental support group that met biweekly at the center, where they were given factual information a child's growth and development. By age three, the infants in the experimental group had significantly higher measured IQs and significantly fewer behavioral problems than those in the control groups, and the gains were greatest for the infants who had the most disadvantaged mothers[53]

Preschool programs be expanded, especially in the poorest neighborhoods, so that many more of the eligible three- and four-year-olds can participate. One program for which there is strong evidence for positive long-term effects is the Perry Preschool in Ypsilanti, Michigan. It enrolled 123 poor black children who were living in father-absent homes; half of them were randomly assigned to a control group; and both groups were followed until they were nineteen years old. Those who had been enrolled in the preschool program were less likely to drop out before finishing high school, less likely to go on welfare, more likely to be working, and less likely to have an arrest record.[54] The Perry Preschool results were not coincidental; the graduates of this preschool did well because the teachers received extensive training, and there was a ratio of one teacher to every five or six students. This program also went beyond the boundaries of the classroom and had sustained contact with the mothers via home visits once a week of about an hour and a half.

Quality day care is an invaluable resource that is rarely affordable for working mothers living in poverty neighborhoods. The federal government should subsidize low-income families by refunding an amount equal to the existing tax credit for day care services to families whose incomes are too low to permit taking a credit. Subsidies of this kind have been shown to be sound investments in the future, for they reduce the heavy social costs of dealing with arrested physical, emotional, and intellectual growth.

Adolescents and young adults, both parents and nonparents, are also in dire need of an expanded network of support services. Every effort must be made to prevent teenagers from becoming pregnant by providing comprehensive family planning and reeducation services and making them accessible to those teenagers most in need of them. Outreach efforts should be aimed at adolescents who are at risk for repeat pregnancies. Because we know that leaving school, teenage parenthood, unemployment, and welfare dependency are interrelated, Congress should maintain or restore adequate funding for programs aimed at disadvantaged adolescents, including the Job Training Partnership Act, the Job Corps, the Summer Youth Employment Program, and Chapter 1 of the Education Consolidation and Improvement Act. Interagency youth councils should be directed to leverage local action in neighborhoods of concentrated poverty with a sustained and concerted attack on the problems of young people who are at risk of becoming parents and failing to make the school-to-work transition. Schools should be used as the centers for delivering comprehensive and integrated services to adolescents.

More Innovative Approaches to Foster Care New approaches to caring for children placed in foster care must be developed and implemented, in that the number of foster parents are falling while the caseloads are growing sharply, especially among African-Americans. Not only are African-American children harder to place, but children who come from the inner city and have been molested, beaten, or abandoned also have difficulty finding places in foster homes. Few foster parents are willing to take in children who have experienced such despair in their lives.

A pioneering two-year old program has given foster children who stood little chance of being placed the opportunity to be placed permanently in a family.[54] Professor Brenda Krause Eheart in southern Illinois purchased sixty-three duplex apartments on twenty-two acres, formerly part of an air force base, and recruited and hired foster parents who live there rent-free. The program pays one parent in each family $18,000 a year to stay home with the children. The group also recruited middle-aged and elderly people who serve as "honorary grandparents." They receive subsidized rents in exchange for volunteering eight to ten hours a week as crossing guards, crafts instructors, and maintenance workers. But their principal value, according to Eheart, comes in simply being part of the lives of the children, playing ball, lending an ear, and telling stories about the old days. There are currently twelve families, with about fifty children, twenty-five of them foster children.

One set of foster parents is Mr. and Mrs. Owen. They became foster parents so that Mrs. Debbie Owen could stay home with her own three children. They were assigned three foster children. One is Marc, who has cerebral palsy. Another is a two-year-old boy who was born to an alcoholic mother and showed signs of fetal alcohol syndrome. A third was a six-year-old girl who has sickle-cell anemia and who had gotten so little love, Mrs. Owen said, that she "seemed to have shut down her emotions. You looked into her eyes and they were empty. She didn't cry. She didn't laugh." Little by little she opened up, but even after two months she had never cried or laughed. Then one night when she was playing in the basement with other children, she watched her new sister in a comical dance and finally she began to laugh. The parents were upstairs when they heard the laughter; they started to cry. Mrs. Owen said, "You know, with a little love, some good food, and a little medical care, you can turn a child around."

The older residents seem to enjoy the children as well. For one older couple who had never had children of their own, having children around gives them a special feeling they have always wanted. According to one honorary grandmother, "A little boy came upstairs the other day and said, 'Grandma, can I have some juice?' " She said it made tears come to her eyes; she had never been called grandma before.

While there have been successes in this program, it is too soon to say whether such a community can provide over the long term the kind of supportive environment that can be found in an ordinary neighborhood. What is clear, however, is that it is currently providing an alternative placement for many African-American children who were previously living in deplorable neighborhoods and had little or no chance of being placed anywhere.

Inner-City Revitalization and Job Creation If Americans are serious about "making work pay," there are two concepts that would improve conditions in deteriorating neighborhoods while simultaneously creating jobs: enterprise zones and community development corporations (CDCs).

The creation of enterprise zones, first proposed during the Reagan years and later endorsed by the Clinton administration, requires state and local governments to propose a "course of action" for small designated areas in depressed neighborhoods. If the proposal is deemed acceptable, the federal government will reduce specific taxes and significantly relax many regulations in these zones, to encourage low-income residents to start new businesses.

When combined with the transfer of government-owned housing, an enterprise zone could be a means of strengthening communities through resident ownership. Many cities have had success with various versions of "homesteading": City-owned housing units are sold to families for a meager sum, and the new owners agree to live in the units and rehabilitate them up to a certain standard, either by investing money or by doing the work themselves as part of a "sweat equity" arrangement. In Kentucky, for example, as part of the state's enterprise zone legislation, a long lease on derelict buildings and vacant land owned by the city in a neighborhood can be given, free of change, to a neighborhood organization or a special corporation comprising residents of the area. In this way, the community can gain control of a capital asset in the neighborhood and benefit from any improvement that takes place. This is a variation on the plan used by the CHU when it hired welfare mothers to restore, repair, and refurbish public housing.

One effective way to organize the poor in distressed neighborhoods is through CDCs. The Watts Labor Community Action Committee in Los Angeles, Chicanas Por La Causa in Phoenix, and the Tocolcy Economic Development Corporation in Liberty City (Miami) have mobilized residents to make improvements in housing, street frontages, and neighborhood safety. CDCs have played an important role in experiments that use tax incentives or tax credits to encourage the construction of various levels of affordable housing in distressed neighborhoods.

The goal of CDCs is to create an environment that promises renewal instead of continued decay and disintegration. Their efforts to improve communities can reinforce the "empowerment" efforts of individuals, families, and communities. They provide an organizational structure for local community leaders to control capital, run social programs, and rekindle people's hopes. They have the potential to provide visible results that can help attract new funds and new residents to deteriorated neighborhoods. It should be noted, however, that some of these neighborhoods are so run-down that they will have to be completely dismantled and rebuilt from scratch.

Black Self-Help across the Class Divide A complex set of social and economic problems have plagued African-Americans ever since they arrived on ships from Africa and then migrated to cities to take low-skilled jobs in the manufacturing sector and relatively higher-paying domestic work. With changes in the global economy that have brought a wave of plant closings and layoffs, the service sector that has arisen to replace industrial work has generated higher-paying jobs for the few blacks with advanced education and poorly paid jobs and joblessness for the rest.

These changes have had an impact on all Americans, not just African-Americans. According to Robert Reich, Clinton's secretary of labor, "Almost all growth in family incomes during the past 15 years has gone to the top 20 percent, while the typical American family is living on less than it did 15 years ago, accounting for inflation."[56] But the results are most apparent among African-Americans whose community has split into a more prosperous class whose fortunes have improved and a poverty class whose position in the economy has steadily declined.

The efforts of the black community for self-improvement are most clearly reflected in their percentage growth as managers and/or professionals and in their advances in educational attainment. For example, in 1950 only 5 percent of black workers were classified as professionals or managers, today that figure is greater than 20 percent. In 1970 only one in ten blacks had attended college, today that figure is one in three. On the other hand, even college-educated blacks have experienced a decline in prosperity. While the number of blacks attending college increased exponentially, the proportion of chronically jobless and part-time workers among black college graduates also increased even more quickly during these years.[57]

In spite of these setbacks for the black middle class, during the 1980s blacks in leadership positions began trying to reach across the class divide to address the poverty and despair found in urban ghettos. One of the important efforts of this type occurred in 1986, when John Hope Franklin and Eleanor Holmes Norton brought together approximately thirty black leaders and prepared a report entitled *Black Initiative and Governmental Responsibility*. It concluded with the following statement:

1. The black community has always been an agent for its own advancement.
2. The "self-help" tradition is so embedded in the black heritage as to be virtually synonymous with it.
3. We must reach more broadly and more deeply to levels of participation

that include the poorest blacks and that draw them closer to blacks who have been more fortunate.

4. Persistent poverty has eroded but not destroyed the strong, deep value framework that for so long has sustained black people.

5. The black community must take the lead in defining the new and continuing problems it faces, in communicating the urgency of these problems, and in both prescribing and initiating solutions.

6. Many fruitful strategies are in place and should be expanded.

7. Many of the most pressing problems of the black community are well beyond its capacity or that of any community to resolve.

8. We urge a concentrated effort by government to invest first in models and then in programs and strategies for human development that will facilitate economic independence and encourage the poor to take charge of their own lives.

9. The inexcusable disparities between blacks and whites . . . can be eradicated only if the government assumes its appropriate role in a democratic, humane, and stable society.[58]

African-American communities have a multiplicity of organizations that are committed to the provision of either direct or indirect services to the black family. In addition, some of the nation's oldest and largest black organizations—such as the NAACP, the National Urban League, and the National Council on Negro Women—have emphasized the importance of the black family by sponsoring family summits and annual black family reunion celebrations. African-Americans have also moved into leadership roles in the family restoration efforts of several national nonprofit organizations—the National Education Association, the Planned Parenthood Federation of America, Family Service America, and the National YWCA, to name a few. What this means is that Level III and IV families on the family assessment scale are reaching back to help families in Levels 1 and II.

National Greek letter sororities have targeted African-American single mothers and adolescent girls in their efforts to strengthen the black family. Delta Sigma Theta, Inc., under the leadership of Hortense G. Canady, who grew up in a single-mother household, came up with the idea for a summit entitled "A Call to Action in Support of Black Single Mothers," in January 1984. Canady indicated that this summit was a response to the rise in the number of black families headed by single women and was intended to address the way these women were often inaccurately and negatively portrayed in the media. She went on to say, "If you want to discredit a whole family or a whole people, discredit the mother." One hundred twenty-eight chapters participated in this project, and the idea was for them to host summits that would give single mothers opportunities to talk about their particular needs but the primary objective was to link single mothers to appropriate agencies and services. Summit follow-ups were held, and the organization created a network of about 100 lawyers who focused on the issues that were raised at the summit.

Alpha Kappa Alpha (AKA), on the other hand, has taken a more preventive and service-oriented approach to the problem of single black parents by targeting adolescent girls in long-range efforts to promote self-esteem, develop marketable skills, and ultimately reduce the number of babies born to unmarried adolescent mothers. Chapters of AKA in urban and suburban communities such as Hamden, Connecticut, Plainfield, New Jersey, and Los Angeles, California, have ongoing mentor programs in which young girls are assigned personal mentors committed to working closely with them over a number of years. For example, the Plainfield, New Jersey, chapter provides mentors and an enrichment program to African-American and Hispanic eighth-grade girls in two middle schools. Program components include tutorial assistance to increase academic achievement, college campus visits, and exploration of the arts through field trips to museums, plays, concerts and cultural festivals, guest speakers, and workshops. At the heart of the program, however, is the personal commitment of chapter members, who are themselves college graduates with active careers and are expected to be a support and role model for their mentees for five years—from eighth grade until the completion of high school. Parents are encouraged to participate in the program, and family members are frequently invited to activities.

One of the more innovative programs has been developed by the Inglewood, California, chapter of Links, Inc., a national black women's service organization. This organization has developed a collaborative partnership with a family service agency. Members of the organization were matched with young women who had been referred to the agency for a wide range of family problems. Some were already single parents while others were "at risk" of dropping out of school and increasing family dysfunction. The young women have been provided with a variety of educational and cultural experiences, including exposure to a wide variety of options for careers or vocations. The emphasis is placed on increasing their awareness of opportunities and how to take advantage of them. Several of the young women have not only completed high school without becoming pregnant but have been admitted to and graduated from community colleges and four-year universities.

There are similar mentoring programs for young black men. One model program in the Washington, D.C., area is the Alliance of Concerned Men, a small group of middle-aged black men who have seen and survived lives of drugs and crime. They bring together children with their fathers who are serving time in prison. These big brothers serve as role models and provide a kind of emotional bonding to younger men who do not have male father figures in their lives.

One mentoring program has even been started by the individual initiative of a physician in Los Angeles, California. Donald Ware, a cardiologist, wanted black inner-city youth to know that they can succeed in life, but he knew that many of the young people did not have role models. He started Youth Empowered for Survival (YES), a program that teams up black students from South Los Angeles high schools with black professionals. One of Ware's goals for the YES program is to set up a camp where students who have at least a 3.0 grade point average but score only moderately on college entrance exams can learn how to improve their performance on these tests.[59]

Two early intervention programs are particularly noteworthy. The Chicago Urban League has started an innovative prevention program targeting young black males. This program, called the Male Responsibility Program, is conducted in the Chicago public elementary schools. Funded by the State of Illinois, its focus is on teaching self-esteem, values, and conflict resolution. Operation People United to Serve Humanity (PUSH), in Chicago, has developed a rites of passage program and conducts sessions to teach young black boys how to be responsible young men. This program provides the opportunity for responsible black men to meet with young black men and talk with them about how to deal with the situations they encounter at home, in school, and on the street. The second phase of the program is to encourage churches in the community to adopt a black young man. The church agrees to intercede on the youth's behalf when he is dealing with problems that are a threat to his safety, health, or self-esteem.

Another group of programs, which can be classified as manhood development programs, focus on group rather than dyadic interactions between men and boys. A group with a formal organization sets an agenda of meetings and activities that permits members of the organization to teach the recruits about values, discipline, responsibiity, personal development, and relations with others. There are the Five Hundred Black Men in Chicago, the One Hundred Black Men in California, Brother Organization of a New Destiny (BOND) in New York, and Save Our Sons (SOS) in Chicago. It is critically important that evaluation programs be set up to measure the effectiveness of these programs.

Conclusion

The efforts of more affluent African-Americans will go a long way in enhancing the lives of blacks isolated in ghetto neighborhoods. However, poverty in urban ghettos will only be abated when federal authorities become directly involved in promoting open housing, creating jobs, and enforcing policies that will minimize the drug trade in poor black communities and bring about equal opportunity in the pursuit of those jobs. Economic opportunity is paramount. In the current political climate, as long as the poorest blacks are warehoused in urban ghettos, the political support necessary to bring jobs and services to the ghetto will probably not be forthcoming.

The need for this kind of government intervention was clearly demonstrated in Atlanta, a city that has been viewed as a mecca of economic empowerment for blacks. Although commercial projects brought economic growth and development to that city, blacks residing in ghetto neighborhoods were shut out of the emerging job markets. That is, rising tides did not lift boats in Atlanta's inner cities. The jobs were found in outlying areas and drew on workers who did not reside in neighborhoods of concentrated poverty. In summarizing their Atlanta study's findings, Gary Orfield and Carol Ashkinaze asserted, "If economic expansion and a tight labor market could create equal opportunity without targeted government action, it should have happened in the Atlanta area."[60] The significance of these findings is that if an efforts to fight against urban blight and poverty are to be effective, government endeavors directed specifically at the inner cities will be critically important.

Clearly, the scope for new government spending will be limited in the years immediately ahead. But as we plan for the future, we must remember that what we save today by cutting spending on behalf of the poor will seem small tomorrow, compared with what we will be spending to combat ghetto-generated crime and to pay for all the other consequences of economic failure, such as incarceration and the rehabilitation of millions whose physical, emotional, and intellectual development has been stunted by grinding poverty. The social welfare of the poorest African-American families is properly the concern of all Americans, not only because we will all stand to benefit from the gains in human capital, but because the moral integrity of our society will be measured by our ability to unite behind this cause.

Notes

1. Kristen Moore, Martha J. Zaslow, Mary J. Coiro, Suzanne M. Miller, and Ellen B. Magenheim, "How Well Are They Faring: AFDC Families with Preschool-Aged Children in Atlanta at the Outset of the JOBS Evaluation," Department of Health and Human Services, U. S. Department of Education, prepared under subcontract to the Manpower Demonstration Research Corportion, February 1996. Ninety-six percent of the respondents were African-American. This information comes from mother self-reports; therefore it is possible that the contacts are underreported.

2. Reported in Karly H. Keene and Everett C. Ladd, eds., "Public Opinion and the Demographic Report," *American Enterprise* 3 (September–October 1992): 85–86.

3. William J. Wilson, *The Truly Disadvantaged: The Inner City, the Underclass, and Public Policy* (Chicago: University of Chicago Press, 1987).

4. For a perspective that argues that single motherhood diminishes the prosocial purposes of fatherhood, deprives children of privilege, and has an adverse impact on society, see David Blankenhorn, *Fatherless America: Confronting Our Most Urgent Social Problem* (New York: Basic Books, 1995).

5. For criticism that Wilson has missed the historically conditioned changing meaning of family, see Adolph Reed, Jr., "The Liberal Technocrat," *Nation*, February 6, 1988, 167–70. Others have argued that the increasing rates of joblessness among black men would seem a logical reason for declining marital rates among African-American men and women in lower income groups. Two studies have concluded that the unemployment of black men explains only a small portion of the decline in marriage rates: Mark Testa, "Male Joblessness, Nonmarital Parenthood, and Marriage," paper presented at the Conference on Urban Poverty and Family Structure, University of Chicago, October 1991; Christopher Jencks, "What Is the Underclass—and Is It Growing?" *Focus* 12 (Spring-Summer 1989): 14–26.

6. For variations on this argument, see, for example, Barbara Bergman, *The Economic Emergence of Women* (New York: Basic Books, 1986); Heidi Hartman, "The Political Economy of Comparable Worth," Paper presented at the Conference on Alternative Approaches to Labor Markets, University of Utah, Salt Lake City, October 1985.

7. Wendy Sarasy and Judith Van Allen, "Fighting the Feminization of Poverty: Socialist-Feminist Analysis and Strategy," *Review of Radical Political Economics* 16 (1984): 89–110.

8. For a careful analysis of how white employers view the race dimension, see Joleen Kirschenmann and Kathryn M. Neckerman, " 'We'd Love to Hire Them but . . . ': The Meaning of Race for Employers," in *The Urban Underclass*, eds. Paul Peterson and Christopher Jencks, (Washington, D.C.: Brookings Institution 1991): 203–34. For other analyses of race and gender, see Julianne Malveaux, "The Economic Interests of Black and White Women: Are They similar? *Review of Black Political Economy* 14 (Summer 1985): 5–29; Donna Franklin, "Feminization of Poverty and African American Families: Illusions and Realities," *Affilia* 7 (Summer 1992), 142–55.

9. Judith Stacey, "Are Feminists Afraid to Leave Home? The Challenge of Conservative Pro-family Feminism," in *What is Feminism?* ed. J. Mitchell and A. Oakley, (New York: Pantheon, 1986), 208–237; and Sylvia Hewlett, *A Lesser Life: The Myth of Women's Liberation in America* (New York: William Morrow, 1986).

10. Quoted in Hewlett, *Lesser Life*, 125.

11. Sara McLanahan and Gary Sandefur, *Growing Up with a Single Parent: What Hurts, and What Helps* (Cambridge, Mass.: Harvard University Press, 1994), 1. For more on the research evidence from father absent families see David Popenoe, *Life Without Father* (New York: Martin Kessler Books, 1996); Frank F. Furstenberg, Jr., and Andrew J. Cherlin, *Divided Families: What Happens to Children when Parents Part* (Cambridge, Mass.: Harvard University Press, 1991).

12. Deborah Prothrow-Stith, with Michele Weissman, *Deadly Consequences* (New York: Harper Collins, 1991).

13. Mercer Sullivan, "Crime and Social Fabric," in *Dual City: Restructuring New York,*

ed. John Hull Mollenkopf and Manuel Castells (New York: Russell Sage Foundation, 1991), 225–44.

14. Aurora P. Jackson, "Black, Single, Working Mothers in Poverty," *National Association of Social Workers* 38 (January 1993): 26–33.

15. Jane Mattes, *Single Mothers by Choice: A Guidebook for Women Who Are Considering or Have Chosen Motherhood* (New York: Times Books, 1994).

16. Carol Jouzaltis, "Unwed Mothers a Common Target in Welfare Debates," *Chicago Tribune*, July 18, 1994, A3.

17. Valerie Polakow, *Lives on the Edge: Single Mothers and Their Children in the Other America* (Chicago: University of Chicago Press, 1993); Linda Gordon, *Pitied, but Not Entitled: Single Mothers and the History of Welfare* (New York: Free Press, 1994); Sheila Kamerman, "Women, Children and Poverty: Public Policies and Female Headed Families in Industrialized Countries," in *Women and Poverty*, ed. Barbara C. Gelpi et al. (Chicago: University of Chicago Press, 1986).

18. Sheppard G. Kellam, Margaret E. Ensminger, and R. J. Turner, "Family Structure and the Mental Health of Children," *Archives of General Psychiatry* 34 (September 1977): 1012–22.

19. For more on the socialization patterns of resilient children, see Emmy E. Werner, "Children of the Garden Island," *Scientific American*, vol. 206 (April 1989): 106–8; Emmy E. Werner and Ruth S. Smith, *Overcoming the Odds: High-Risk Children from Birth to Adulthood* (Ithaca, N.Y.: Cornell University Press, 1992).

20. Quoted in Ruth Rosen, "Which of Us Isn't Taking 'Welfare'?," *Los Angeles Times*, December 27, 1994, Commentary, B5.

21. Quoted in Ronald Brownstein, "Welfare Debate Puts Blame on Poverty Mainly on Poor," *Los Angeles Times*, March 25, 1995, A1. In this statement, Bill Archer is presenting the explanation that Charles Murray, George Gilder and other conservatives have made for inner-city decline. They blamed the liberal welfare state of the 1960s for reduced incentives to marriage, decreased incentives for low-wage work, and increased benefits of bearing children without marriage. For some of the more persuasive refutations to this argument, see David Ellwood, *Poor Support: Poverty in the American Family* (New York: Basic Books, 1984); Frank Levy, *Dollars and Dreams: The Changing American Income Distribution* (New York: Norton, 1988); Douglas S. Massey and Nancy A. Denton, *American Apartheid: Segregation and the Making of the Underclass* (Cambridge, Mass.: Harvard University Press, 1993).

22. Lisa Richardson, "Ethics of State Welfare Fraud Study Questioned," *Los Angeles Times*, August 20, 1995, A1.

23. Ruth Rosen, "All's Not Fair When It Comes to Families," *Commentary*, March 21, 1995, B8. For more on the politics of motherhood, see Jill Quadagno, *The Color of Welfare* (New York: Oxford University Press, 1994), ch. 6; Mary Frances Berry, *The Politics of Parenthood: Child Care, Women's Rights, and the Myth of the Good Mother* (New York: Viking, 1993).

24. Herbert J. Gans, *The War against the Poor: The Underclass and Antipoverty Policy* (New York: Basic Books, 1995), 117–18.

25. A study by the Manpower Demonstration Research Corporation of case files for AFDC recipients in four programs in different states found that welfare-reduction rates varied widely and that they were more likely to be lower than many observers expect. Daniel Friedlander and Gary Burtless, *Five Years Later: The Long Term Effects of Welfare-to-Work Programs* A Manpower Demonstration Research Corporation Study (New York: Russell Sage Foundation, 1995), 199.

26. Sheldon Danziger, Robert Haveman, and Robert Plotnick, "How Income Transfer Affects Work, Savings, and the Income Distribution: A Critical Review," *Journal of Economic Literature* 19 (September 1981):975–1028.

27. Massey and Denton, *American Apartheid,* 222.

28. Figures from Bob Herbert, "The Real Welfare Cheats," *New York Times,* OP-ED. April 26, 1996, A31. For a more in depth analysis of job shortages, see Alan Finder, "Welfare Clients Outnumber Jobs They Might Fill, *New York Times,* August 25, 1996, A1.

29. For the most comprehensive analysis of the disappearance of jobs in inner-city ghettos, see William J. Wilson, *When Work Disappears: The World of the New Urban Poor* (New York: Knopf, 1966).

30. Quadagno, *Color of Welfare,* 197.

31. Ibid., 178.

32. Quoted in Guida West, *The National Welfare Rights Movement* (New York, Praeger, 1981), 92.

33. Leonard Goodwin, *Do the Poor Want to Work? A Social-Psychological Study of Work Orientations* (Washington, D.C.: Brookings Institution, 1972).

34. Ibid., 52.

35. Moore, Zaslow, Coiro, Miller, and Magenheim, "How Well Are They Faring?"

36. Bob Sector, "Flight to the Suburbs Is Proving Worthwhile," *Los Angeles Times,* 109, May 30, 1990 A5; James E. Rosenbaum, Susan Popkin, Julie Kaufman, and Jennifer Rusin, "Social Integration of Low-income Black Adults in Middle-Class White Suburbs," *Social Problems* 38 (November 1991).

37. Isabel Wilkerson, "Taste of Middle-Class Pay for Welfare Mothers," *New York Times,* February 10, 1994, A1.

38. Jon Nordheimer, "Welfare-to-Work Plans Show Success is Difficult to Achieve," *New York Times,* September 1, 1996, A1.

39. Friedlander and Burtless, *Five Years Later,* 201.

40. Stuart Butler and Anna Kondratas, *Out of the Poverty Trap* (New York: Free Press, 1987), 145.

41. Friedlander and Burtless, *Five Years,* 199.

42. Nordheimer, *New York Times,* A1, 10.

43. In this typology I have modified an idea that was first presented by Larry Lynn in his persuasive article, "Ending Welfare as We Know It," *American Prospect* (Fall 1993): 83–92. In addition, I have scrutinized the findings of studies that have examined the characteristics of black women on welfare: Margaret E. Ensminger, "Welfare and Psychological Distress: A Longitudinal Study of African American Urban Mothers," *Journal of Health and Social Behavior,* 36 (December 1995): 346–59; this study found that women who grew up

receiving welfare were more likely to report psychological distress and lower self-esteem later in life; Linda Burton, "Teenage Childbearing as an Alternative Life-Course Strategy in Multigenerational Black Families," *Human Nature* 2 (1990): 123–43; this study found multigenerational, age-condensed families with women who became mothers as teenagers and have lived on welfare; Moore, Zaslow, Coiro, Miller, and Magenheim, "How Well Are They Faring?"

44. When *Frontline* focused on Hillary Clinton's class at Wellesley, one of the most striking differences between her black and white classmates was that the black women were better equipped to juggle the dual responsiblities of work and motherhood, in that they had observed their black mothers, who had worked outside the home. The black women talked with ease about combining both roles, whereas the white women's level of frustration and anxiety was apparent. This generation of white women was one of the first to work outside the home, and they had no role models. Many had left very promising careers because they just could not do both effectively. The same kind of consideration and compassion must be given to multigenerational welfare mothers.

45. Kellam, Ensminger, and Turner, "Family Structure and the Mental Health of Children."

46. P. Lindsay Chase-Lansdale, Jean Brooks-Gunn, and E. S. Zamsky, "Young African-American Multigenerational Families in Poverty: Quality of other and Grandmothering," *Child Development*, 65(April, 1994): 373–94.

47. Laurie Becklund, "Opening a Closed Door," Teen Birth Explosion Series, pt. 3, *Los Angeles Times*, March 16, 1993, E1, 10. This article quotes Tom Kring, executive director of the Los Angeles Regional Planning Council: "Ironically, in wealthy neighorhoods that can better afford private care, it is easier to find [subsidized] clinics."

48. L. M. Gutierrez, "Working with Women of Color: An Empowerment Perspective," *Social Work* 2 (February 1990): 149–53.

49. The "classic" work on family-centered interventions with the poor is Salvador Minuchin, Braulio Montalvo, Bernard G. Guerney, Jr., Bernice L. Rosman, and Florence Schumer, *Families of the Slums: An Exploration of Their Structure and Treatment* (New York: Basic Books, 1967); Other family approaches include: Sally Provence and Audrey Naylor, *Working with Disadvantaged Parents and Their Children* (New Haven: Yale University Press, 1983); John S. Weltner, "A Structural Approach to the Single- Parent Family," *Family Process* 21 (June 1982): 203–10. The "classic" guide for working with black individuals, groups, and families is Barbara Bryant Solomon, *Black Empowerment: Social Work in Oppressed Communities* (New York: Columbia University Press, 1976). For therapeutic approaches with individual mothers, see L. P. Thurston, "Women Surviving: An Alternative Approach to "Helping" Low-Income Urban Women, *Women and Therapy* 8 (1989): 109–27; E. S. Uehara, "The Influence of Social Network's 'Second-order Zone' on Social Support Mobilization: A Case Example," *Journal of Social Relationships* 11 (May 1994): 277–94; B. Whittington, "Life Skills for Single-Parent Women: A Program Note," Women and Women Health, *Canadian Journal of Community Mental Health* 16, special issue(1986): 41–54.

50. A standardized instrument developed by W. R. Beaver and his associates, measures the concept of family competence and places it on a progressive continuum ranging from

healthy family functioning to severely dysfunctional; this concept has been modified and applied to black families. W. R. Beavers, Y. F. Hulgus, and R. B. Hampson. *Beavers System Model of Family Functioning: Family Competence and Family Style Evaluation Manual* (Dallas: University of Texas Health Science Center, 1988).

51. See Moore, Zaslow, Coiro, Miller, and Magenheim, "How Well Are They Faring?".

52. J. S. Weltner, "Matchmaking: Choosing the Appropriate Therapy for Families at Various Levels of Pathology," in *Handbook of Adolescents and Family Therapy*, ed. M. Mirkin and S. L. Koman (New York: Gardner Press, 1985), 53.

53. Infant Health and Development Project, "Enhancing the Outcomes of Low Birth Weight, Premature Infants," *Journal of the American Medical Association*, 263 (June 13, 1991):3035–42.

54. John R. Berrueta-Clement, et. al., *Changed Lives: The Effects of the Perry Preschool Program on Youths Through Age 19* (Ypsilanti, Mich.: High/Scope, 1984).

55. Dirk Johnson, "Program Creates Community for Foster Care," *New York Times,* April 1, 1996, A1.

56. Robert B. Reich, "Meet the Frayed-Collar Workers Getting the Boot," *Los Angeles Times,* September 4, 1995, Commentary, B5. For an in-depth analyses of how and why these changes have occurred in the economy, see Frank Levy, *Dollars and Dreams: The Changing American Income Distribution* (New York: Norton, 1988).

57. According to Mark J. Stern, during the 1970s alone the proportion of college-educated African-Americans who did not work, were chronically jobless, or worked part-time doubled; "Poverty and Family Composition since 1940," in *The "Underclass" Debate: Views from History* ed. Michael B. Katz (Princeton: Princeton University Press, 1993), 220–53. This conclusion is supported by Phillip Moss and Chris Tilly, "Why Black Men Are Doing Worse in the Labor Market: A Review of Supply-Side and Demand-Side Explanations," paper prepared for the Social Science Research Council Subcommittee on Joblessness and the Underclass, 1991.

58. John Hope Franklin and Eleanor Holmes Norton, *Black Initiative and Governmental Responsibility: A Policy Framework for Racial Justice* (Washington, D.C.: Joint Center for Political Studies, 1987), 4–15.

59. Maki Becker, "Students Say Yes to Success," *Los Angeles Times,* March 6, 1996, B2.

60. Gary Orfield and Carol Ashkinaze, *The Closing Door* (Chicago: University of Chicago Press, 1991), 4.

INDEX